In *Chronoschisms: Time, Narra*[...]
explores the way in which devel[...]
tion and information technologies have led to the emergence of a new
culture of time in Western societies. The radical transformation in our
understanding and experience of time has also profoundly affected the
structure of the novel. Heise argues that postmodern novels are centrally
concerned with the possibility of experiencing time in an age when
temporal horizons have been drastically foreshortened. Drawing on
theories of postmodernism and narratology, she shows how postmodern
narratives break up plot into a spectrum of contradictory story lines. The
coexistence of these competing experiences of time allows new conceptions of history and posthistory to emerge, and opens up comparisons
with recent scientific approaches to temporality. This wide-ranging study
offers new readings of postmodernist theory and fresh insight into the
often vexed relationship between literature and science.

Chronoschisms

Literature, Culture, Theory

General editor

RICHARD MACKSEY, *The Johns Hopkins University*

Chronoschisms

Time, Narrative, and Postmodernism

❖❖

URSULA K. HEISE

Columbia University, New York

CAMBRIDGE
UNIVERSITY PRESS

PUBLISHED BY THE PRESS SYNDICATE OF THE UNIVERSITY OF CAMBRIDGE
The Pitt Building, Trumpington Street, Cambridge CB2 1RP

CAMBRIDGE UNIVERSITY PRESS
The Edinburgh Building, Cambridge, CB2 2RU, United Kingdom
40 West 20th Street, New York, NY 10011–4211, USA
10 Stamford Road, Oakleigh, Melbourne 3166, Australia

First published 1997

Printed in the United Kingdom at the University Press, Cambridge

Typeset in Palatino 10/12$\frac{1}{2}$

A catalogue record for this book is available from the British Library

Library of Congress Cataloguing in Publication data
Heise, Ursula K.
Chronoschisms: time, narrative, and postmodernism / Ursula K. Heise.
p.   cm. – (Literature, culture, theory; 23)
Based on the author's thesis – Stanford University; parts of the work were first
presented as conference papers, 1991–1995; ch. 4 is a revision of an article
previously published 1992.
Includes bibliographical references and index.
ISBN 0 521 55486 1 (hardback) – ISBN 0 521 55544 2 (paperback).
1. Time in literature. 2. Postmodernism (Literature)
3. Literature and science. 4. Literature, Modern – 20th century –
History and criticism.
I. Title. II. Series.
PN56. T5H45   1997
809'.9338–dc20   96-36668 CIP

ISBN 0 521 55486 1 hardback
ISBN 0 521 55544 2 paperback

CE

Für Brigitte und Horst Wolfgang Heise

Contents

Acknowledgments

Chronoschisms started out as a dissertation at Stanford University, and the book was completed at Columbia University; many more teachers and colleagues at both institutions contributed to its gradual development than I can easily acknowledge. I am particularly indebted to my advisor at Stanford, Shirley Brice Heath, and the members of my reading committee, Marjorie Perloff and David Halliburton, for their encouragement, enthusiasm, and their unfailing intellectual support and advice during the completion of the dissertation. Special thanks are also due to my advisors from outside Stanford, who allowed me to take advantage of their expertise in narrative theory across departmental and institutional boundaries. Garrett Stewart from the University of Iowa, and William Mills Todd III from Harvard University generously offered their time and comments on every chapter of the original manuscript.

David Damrosch, George Stade and Bianca Theisen discussed various dimensions of the book with me at different stages of its development and offered detailed comments that proved extremely helpful in rethinking and revising the manuscript; I would like to thank them for the time they took to discuss my ideas and convey their insights to me. My greatest intellectual and personal debt outside the field of literature is to Rafael Pardo Avellaneda, who not only gave me his support through all the years it took to complete the book, but also first awakened my interest in the connections between art and contemporary information technologies. I have profited immensely from his lucid comments on sociological approaches to postmodern society and culture, as well as on the more theoretical parts of my argument. Needless to say, however much the book has benefited from the ideas and insights of those who discussed it with me, its weaknesses remain exclusively my own.

Acknowledgments

Material support for the completion of the book was provided to me through a Theodor H. and Frances K. Geballe Fellowship, which gave me the opportunity to focus fully on research and writing at the Stanford Humanities Center in 1990–91, and a Mabelle McLeod-Lewis dissertation fellowship in 1992–93, which allowed me to complete the original manuscript. Summer fellowships granted by the Columbia University Council for Research in the Humanities in 1994 and 1995 made it possible for me to develop the project further toward its final shape. I am grateful to all three institutions for their generous support. My thanks also go to Nicole Waller for her diligence and care in helping me edit the manuscript.

Parts of the argument were first presented as papers at the International Conference on Narrative, 1991, the American Comparative Literature Association Annual Meeting, 1995, and the Convention of the Society for the Study of Narrative Literature, 1995. Chapter 4, "Print Time: Text and Duration in Beckett's *How It Is*," was previously published under the title "*Erzählzeit* and Postmodern Narrative: Text as Duration in Beckett's *How It Is*," *Style* 26 (1992): 245–69. I thank the editors of *Style* for allowing me to include it here in somewhat different form. I would also like to thank Carcanet Press for the permission to quote from Christine Brooke-Rose's novel *Out*.

Finally, I would like to thank my parents, without whose material, emotional and intellectual support over many years this project, like so many others, could not have been completed. This book is dedicated to them.

Introduction

Analyzing the temporality of contemporary novels may seem like an attempt to find modernist concerns in postmodernist literature. Whereas the interest of many high-modernist writers, artists and philosophers in the experience of time and its problems is not in critical dispute, postmodernist culture has often been analyzed as relying primarily on spatial categories. The shift in emphasis from time to space, according to these theories, is accompanied by a drastic weakening of historical consciousness with far-reaching social and political implications. Unquestionably, the culture of time has changed since the early twentieth century, and postmodernist texts and artworks do not usually celebrate the interlacing of memory and expectation in the individual's experience of time, Jamesian flow, Bergsonian *durée*, or cyclical returns of history as one finds them in the works of high-modernist artists and writers. But time and its problems have not simply disappeared from the contemporary cultural scene, while concerns with space have taken its place. Temporality, this book will argue, constitutes a major concern of postmodernist theory and art, although it is envisioned in terms that differ fundamentally from those of high-modernist culture.

It is doubtful, at any rate, that a fundamental reconceptualization of space could occur without corresponding changes in the notion of time, since time and space are not really so much conceptual opposites as complementary parameters of experience. Metaphorical usage, to be sure, can make them appear to be binary opposites, and it is perhaps the postmodernist predilection for spatial metaphors – from the "web sites," "cyberspace" and "information super-highway" of computer technology to the "sites of resistance," "textual boundaries" and cultural "borderlands" of literary and cultural theory – that most strongly impresses one with the sense that postmodernist culture extends

1

in space rather than in time. Such metaphors tend to obscure the fact that in the late twentieth century, conventional notions of both time and space are in crisis, and cultural artifacts, to the extent that they depend upon or address temporal and spatial experiences, participate in their reconceptualization. Given this cultural framework, it is the specific contention of this book that postmodernist novels are centrally concerned with the possibility and modalities of experiencing time in the age of posthistory and the nanosecond culture, and that their experiments with narrative structure can only be properly understood with this concern in mind.

The argument proposed here focuses on narrative as the literary genre that is most directly dependent on its deployment in and as time, and where changes in the cultural conception of temporality can therefore be expected to play themselves out most visibly and with the greatest impact on literary form. The theoretical argument as well as the readings of individual texts are based on the assumption that there is indeed such a category as the "postmodern novel" that can be distinguished in its narrative strategies from the modernist novel of the early twentieth century, and *Chronoschisms* is meant to contribute to the mapping of this faultline. It is, obviously, not the first attempt to outline this transition. But earlier studies have either focused exclusively on "historiographic metafiction," which plays with historical figures and events in such a way that the boundary between fiction and history is blurred, or have restricted themselves to the formal description of postmodernist novels without any consideration of the cultural context in which they participate.[1] *Chronoschisms* pursues a broader objective: it is designed to show how the narrative organization of postmodern novels reconceives temporality regardless of whether their subject matter involves explicit references to history or not, and how these formal strategies form part of a restructuration of time that

---

[1] "Historiographic metafiction" is Linda Hutcheon's phrase; she discusses this genre in *A Poetics of Postmodernism: History, Theory, Fiction* (New York: Routledge, 1988), esp. Chapters 6 and 7. Her earlier *Narcissistic Narrative: The Metafictional Paradox* (London: Routledge, 1991; originally published in 1980), belongs to the more formal studies, as do Brian McHale's *Postmodernist Fiction* (New York: Methuen, 1987) and Alan Thiher's *Words in Reflection: Modern Language Theory and Postmodern Fiction* (Chicago: University of Chicago Press, 1984).

goes far beyond literature and affects a broad range of cultural and social practices.

The category "postmodern fiction," however, is harder to define in the 1990s than it was at the beginning of the 1980s, since the term now includes two quite different sets of texts. In its first acceptation, "postmodern fiction" refers to texts primarily from the 1960s and 70s that emphasized narrative experiment and introduced new ways of handling character, description, dialogue and plot: American "metafiction," the French *nouveau roman*, *nouveau nouveau roman* and the works of the *Ouvroir de Littérature Potentielle* (OULIPO), as well as some of the Latin American fiction of the so-called "boom," to name only the most important movements. But in the United States, "postmodern fiction" now also refers quite frequently to the kind of novel which came to prominence in the 1980s, and whose primary objective is not so much formal innovation as the publicization of those alternative histories of women, cultures colonized by Western powers, or racial and ethnic minorities that had been ignored or repressed in mainstream historiography. Quite a few of these novels also experiment with narrative forms and strategies in highly innovative ways, but some have reverted to either modernist or even pre-modernist forms of storytelling. "Postmodern fiction" has therefore become an ambiguous term that can refer to very different types of narrative. Since the present study is mainly concerned with the reinvention of narrative time in the wake of modernism, it focuses primarily on novels from the 1960s and 70s, the moment when the first radical break with high-modernist storytelling procedures took place. The cultural analysis that frames the analysis of these novels, however, describes a chronologically somewhat broader scenario that reaches from the 1960s up to the present, since many novels that belong to the "second wave" of postmodern fiction take up and elaborate the metafictional techniques discussed here that were developed in the "first wave."

The novels selected for detailed analysis are, with the exception of Christine Brooke-Rose's *Out*, canonical texts as far as contemporary literature is concerned. Clearly, there is a very large number of other texts, some canonical, some less canonical, and some virtually unknown, that could have served as examples for the conceptual development *Chronoschisms* outlines, and I make reference to some of these other texts in the theoretical discussion. But since the objective of this study is to compare the "mainstream" of modernist fiction with what has become "mainstream" in the postmodern period, I have found it preferable to rely on texts that many readers are likely to be familiar with, either specifically or in terms of their authors' typical narrative choices and strategies. This procedure allows me to situate these texts and authors in and explain their contribution to the broader cultural transformation of time that is the main object of my discussion. In this framework, Julio Cortázar's *Rayuela*, as analyzed in Chapter 2, emerges as a novel on the borderline between modernism and postmodernism since it deploys typically postmodernist narrative strategies for modernist effects. Alain Robbe-Grillet and Samuel Beckett are both authors whose early work is informed by modernist – or perhaps "late modernist" – assumptions, whereas their later texts clearly move beyond these parameters. As examples of this later work, Robbe-Grillet's *Topologie d'une cité fantôme* and Beckett's *How It Is* fracture time into multiple versions of itself by means of intricate structures of repetition and quotation, leaving neither characters nor readers with a firm hold on past or present. All these novels, analyzed in the section "Time Loops," deal mainly with the temporal disintegration of the individual, whereas the two texts that follow in the section entitled "Posthistories" specifically address the question of the relationship between time and history understood as a social and not only individual parameter of experience. Thomas Pynchon's *Gravity's Rainbow* has become a classic – perhaps *the* classic – of postmodern literature precisely because of its fantastic transformations of twentieth-century history and its multi-dimensional exploration of temporality and causation. Christine Brooke-Rose's *Out* pursues a similar project, but does so with very different means, since *Out* is set in a fictional future rather than a semi-fictional past, and operates with an extremely limited inventory of characters and episodes that sharply contrasts with Pynchon's abundance of figures and plots. Exploring problems of time and causation by means of an unfamiliar fictional universe in combination with unfamiliar narrative strategies, *Out* accomplishes the perhaps most difficult task an experimental text can carry out. The epilogue, finally, briefly presents a more mainstream science-fiction text, Bruce Sterling's cyberpunk novel

Schismatrix, so as to indicate one of the directions more recent fiction has taken in its dealings with time and causation: the integration of literature and certain aspects of the branch of scientific exploration that has come to be popularly known under the label of chaos theory.

Through the analysis of these novels as well as the theoretical discussion, *Chronoschisms* aims at showing the relationship between their innovative narrative structures and a broader transformation in the Western culture of time that has taken place since the 1960s and involves changes in science, technology, and socio-economic structures as well as in aesthetic practices. Claiming that such a relationship exists does not, however, imply that the literary texts "reflect" or "respond to" social, economic or material changes in any simple sense. Such a response hypothesis is implausible, to begin with, for chronological reasons: as I will show in Chapter 1, some of the texts that first modeled the narrative structures to emerge in the 1960s – most crucially, those of Jorge Luis Borges – were published in the 1940s, well before the revolutions in transportation, information and communication technologies that most strikingly transformed the Western time sense between the 1960s and the 1980s. Even if one disregards the perhaps exceptional case of Borges, however, the contemporaneity of these revolutions with the emergence of new aesthetic and, more specifically, literary forms is not in and of itself a convincing argument for a causal connection between the two sets of phenomena, especially since one would expect an at least minimal time lapse to occur before socio-economic and technological changes are translated into literary structures.

But perhaps more importantly, what complicates this analysis of the relation of literary forms to their social and cultural context is that postmodern literature interacts not only with its contemporary environment, but must also engage with its own genre-specific history: in the case of narrative, postmodernist texts cannot be understood only within the cultural framework of the last four decades, but must also be viewed in the context of their engagement with their high-modernist predecessors. In Chapter 1, I will outline the ways in which postmodernist texts develop and transform some of the most important high-modernist narrative techniques so as to create a very different sense of time that in its discontinuity, its fragmentation into multiple temporal itineraries and its collisions of incommensurable time scales highlights and hyperbolizes certain characteristics of a culture of time that is shared by a whole range of other, non-literary discourses and practices. My argument is that whereas one can discern a certain logic in the literary foregrounding of these and not other features of the contemporary time sense, this choice was by no means inevitable or uniquely dependent on non-literary practices; in other words, while recent developments in science, technology, media, modes of production and social interaction help to explain the formal experiments postmodern novelists undertake, postmodern novels in their turn help to create the cultural lenses through which we perceive and interpret social and technological developments. To make this argument somewhat more concrete, one can claim, for example, that the fragmented plots of many postmodernist novels are to some extent conditioned by the accelerated temporal rhythms of late-capitalist technologies of production and consumption, which tend to make long-term developments more difficult to envision and construct; but it is arguably equally valid that fragmented narrative plots in conjunction with theories about the demise of "master narratives" tend to shape our perception of production and consumption in the late twentieth century in such a way that the latter come to appear as obstacles that impede more long-term constructions of time. In this perspective, both economic and aesthetic practices contribute to the emergence of a culture of time which focuses on drastically shortened temporal horizons at the expense of long-term planning and coherence; and while both sets of practices can and should be understood to have some impact upon each other, neither is uniquely dependent on the other. The analysis proposed in Chapter 1 follows this model, emphasizing convergences of trends in different social and cultural domains rather than unidirectional vectors of causation.

For the novel, as a genre whose organizational structures necessarily embody specific conceptions of time, two developments in particular present a serious challenge to conventional models of narrative and causation: the shortening of temporal horizons in the late twentieth century, and public awareness, in Western societies, of the co-existence of radically different time scales from the nanoseconds of the computer to the billions of years in which contemporary cosmology calculates the age of the earth and the universe. But these challenges also existed, albeit to a lesser extent, in the heyday of the high-modernist novel, and were met with innovative narrative strategies that enabled writers and readers to explore individual and psychological temporality, whose peculiar sequential logic could be held up as a counter-model to what were perceived to be the repressive implications of official history and public time. Perhaps the most fundamental challenge to the postmodern novel, therefore, is the demise of character, of human experience as the central organizing parameter of narrative. If plot in the conventional sense was already substantially weakened in high-modernist novels, narrative voice and fictional character remained and were even reinforced as crucial supporting pillars of the fictional universe. One of the most striking developments in the transition from the modernist to the postmodernist novel is the disintegration of narrator and character as recognizable and more or less stable entities, and their scattering or fragmentation across different temporal universes that can no longer be reconciled with each other, or justified by recurring to different psychological worlds. Whether it is the demise of identifiable characters that causes time to fracture, or the fragmentation of time that sets an end to character, is not easy to decide; what is clear, however, is that the time of the individual mind no longer functions as an alternative to social time. Neither is social time any longer perceived as a threat to psychological *durée*, memory and the flow of conscious-ness; on the contrary, it is subject to the same divisions and fragmentations that affect the worlds and identities of individual characters. The weakening of individual as well as social and historical time as parameters for organizing narrative is the most crucial problem the postmodern novel articulates in its multiple formal experiments as well as many of its thematic concerns. *Chronoschisms* is an attempt to map this problem in its various literary dimensions, its parallels in and implications for other types of social and cultural discourses and practices, and its narrative solutions as they are proposed in the postmodernist novel.

I

Chronoschisms

Chromosomes

1

From soft clocks to hardware: narrative and the postmodern experience of time

❖❖

Time is obsolete. History has ended. This seemingly implausible claim has haunted theories of European and American culture since World War II, and has appeared with equal frequency in characterizations of the postmodernist novel over the last thirty years. The notion that Western societies in the late twentieth century have entered a stage of "posthistory" or a "crisis of historicity" may seem to align with a whole set of concepts such as postmodernism, postindustrialism, posthumanism or post-structuralism, whose usage in sociology, cultural theory and literary criticism has come to indicate the demise of historically important processes and phenomena. But the term "posthistory" implies a considerably larger claim in that it refers not to specific historical developments, but to the process of history and the understanding of temporality itself.[1] Aside from its obvious interest for the historian and sociologist, such a claim is also of crucial concern to cultural and literary analysis since it has the potential to shape the way we look at contemporary cultural currents and works of art. This concern imposes itself with even greater urgency in so far as some theories and practices of postmodernist art and literature specifically question the rele-vance of temporality and historicity for aesthetic production in the late twentieth century.

Obviously, although the term "posthistory" or "posthistoire" is a relatively recent coinage, the idea that history has come to an end is not new in Western thought, and is not limited to those

---

[1] Lutz Niethammer, *Posthistoire: Ist die Geschichte zu Ende?* (Reinbek: Rowohlt, 1989), 7.

who consider themselves part of the artistic or art-critical avant-garde. Philosophers and politicians throughout the nineteenth and twentieth centuries have been interested in the idea of historical closure, from Hegel, who considered history to have ended in the early years of the nineteenth century, to a variety of right- and left-wing intellectuals who believed history had come to a close in the aftermath of World War II. The crisis of historicity that theorists of postmodernism refer to, and that I will explore in detail here, is of a somewhat different nature: it is claimed to have brought about not so much a closure of the historical process in the conventional sense as a speed-up of temporal experience that tends to erase historical differences and to open the present up to a multitude of historical moments. The first section of this chapter will define and analyze these differing approaches.

In the analysis of some of the major arguments about the crisis of historicity, the question imposes itself whether these claims differ substantially from the historical breaks which avant-garde movements frequently declare so as to mark their own entrance on the cultural scene. Avant-garde groups tend to position themselves in relation to the mainstream culture by means of a "language of rupture" that stresses the importance of innovation and the desirability of radical breaks with the past: the essays and manifestos of the modernist avant-garde of the early twentieth century give ample testimony of this tendency.[2] One must therefore ask whether the notion of "posthistory" is merely another way of announcing a desired historical break not only with the aesthetic, but also with the literary-critical conventions of high modernism, or whether the experience and conceptualization of time and history has indeed fundamentally changed between the early and the late part of the twentieth century. In the second and third sections of this chapter, I will compare the temporal experience that informs postmodernism to that which shaped aesthetic production during the high-modernist period, and expand this reflection by examining not only the question of historical continuity but also its connection with the experience of different time scales. I will argue that a

[2] This phrase is taken from Marjorie Perloff's analysis of futurism in *The Futurist Moment: Avant-Garde, Avant Guerre, and the Language of Rupture* (Chicago: University of Chicago Press, 1986).

fundamental change in the Western culture of time has indeed taken place, and that the question of posthistory and the narrative practices which have accompanied it can therefore not simply be relegated to the realm of hyperbolic avant-gardist self-representation.

Section 4 moves into the more specifically literary questions related to these practices by tracing the relationship between the experience of time and changing forms of narrative from the nineteenth- to the late twentieth-century novel. At each of the three stages of this historical analysis – from realism to modernism and postmodernism – the argument focuses on the ways in which narrative form fits into, responds to and helps to shape broader cultural conceptions of time. This more long-term historical assessment, rather than the more narrow and binary comparison between modernism and postmodernism, is necessary for a proper understanding of postmodern experiments with narrative temporality and their cultural implications. As I will show, the faultlines between different historical forms of the novel can be traced in terms of the concepts of time and causation that shape them. The difference between high-modernist and postmodernist texts is particularly striking in this respect: if novelists such as Proust, Mann, Joyce, Woolf, Stein and many others reinvented narrative structures so as to explore the flow of memory, duration and expectation in human consciousness, writers such as Beckett, Calvino, Robbe-Grillet and Brooke-Rose design narrative forms that deliberately make temporal progression difficult or impossible to conceive. The comparison between realist, high-modernist and postmodernist novels (with particular emphasis on the latter transition), and the reasons for this conspicuous shift in the treatment of narrative time are the primary concerns of the theoretical analysis as well as the readings of individual postmodernist texts proposed here.

Section 5 of this chapter, finally, will take a step back from the specific consideration of the novel to examine the implications of "historicizing posthistory," that is, the attempt to analyze historically a culture that resists the very notion of history. While there is no easy way of avoiding this paradox, the postmodernist resistance to history may help to reshape historical analysis without leading it to abandon history completely.

1. Posthistory: standstill or speed-up?

Theories and practices of the postmodern over the last thirty years manifest extremely divergent attitudes with regard to issues of time. Whereas some theorists – from the political right as well as the political left – see the distinctiveness of post-modernism in its emphasis on categories of space rather than time, other critics claim on the contrary that the re-emergence of historicity after what they perceive to be the ahistoricity of high modernism most crucially characterizes the postmodern move-ment. Sociologist Daniel Bell, for example, claims that "[t]he organization of space, whether it be in modern painting, architec-ture, or sculpture, has become the primary aesthetic problem of mid-twentieth-century culture, as the problem of time (in Bergson, Proust, and Joyce) was the primary aesthetic concern of the first decades of this century."[3] Similarly, Fredric Jameson, in his Marxist approach to contemporary culture, describes the "waning of the great high modernist thematics of time and temporality, the elegiac mysteries of *durée* and memory" and argues that "our daily life, our psychic experience, our cultural languages, are today dominated by categories of space rather than by categories of time."[4] But this view is by no means shared by all theorists of postmodernism; especially since the late 1980s, one finds an increasing emphasis on the re-emergence of histor-ical interest, although most critics agree that this renewed interest does not imply a simple return to conventionally understood historicity, but on the contrary a questioning of traditional notions of history and historiography. Linda Hutcheon formu-lates this viewpoint when she claims that "[t]he postmodern . . . effects two simultaneous moves. It reinstalls historical contexts as significant and even determining, but in so doing, it problema-tizes the entire notion of historical knowledge."[5] One could argue that this questioning of historical knowledge is itself a symptom of the crisis of historicity that Jameson and others see enacted in

---

[3] *The Cultural Contradictions of Capitalism* (New York: Basic, 1976), 107.
[4] *Postmodernism, or, The Cultural Logic of Late Capitalism* (Durham, NC: Duke University Press, 1991), 16.
[5] *A Poetics of Postmodernism: History, Theory, Fiction* (New York: Routledge, 1988), 89. See also Paul Alkon, "Alternate History and Postmodern Temporality," *Time, Literature and the Arts: Essays in Honor of Samuel L. Macey* (Victoria: English Literary Studies, 1994), 65–85.

contemporary culture, but Hutcheon is nevertheless right in stressing that questions of history have come to the fore again in the most recent forms of art and literature. Andreas Huyssen sums up this paradox by pointing out that the co-existence of these two tendencies has "led to a major and puzzling contradiction in our culture. The undisputed waning of history and historical consciousness, the lament about political, social and cultural amnesia, and the various discourses, celebratory or apocalyptic, about *posthistoire* have been accompanied in the past decade and a half by a memory boom of unprecedented proportions."[6]

Part of the problem in considering this contradiction between different theories of the postmodern is the relation between the concepts of "time" and "history," which are unquestionably entangled with each other, but not necessarily identical. Sociocultural changes in the management, representation and means of measuring time can be accompanied by transformations in the conceptualization of history; but such reconceptualizations need not be uniform or stable. Once we take this distinction into account, it becomes possible to describe changes in the culture of time as they have taken place over the last thirty or forty years, and to specify how they resemble or differ from those that occurred in the early twentieth century. These transformations can then be related to changes in historical thought and narrative reasoning, leaving open the possibility that such changes can also evolve to a certain extent independently, and that they can involve a range of different developments rather than a single one. This perspective, which I will take in the following analysis, enables a description of the postmodern that includes material innovations in the Western time sense as well as the crisis in conceptualization that has arisen along with them, a crisis that has led variously to rejections of history and to qualified returns to historical reasoning. Both types of reaction are related to each other; I will here focus on the former because I believe that some of the most crucial concepts that have informed theories of "posthistory" or a "crisis of historicity" have also shaped the

---

[6] *Twilight Memories: Marking Time in a Culture of Amnesia* (New York: Routledge, 1995), 5.

conditions under which writers and artists could subsequently return to some form of historical reasoning.

Since the translation of *La condition postmoderne* into English in 1984, Jean-François Lyotard's claim about the demise of "grand narrative" has become a basic element of most theories of postmodernism. Addressing primarily the situation of the natural sciences, Lyotard's report quickly made its way into cultural and literary theory, where it generated a much more lively response than among scientists. His thesis that the overarching narratives of legitimation which justified scientific activity in the past have lost credibility in the late twentieth century and caused scientific disciplines to splinter into numerous specialized "language games," proved of interest to cultural and literary critics because the legitimization narratives Lyotard refers to are related to the great nineteenth-century philosophies of history: the humanist narrative of progress according to which science functions as an instrument of emancipation and liberation for the individual, and the idealist narrative of the gradual "becoming" of spirit, which manifests itself in scientific progress among other achievements. Cultural critics argued that these large-scale philosophies of historical development have lost authority not just for the natural sciences, but more generally as narrative patterns through which Western societies and cultures define themselves. The rapidly decreasing belief in narratives of progress, enlightenment, emancipation, liberation or revolution, especially since the 1960s, has become one of the hallmarks of postmodernist culture that, in the view of many theorists, mostly clearly marks its difference from modernist thinking.

But if the interest in large-scale, abstract theories of universal historical development has diminished in the last thirty years, interest in histories understood as more local and concrete narratives has proliferated. The receding importance of those stories that formed the backbone of Western historical self-awareness has opened the way for the articulation of other stories that had been repressed, or had seemed too marginal or too deviant to find an audience before. Historians, anthropologists and social scientists, as well as fiction writers of the most varied kinds, have publicized histories of non-Western cultures, women, ethnic, racial and sexual minorities, and victims of structural or physical violence that had not been brought to public awareness before;

16

often, these histories have been voiced in the context of claims to emancipation, liberation and individuality that are rooted in Enlightenment thought and sometimes rest uneasily with the critique of Enlightenment rationality and imperialism that also forms part of this radically pluralist project. The proliferation and multiplication of histories since the 1960s, and the theoretical reflection on their status and their relationship to mainstream history as well as to the Enlightenment and to poststructuralist critiques of Enlightenment thought since the 1980s, has come to form part and parcel of postmodernist culture just as much as Lyotard's analysis of the demise of grand narrative.[7]

If the cultural and intellectual transition from grand History to the multiplication of histories marks one of the trajectories of postmodernist thought, theories of a movement from history to posthistory define another trend of the postmodern. These theories question the possibility of history more radically than critiques of metanarrative; rather than postulating merely a shift from the universal to the specific, or from global to local narrative, they examine the structures of temporality that make *any* kind of narrative possible, and reflect on the present and future viability of the particular type of temporal organization that narrative is based on. From this perspective, local narratives and specialized language games are not in principle any less problematic than universalizing narratives, since it is the very genre of narrative and the temporal philosophy that informs it which comes into question. As Paul Virilio observes, "[t]he crisis of the grand narrative that gives rise to the micro-narrative finally becomes the crisis of the narrative of the grand and the petty."[8] Such reflections obviously have important implications both for historiography and for literary storytelling.

However, theories that point to a crisis of historicity in the late twentieth century are themselves far from uniform. Generally speaking, they fall into two very different types. The first type postulates that history as a dialectic interplay of opposing forces has exhausted itself and led society to a stage in which all that

---

[7] Hans Bertens gives an excellent account of the changing associations of the term "postmodern" with various aesthetic and political projects from the 1960s to the 1980s in *The Idea of the Postmodern: A History* (London: Routledge, 1995), 3–19.

[8] *The Lost Dimension*, trans. Daniel Moshenberg (New York: Semiotext(e), 1991), 24.

can be expected of the future is a continuing replay and spread of already familiar modernization processes. The end of history in such theories is not a cataclysmic or apocalyptic event in the conventional sense, as Lutz Niethammer has shown; rather, it is envisioned as a process of petrification or crystallization which turns society into a machine-like aggregate that stubbornly reproduces its own structures without allowing any meaningful human intervention. Considering that these theories were for the most part conceived during the period of the Cold War, it may be rather surprising that they would stress society's ability for self-preservation rather than its potential for self-destruction; nevertheless, in contrast to other political and philosophical currents which foregrounded the threat of nuclear annihilation and, somewhat later, that of environmental collapse, European theorists of posthistory from the 1950s to the 1970s saw the principal danger for Western society in the rigidification and unending self-reproduction of its own internal structures.[9] In his study *Posthistoire: Ist die Geschichte zu Ende? (Posthistory: Has History Come to an End?)*, Niethammer traces this type of thought from mostly (though not exclusively) right-wing intellectuals in the 1950s to leftist thinkers in the 1970s, arguing that it typically emerged in the aftermath of the collapse of important political ideologies – Nazism, Stalinism, and the failure of the 1968 uprisings. One of the approaches he briefly discusses in this context, and which may serve as an example here, is Horkheimer and Adorno's *Dialektik der Aufklärung* (Dialectic of Enlightenment), which has become more widely known in the U.S. than most of the other works he examines. Emerging from the experience of German Nazism, Horkheimer and Adorno's central concern is the "Selbstzerstörung der Aufklärung" (self-destruction of the Enlightenment), which in their view manifests itself in a rationality that has developed to the point where it turns against the individuals it was originally intended to liberate and emancipate, disempowering and indeed erasing them. Obviously, such an analysis challenges not only the primacy of scientific rationality, but also the conceptions of linear historical development and progress that usually accompanied it. To the extent that this argument

---

[9] Although all of these theorists consider the possibility of a closure of the historical process, not all of them specifically use the term "posthistory," as my example below will show.

criticizes some of the central concepts of Western modernity and modernization, it prepares the way for later and even more fundamental attacks on the project of the Enlightenment that lie at the core of much postmodernist thought, and thereby connects posthistorical and postmodernist reasoning. Indeed, the question of whether the Enlightenment project has reached a logical impasse in the twentieth century, or whether, as Jürgen Habermas maintains, it is an "incomplete project" which continues to realize itself gradually, and must continue to do so for the well-being of society, is one of the crucial issues in debates over the implications of postmodernism in the 1980s.[10] Niethammer emphasizes the way in which Horkheimer, Adorno and many others turn against nineteenth-century concepts of historical progress, and therefore interprets the idea of *posthistoire* as essentially "ein enttäuschtes Postskript zur Geschichtsphilosophie des 19. Jahrhunderts" (a disillusioned postscript to nineteenth-century philosophy of history).[11]

Most of the European intellectuals whose work Niethammer analyzes form part of one of the traditions of Hegelian thought. For Hegel, however, the end of history was not inscribed in a general framework of cultural pessimism: his well-known identification of Napoleon with the "Weltseele" on the eve of the battle of Jena in 1806, signalling the approaching conclusion of history, is framed by the assumption that the *Weltgeist* has finally found itself through the intermediary of the philosophical observer, and that history has attained its full and perfect shape. The mostly German and French intellectuals Niethammer studies invert this pattern and pessimistically describe the end of history as an event that erases human freedom and individuality.[12] The most recent American avatar of this tradition, however, Francis Fukuyama's *The End of History and the Last Man* (1992), takes a more optimistic stance. Fukuyama, whose earlier article on the same question had

[10] For Habermas' argument, see his article "Modernity versus Postmodernity," *New German Critique* 22 (1981): 3–14, reprinted under the title "Modernity – An Incomplete Project" in *The Anti-Aesthetic: Essays on Postmodern Culture*, ed. Hal Foster (Seattle: Bay Press, 1983), 3–15. A concise assessment of Habermas and problems of historicity in postmodernity is Hans-Ulrich Gumbrecht's essay "Posthistoire Now" in *Epochenschwellen und Epochenstrukturen im Diskurs der Literatur- und Sprachhistorie*, ed. Hans-Ulrich Gumbrecht and Ursula Link-Heer (Frankfurt: Suhrkamp, 1985), 34–50.

[11] Niethammer, *Posthistoire*, 170.

[12] *Ibid.*, 67–71.

provoked great interest and controversy both in the U.S. and Europe, relies on Alexandre Kojève's reading of Hegel to suggest that the end of the Cold War implies the closure of the historical process itself. In his view, the late twentieth century has proven the non-viability of the two major challenges to liberal democracy, fascism and communism, and no other concept of the state has emerged at least in the form of an ideal that could compete with democracy. This ideal, he believes, will continue to impose itself globally. Although he concedes that re-emerging nationalisms and religious fundamentalisms may threaten the development of democracy in some parts of the world, they do not imply any fundamental challenge to democracy as a political ideal. The more basic question, he claims, is whether liberal democracy itself can in the long run satisfy humans, or whether it has inherent flaws that will in their turn have to be overcome by a different form of political organization; if so, this would amount to a new beginning of the historical process. Rejecting the leftist critique that capitalist democracies perpetuate certain forms of economic inequality, he suggests instead that it is precisely the democratic emphasis on equality that may ultimately lead individuals and groups to search for different forms of society. But even though this possibility exists, Fukuyama emphasizes that in his view, liberal democracy currently has no serious rivals as a political ideal, and that in this sense at least the historical process is concluded.

Fukuyama's optimism, however, is exceptional in contemporary theories of posthistory. Most of these theories find great difficulty in assigning meaning to contemporary events: "Die Problemstellung der Posthistoire-Diagnose ist nicht das Ende von Welt, sondern das Ende von Sinn" (The issue for diagnoses of posthistory is not the end of the world, but the end of meaning).[13] This difficulty links European theories of *posthistoire* with an otherwise very different type of approach to the crisis of historicity, which foregrounds changes in the cultural time sense that have been prompted by the technological, economic and social innovations of late twentieth-century capitalism. According to this second type of theory, the problem for contemporary historical awareness is not a standstill of conventional

[13] *Ibid.*, 9.

patterns of conflict and development, but on the contrary the enormous speed-up in the existential rhythm of individuals as well as societies over the last three or four decades. This acceleration led Alvin Toffler in 1970 to speak of a "future shock" that forces large numbers of individuals in Western societies to live in an economic, technological and social culture alien to them because they are unable to keep up with its pace of change.[14] Some Marxist analysts relate this acceleration to the dynamics of capitalist development; David Harvey, most prominently, claims that the current crisis of historicity in the West is due to a phase of intense "time-space compression." Such phases, he argues, have occurred periodically in the history of capitalism and have triggered each time a crisis in the representation of time and space through "processes that so revolutionize the objective qualities of space and time that we are forced to alter, sometimes in quite radical ways, how we represent the world to ourselves."[15] Such moments of representational rupture affect science, philosophy and the arts in everything from theories about the cosmos to map-making and literary or pictorial techniques.

In Harvey's analysis, crises in representation are related to the two basic goals of capitalist economic activity: overcoming spatial barriers so as to open up new markets, and accelerating the turn-over time of capital (that is, the time it takes for invested capital to return in the form of profit). These two tendencies have reached new historic heights in the "long boom" of Western economies from 1945 to 1973, but particularly since the early 1970s. Partly due to innovations in transportation technology in the 1960s, the capitalist market has spread for the first time to the entire globe.[16] Concurrently, the emphasis of economic activity has shifted from the goods to the services industry, where accumulation and turn-over are virtually unlimited, and change through product fashions has sped up and spread into markets that were not traditionally subject to them. The evolution of a product from its first design and development to its eventual

---

[14] Alvin Toffler, *Future Shock* (New York: Random House, 1970), 11–19.
[15] David Harvey, *The Condition of Postmodernity: An Enquiry into the Origins of Cultural Change* (Oxford: Blackwell, 1990), 240.
[16] See Peter Dicken, *Global Shift: Industrial Change in a Turbulent World* (London: Chapman, 1988), 107.

obsolescence, a time span referred to in marketing as the "product life cycle," is becoming shorter and forcing companies to innovate at a much faster rate, and to change their organizational structures so as to increase their flexibility and ability to respond to their environment.[17] Harvey comments:

The first major consequence has been to accentuate volatility and ephemerality of fashions, products, production techniques, labour processes, ideas and ideologies, values and established practices. The sense that 'all that is solid melts into air' has rarely been more pervasive period . . . In the realm of commodity production, the primary effect has been to emphasize the values and virtues of instantaneity (instant and fast foods, meals, and other satisfactions) and of disposability (cups, plates, cutlery, packaging, napkins, clothing, etc.). . . . It mean[s] more than just throwing away produced goods . . . but also being able to throw away values, lifestyles, stable relationships, and attachments to things, buildings, places, people, and received ways of doing and being.[18]

Under these circumstances, long-term planning diminishes in importance, whereas the ability to make use of the phases and fashions of the market becomes crucial.

Harvey here rightly points to parallel developments in the realm of production and consumption and the more general cultural domain. It is less clear, however, whether the cultural changes have been prompted unidirectionally by changes in the production-consumption cycle. The new information technologies that emerged in the 1960s and 70s, for example, were not originally invented by industrial companies intent on rationalizing, coordinating and accelerating their economic activities; on the contrary, companies took considerable time in assimilating them into their organizational structures.[19] Causal relations

---

[17] Dicken, *Global Shift*, 98–99; Thomas W. Malone and John F. Rockart, "Computers, Networks and the Corporation," *Communications, Computers and Networks*, Special issue of *Scientific American* 265.3 (1991): 98; Michael L. Dertouzos, Richard Lester and Robert Solow, *Made in America* (Cambridge, MA: MIT Press, 1989), 70ff; James P. Womack, Daniel T. Jones and Daniel Roos, *The Machine That Changed the World* (New York: Rasson, 1990), 48ff; and Bennett Harrison, *Lean and Mean: The Changing Landscape of Corporate Power in the Age of Flexibility* (New York: Basic, 1994).

[18] Harvey, *Condition of Postmodernity*, 285–86.

[19] Rafael Pardo Avellaneda, "Globalización, innovación tecnológica y tiempo," *Información comercial española* 695 (1991): 78; Paul Ceruzzi, "An Unforeseen Revolution: Computers and Expectations, 1935–1985," *Imagining Tomorrow: History, Technology and the American Future*, ed. Joseph J. Corn (Cambridge, MA: MIT Press, 1986), 189–90. Regarding the impact of computers on corporations

between industrial production and the new information technologies, therefore, are complex and multidirectional.[20] As far as changes in the cultural awareness of time are concerned, it therefore makes more sense to trace the structural analogies that emerge between the cultural and other social realms in their mutual interdependence, than to postulate a unidirectional causality that cannot really be substantiated in empirical terms.

On this basis, it is nevertheless worth pursuing the role of technological innovation in the formation of the postmodern time sense. Certainly, the most significant changes in the last thirty years have taken place in transportation and communications – especially telecommunications and information technologies – sectors that have developed at a rate unprecedented in the history of Western technology, increasing services and drastically reducing prices. Innovations in these areas and, in particular, the fusion of computers and telecommunications have foregrounded mainly two temporal values: simultaneity and instantaneity.[21] In the realm of business, the introduction of new devices such as telex, fax, electronic mail and, in general, computerized bookkeeping and communication have created a global space in which information can be circulated among physically remote places such as New York, London, Tokyo or Melbourne virtually without any temporal delay. As a consequence, the interdependence of the net has increased to such an extent that changes or crises immediately translate to the network as a whole rather

and their organizational structure, see also the essays in Michael S. Scott Morton, ed., *The Corporation of the 1990s: Information Technology and Organizational Transformation* (New York: Oxford University Press, 1991).

[20] J. David Bolter makes a similar point in *Turing's Man: Western Culture in the Computer Age* (Chapel Hill: University of North Carolina Press, 1984): "Did the Europeans invent weight-driven clocks because of their desire to know the precise hour, or did the clocks, once invented, change their way of scheduling business and social activities? The answer is likely to be yes to both questions. Some cultural value must have driven the Europeans to perfect a device that no other culture had cared much about. Yet once the new technology was called forth, it proceeded with its own relentless logic and eventually helped to reorder the values of the whole culture. Did we invent computers because we needed very fast calculators, or did the calculators suggest to us the importance of solving problems that require such speed? In either case, our appreciation and our evaluation of the passage of time is changing in the computer age" (100).

[21] Barbara Adam, "Modern Times: The Technology Connection and Its Implications for Social Theory," *Time and Society* 1 (1992): 177, and *Timewatch: The Social Analysis of Time* (Cambridge: Polity Press, 1995): 114.

than remaining within a particular local environment.[22] Although this change of pace may be particularly perceptible in the international centers of finance and business, it is also affecting a steadily growing number of employees in the industrialized nations, and, of course, the average consumer, who increasingly relies on computerized systems of banking, shopping, health, entertainment, information and other services.[23] Over the last two or three decades, individuals have therefore become, consciously or unconsciously, more and more involved in global networks of information and communication that they have no real possibility to survey or comprehend, let alone control.[24]

But whereas devices such as the fax machine or the computer may relate individuals to these networks mainly during their working hours, global simultaneity has also taken a firm hold on private life through another recent technological revolution: satellite television. B. Taylor characterizes television as " 'the first cultural medium in the whole of history to present the artistic achievements of the past as a stitched-together collage of equi-important and simultaneously existing phenomena, largely divorced from geography and material history and transported to the living rooms and studios of the West in a more or less uninterrupted flow'."[25] The contemporary television viewer's routine procedure of "flipping through the channels" juxtaposes radically disjunct times and spaces in visual simultaneity, creating a " 'perception of history as an endless reserve of equal events'."[26] Twenty-four-hour news and weather channels ensure that even minor changes in the international political, economic or meteorological climate are immediately made available to a TV audience that, in terms of sheer numbers and dispersion, far

---

[22] Donald G. Janelle, "Global Interdependence and Its Consequences," *Collapsing Space and Time: Geographical Aspects of Communication and Information*, ed. Stanley D. Brunn and Thomas R. Leinbach (London: Harper Collins, 1991), 49ff; Adam, "Modern Times," 177 and *Timewatch*, 113; Dicken, *Global Shift*, 110; Malone and Rockart, "Computers," 98.

[23] Dicken, *Global Shift*, 114.

[24] In his interpretation of the architectural lay-out of the Los Angeles Bonaventure Hotel in *Postmodernism*, Fredric Jameson has shown how this difficulty of "cognitive mapping" is re-created in contemporary art: in this case, in the labyrinthine design of a supposedly functional building (39–44). On global networks of communication, see Linda M. Harasim, ed., *Global Networks: Computers and International Communication* (Cambridge, MA: MIT Press, 1993).

[25] Quoted in Harvey, *Condition of Postmodernity*, 61.

[26] B. Taylor, quoted *ibid.*, 61. See also Adam, *Timewatch*, 115.

exceeds that reached through computer networks so far: global simultaneity affects both the professional and the private lives of individuals not exclusively in the industrialized nations, but even in a fair number of those cultures where print has not reached all members of society.[27] The paradox of contemporary vision technology, then, is that although it allows the viewers an infinitely more varied and detailed access to places and times the overwhelming majority of which they will never see with their own eyes, it also blurs any sense of genuine distinction or authentic historicity precisely through the detail and apparent realism of its presentation.

The simultaneity of disparate geographical spaces and historical periods in the virtual space of the TV screen has been accompanied by another and closely related feature of the postmodern experience of temporality: the expectation of and desire for instant availability. Already in 1970, Alvin Toffler pointed out the close relation of instant availability and disposability in what he referred to as the "throw-away society."[28] The 1990s have continued this trend, but the demand for instant access has now expanded from products to services. Television itself may again serve as one of the most prominent examples here, since twenty-four-hour programming is now common in almost all Western countries. Technological devices such as the microwave oven, the automatic bank-teller or electronic mail and bulletin boards, in their turn, are sizable expressions of the desire for instantaneity, as are services such as one-hour photo development, twenty-four-hour grocery shopping or toll-free numbers for instant phone-order purchases. All these recent introductions into the service and product market bear witness to the increased demand for quick access to goods and services, independent of daily or weekly business cycles and opening hours.[29]

Many of these new services are facilitated by the large-scale use of the device that is likely to have the most far-reaching impact on Western culture now and in the future – the computer. Through the computer's ability to make available to the user huge amounts of information in often just fractions of seconds,

---

[27] See Dicken, *Global Shift*, 113–14.

[28] Toffler, *Future Shock*, 47–67.

[29] Malone and Rockart, "Computers," 98; Alvin Toffler, *The Third Wave* (New York: Bantam, 1981), 245–54.

instant access to products, services or data has become available in a wide range of areas, from ordering replacement parts for electric household devices or scheduling an express-mail pick-up to checking a credit card balance, reserving a flight ticket or retrieving bibliographic information. It is also beginning to affect the domain of private or semi-private interaction between individuals and groups through electronic mail and bulletin boards, which let even individuals in different continents communicate with each other and transfer large and complex amounts of information practically without time delay.[30] Through this acceleration of normal temporality, computer use immerses the individual in a "hyper-present" of sorts, a hyper-intensified immediacy that focuses the user's attention on a rapid succession of micro-events and thereby makes it more difficult to envision even the short-term past or future. Computer hardware is therefore the most advanced and most conspicuous manifestation of a culture many of whose recent developments contribute to focusing the attention of individuals and groups on the present understood as a narrowly defined time period unhinged from past causes and future extensions or effects.

Most theorists who have analyzed these phenomena and their relation to contemporary society agree that their cumulative effect has been to shorten time horizons "to the point where the present is all there is."[31] Long-term historical coherence becomes harder and harder to envision, whereas the present forces itself increasingly on the attention of individuals and societies.[32] As Paul Virilio argues, "the new technological time has no relation to any calendar of events nor to any collective memory. It is pure computer time, and as such helps construct a permanent present, an unbounded, timeless intensity,"[33] an observation

---

[30] Malone and Rockart, "Computers," 98.

[31] Harvey, *Condition of Postmodernity*, 240.

[32] Lorenzo C. Simpson offers a different interpretation of the connection between time and technology in his *Technology, Time, and the Conversations of Modernity* (New York: Routledge, 1995), arguing that technology is principally a means of planning and controlling the future; to this technological "domestication" of time he opposes Kierkegaardian "repetition" as a mode of experience which accepts time as flux and does not attempt to subdue it. I would argue that this assessment seriously underestimates the extent to which technology's very success in compressing time limits its ability to control the future.

[33] Virilio, *Lost Dimension*, 15. A somewhat different view is proposed by Jean Baudrillard in *The Illusion of the End* (trans. Chris Turner [Stanford: Stanford

which for him implies the obsolescence of the very notion of physical dimension. But evaluations of this new time experience differ widely: whereas some analysts perceive the demise of history as a serious threat to any possibility of political language and action, others see it as a liberation from one of the most totalizing and logocentric concepts of Western philosophy. Fredric Jameson's analysis, representative of the first viewpoint, focuses on the subject's loss of "its capacity actively to extend its pro-tensions and re-tensions across the temporal manifold and to organize its past and future into coherent experience,"[34] which he reads as a pathological symptom with structural affinities to schizophrenia. Not only is the present experienced as cut off from succession in time, but it is lived as a state of heightened perception, since

the breakdown of temporality suddenly releases this present of time from all the activities and intentionalities that might focus it and make it a space of praxis; thereby isolated, that present suddenly engulfs the subject with undescribable vividness, a materiality of perception properly overwhelming, which effectively dramatizes the power of the material – or better still, the literal – signifier in isolation. This present of the world or material signifier comes before the subject with heightened intensity, bearing a mysterious charge of affect, here described in the negative terms of anxiety and loss of reality, but which one could just as well imagine in the positive terms of euphoria, a high, an intoxicatory or hallucinogenic intensity.[35]

Jameson deplores this state of affairs as one which paralyzes the subject in the present without any possibility for meaningful social and political language and action, and which leads to art forms one of whose main features is pastiche, the aleatory combination of fragments from disparate historical moments without any sense of their historicity. Postmodernist culture manifests "an omnipresent and indiscriminate appetite for dead styles and fashions; indeed, for all the styles and fashions of a

University Press, 1994]), where he suggests in his typical hyperbolic and self-cancelling fashion that history has disappeared both because of acceleration (". . . the acceleration of modernity, of technology of events and media, of all exchanges – economic, political and sexual – has propelled us to 'escape velocity', with the result that we have flown free of the referential sphere of the real and of history") and because of the deceleration that results from the inertia of the "silent majorities" (1 and 3–4).

[34] Jameson, *Postmodernism*, 25.

[35] *Ibid.*, 27–28.

dead past":[36] in other words, it practices a "random cannibaliz-
ation of all the styles of the past"[37] which erases critical distance
to the present as well as to other historical periods. Since this
distance is a prerequisite for political intentionality, Jameson
cannot but deplore its loss as one which makes revolutionary
change in the "late capitalist" societies of the West practically
inconceivable.

But not all critics see the demise of history as a socio-political
problem. Elizabeth Ermarth, for example, considers it a cultural
achievement that liberates the individual. Her argument is based
not so much on temporal experience as it is affected by the
material environment, but as it has been constituted by the
Western philosophical tradition. In *Sequel to History*, she argues
that as a "realistic" or "representational" device,

historical time [is] a convention that belongs to a major, generally
unexamined article of cultural faith . . . : the belief in a temporal medium
that is neutral and homogeneous and that, consequently, makes possible
those mutually informative measurements between one historical
moment and another that support most forms of knowledge current in
the West and that we customarily call "science." History has become a
commanding metanarrative, perhaps *the* metanarrative in Western discourse.[38]

According to Ermarth, postmodern culture discards the idea that
time is a medium or container "in" which events occur and
replaces it with "rhythmic" time, which is co-extensive with and
inseparable from the individual event. Neither large-scale narrative sequence nor, indeed, coherent individual identities can be
envisioned in this kind of temporality. Although Ermarth fails to
explore any of the serious theoretical problems that arise in this
analysis of time and subjectivity, her account does capture something essential about the contemporary experience of time: the
sense that time is inherent in the event rather than an abstract
dimension surrounding it, and that it can only be described and
defined by entering into the event's internal structure; in other
words, it has become difficult to abstract any notion such as

---

[36] *Ibid.*, 286.
[37] *Ibid.*, 18.
[38] Elizabeth Deeds Ermarth, *Sequel to History: Postmodernism and the Crisis of
Representational Time* (Princeton: Princeton University Press, 1992), 20; original
emphasis.

"history," "progress" or "entropy" from temporal phenomena that seem to be only randomly related to each other.

In spite of their fundamentally different judgments on the implications of the crisis of historicity, Jameson and Ermarth coincide in emphasizing the overwhelming importance of the present in the contemporary time sense, and in pointing out the difficulties of describing more long-term temporal patterns. Other theorists concur with the basic thrust of this analysis. Helga Nowotny, for example, claims that the concept of the "future" has been replaced in the second half of the twentieth century by that of an "extended present." Since the belief in inevitable and steady progress no longer seems convincing, the future cannot function any longer as the screen for the projection of wish fulfillments; neither can it be used as the space to which existential fears are relegated, because long-term problems increasingly manifest themselves in the present. The notion of an "extended present," therefore, makes a longer time period available for decision-making and problem-solving.[39] Katherine Hayles similarly argues that it has become more and more difficult for Western societies to project a viable long-term future for themselves:

Since the 1960s, the consensus that there is a fixed end point has been eroded by our growing sense that the future is already used up before it arrives. . . . The rhythm of our century seemed predictable. World War I at the second decade; World War II at the fourth decade; World War III at the sixth decade, during which the world as we know it comes to an end. But somehow it did not happen when it was supposed to. By the ninth decade, we cannot help suspecting that maybe it happened after all and we failed to notice. Consequently time splits into a false future in which we all live and a true future that by virtue of being true does not have us in it.[40]

As I will argue later, this notion of a split between alternative temporalities is central to the narrative organization of postmodern novels. Hayles points out that as a consequence of this split present and future, there arises "a feeling that time itself has ceased to be a useful concept around which to organize experi-

[39] Helga Nowotny, *Eigenzeit: Entstehung und Strukturierung eines Zeitgefühls*, 2nd edn (Frankfurt: Suhrkamp, 1989), 47–76, esp. 51–54.
[40] N. Katherine Hayles, *Chaos Bound: Orderly Disorder in Contemporary Literature and Science* (Ithaca: Cornell University Press, 1990), 279–80.

ence. . . . if we cannot envision ourselves in the future without imagining that it has undergone a phase change into a different kind of space . . . then time is not just denatured. It is obsolete."[41]

Theoretical approaches to the crisis of historicity in Western culture, then, differ widely in the analysis they propose (from political standstill to technological and cultural speed-up) as well as in their assessment of its implications (from the political paralysis of the subject to its liberation); in spite of these fundamental differences, however, all of them articulate the sense that in the political, social, cultural and technological realms, time can no longer be understood in terms of the parameters that the modernization processes of the last two centuries have bequeathed to us. All emphasize the contemporary focus on a present that is increasingly conceived as taking over both past and future, and the difficulty of envisioning temporal patterns that transcend the present and allow the observer to view it from a distance. Conventional philosophies of history no longer carry the force of persuasion they did prior to the 1960s and have therefore ceased to offer viable options for such a long-term perspective; indeed, the very possibility of thinking and writing historically has come into question.

But the differences between these theories of the postmodern are as striking as their convergences. If the divergent ideological perspectives and the very different types of evidence and reasoning that they propose nevertheless seem to lead inexorably to the same conclusion, one cannot but suspect that the detail of each theory may be overall less important than the underlying willingness and indeed urge on all sides of the political and theoretical spectrum to declare conventional and high-modernist modes of reasoning about time inadequate and outdated. In some cases, this urge expresses itself in a clear tendency toward the hyperbolic: Jameson's association of the postmodern time sense with schizophrenia, for instance, as well as Ermarth's indiscriminate celebration of "rhythmic time" provide illuminating metaphors rather than descriptions that ask to be taken literally. Indeed, the term "posthistory" itself can in a certain sense be understood as hyperbole, since it evokes the sense of an ending, of cataclysm, even though the historical perspective it refers to

---

[41] *Ibid.*, 281.

would deny the relevance of endings. That theories of postmodern temporality at times indulge in hyperbole, however,
does not imply that they should not be taken seriously. On the
contrary, their rhetoric is itself an important indication that
conventional theoretical language seems inadequate to the task of
articulating the new time sense, and that the new temporal
realities do not seem to fit readily into the vocabulary that non-
technical language puts at the critic's disposal. The proliferation
of theoretically and politically widely divergent attempts in
philosophy, history, cultural and literary theory to account for
the postmodern sense of time and history is therefore itself clear
evidence that the culture of time in the late twentieth century has
evolved faster than the theoretical reasoning which has accompanied it, and which makes up through hyperbole for its own
perceived shortfalls of language.

One would expect such shortfalls of language and the temporal problems they arise from to resonate in reflections on
narrative form and the ways in which it could meet the
challenge of postmodern culture. And indeed, the sense that
time in its conventional definition no longer provides a meaningful way of organizing narrative has been articulated explicitly
by two of the writers who have become prominent sources of
influence on fiction after World War II: Argentinean short-story
writer Jorge Luis Borges and French *nouveau romancier* Alain
Robbe-Grillet. Jorge Luis Borges' essay, "Nueva refutación del
tiempo" (New Refutation of Time), is formulated as a playful
philosophical argument: extrapolating from the idealism of
Berkeley and Hume, Borges argues that if matter, spirit and
space have no reality except as they exist in the mind of the one
who perceives, there are no grounds for claiming that time exists
beyond each individual instant of perception, and hence no
reason to attribute continuity over time to either matter, spirit or
space. Therefore, Borges concludes, time itself cannot be claimed
to exist: "Cada instante es autónomo. . . . Me dicen que el
presente, el *specious present* de los psicólogos, dura entre unos
segundos y una minúscula fracción de segundo; eso dura la
historia del universo. Mejor dicho, no hay esa historia, como no
hay la vida de un hombre . . . cada momento que vivimos existe,
no su imaginario conjunto" (Each instant is autonomous. . . . I
am told that the present, the *specious present* of the psychologists,

31

lasts from a few seconds to a minuscule fraction of a second; so does the history of the universe. In other words, there is no such history, just as there isn't the life of a man . . . each moment we experience exists, but not their imaginary combination).[42] Borges himself admits that he does not believe in this argument, but insists that it haunts him with the force of absolute dogma. In the end, he proposes a paradox that mediates between the existence of a temporal universe and the existence of the perceiver: "El tiempo es un río que me arrebata, pero yo soy el río"[43] (Time is a river which sweeps me along, but I am the river). This concern with the paradoxes of time, as Borges himself indicates, underlies many of his short stories; "Nueva refutación del tiempo" attempts to lay the theoretical foundation for the ideas these texts revolve around, to formulate philosophically (if only tongue-in-cheek) the argument that would account for their turn away from narrative temporality as a medium of continuity and coherence. We may be as disinclined as Borges himself to accept the idealist argument: the concern with the possibility and shape of narrative in the absence of conventional time remains.

Alain Robbe-Grillet, in what has become one of the best-known programmatic characterizations of the *nouveau roman* in particular and the post-war novel in general, observes that "dans le récit moderne, on dirait que le temps se trouve coupé de sa temporalité. Il ne coule plus. Il n'accomplit plus rien. . . . L'instant nie la continuité" (In modern narrative, it seems as if time is cut off from its temporality. It no longer passes. It no longer achieves anything. . . . The moment denies continuity).[44] There is no longer a "story" or "history" external to the written text that can be reconstructed from it, and hence questions of chronology, of "clocks and calendars," have become irrelevant: the only duration is that of the text itself. Therefore, Robbe-Grillet insists, it is erroneous to claim that since the novels of Proust and Faulkner, time has become the main character and agent of fiction. Time forms part of the referential illusion generated by conventional

[42] Jorge Luis Borges, "Nueva refutación del tiempo," *Otras Inquisiciones*, 3rd edn (Madrid: Alianza, 1981), 176; original emphasis.

[43] *Ibid.*, 187.

[44] Alain Robbe-Grillet, *Pour un nouveau roman* (Paris: Minuit, 1963), 133.

narrative, and such illusions are what the most advanced novels work to undermine.[45]

I will pursue the question of what kind of narrative has been generated by these and similar reflections on the novel in more detail later. But Robbe-Grillet's allusion to Proust and Faulkner already hints at a complex set of questions regarding the relationship between contemporary analyses of the crisis of narrative and historicity, and similar claims that were voiced in the early twentieth century.

2. Soft clocks

If we define the concern over the diminished relevance of temporality and historicity to contemporary experience as one of the central features of postmodernist culture, the question arises how this concern relates to the intense interest in questions of time in the early twentieth century. The late nineteenth and early twentieth centuries, as many historians and sociologists have pointed out, already brought about a wave of scientific and technological innovations and a revolution in the awareness of space and time that not only rival those of the last thirty years but indeed might be argued to outweigh them in importance.

In the first decades of the twentieth century, opposing tendencies in the organization and perception of time came to confront each other. Most visibly, efforts to mechanize and standardize time that had been underway since the beginning of the industrial era reached a historical climax:[46] Frederick W. Taylor's studies of work processes, begun in the 1880s and completed in 1911 with

---

[45] Roland Barthes echoed this rejection of time only a few years after the publication of *Pour un nouveau roman* in his seminal narratological essay, "An Introduction to the Structural Analysis of Narrative" (first published in French in 1966): "From the point of view of narrative, what we call time does not exist, or at least it only exists functionally, as an element of a semiotic system: time does not belong to discourse proper, but to the referent. Both narrative and language can only refer to semiological time; 'true' time is only a referential illusion" (trans. Lionel Duisit, *New Literary History* 6 [1975]: 252).

[46] For a by now classical account of the temporal changes brought about by industrialization, see E. P. Thompson's "Time, Work-Discipline, and Industrial Capitalism," *Past & Present* 38 (December, 1967): 56–97. See also Nigel Thrift, "The Making of a Capitalist Time Consciousness," *The Sociology of Time*, ed. John Hassard (Houndmills: Macmillan, 1990), 112–20; and Chris Nyland, "Capitalism and the History of Work-time Thought," *The Sociology of Time*, 130–51.

the publication of *The Principles of Scientific Management*, laid out a plan for the rationalization and acceleration of industrial work by splitting it into small components of motion and determining the standard time for each.[47] Henry Ford's introduction of the assembly-line into his Highland Park car factory in 1913 translated some of these suggestions into a new mode of production that was to revolutionize Western economies and societies. Simultaneously, the development of electric communication devices such as the telephone, telegraph and the radio led for the first time in history to the disjunction of spatial from temporal distance,[48] and therefore to the necessity of coordinating the local times of far-removed regions in a standardized network of global simultaneity. From the establishment of Greenwich as the zero meridian in 1884 to the creation of a global temporal network based on signals sent from the Eiffel Tower in 1913, the modernist period saw a whole series of national and international measures designed to ensure a uniform time frame for the nation and the world.[49] Taken together, these innovations led to a first wave of "time-space compression" in the twentieth century that is arguably at least as important as the one that has occurred since the 1960s.[50]

The acceleration of pace that this time-space compression brought with it prompted some members of the high-modernist avant-garde to proclaim the end of time in terms that at first sight look similar to pronouncements of the postmodernists. "Time and Space died yesterday. We already live in the absolute, because we have created eternal, omnipresent speed," Marinetti declared in "The Founding and Manifesto of Futurism" in 1909.[51] But the resemblance remains superficial, since Marinetti's statement is not meant so much to deny time *per se* as a relevant

---

[47] Stephen Kern, *The Culture of Time and Space 1880–1918* (Cambridge, MA: Harvard University Press, 1983), 92 and 115–16. On the standardization of time as a general feature of historical modernization processes and the ensuing dissociation of time from space, see also Anthony Giddens, *The Consequences of Modernity* (Stanford: Stanford University Press, 1990), 17–21.

[48] See Dicken, *Global Shift*, 107.

[49] Kern, *Culture*, 12–14; Nowotny, *Eigenzeit*, 20–45; Eviatar Zerubavel, "The Standardization of Time: A Sociohistorical Perspective," *American Journal of Sociology* 88 (1982): 4–17; Nigel Thrift, "Capitalist Time Consciousness," 120–28.

[50] See Harvey, *Condition of Postmodernity*, 260–83.

[51] *Let's Murder the Moonshine: Selected Writings*, ed. and trans. R. W. Flint (Los Angeles: Sun & Moon Classics, 1991), 49.

category of human experience, but to reject tradition and the past as relevant to the present. The *antipassatismo* of Italian futurism was the most violent articulation of this rejection in the high-modernist period; but, as Renato Poggioli has pointed out, the rhetoric of rupture with the past is a common feature of most artistic avant-garde movements, even those that chose to express themselves in much less inflammatory language than the futurists.[52] And the futurists themselves showed intense interest in the possibilities and difficulties of representing time in the visual work of art, as Antonio Bragaglia's "photodynamism," sculptures such as Umberto Boccioni's *Development of a Bottle in Space* or paintings such as Boccioni's *Dynamism of a Cyclist* and Giacomo Balla's *Flight of a Swallow*, among others, reveal very clearly. The modernist rhetoric of temporal rupture, then, differs from the postmodernist one in that it questions and rejects the past, but not the notion of time in itself. That is, it does not imply any doubt about the relevance of temporality for the organization of human experience, whereas this doubt is precisely what informs the postmodernist questioning of time. Furthermore, the modernist break with time does not imply any systematic skepticism toward the future, which on the contrary serves as the space into which the aspirations of the avant-garde are projected, whereas the future does become difficult or impossible to envision in postmodernist reflections on time.

Another major difference emerges when we consider that the high-modernist "time-space compression" did not lead most philosophers, artists and writers to either the wholesale rejection of the past or the celebration of technological progress that was typical of the futurist movement. Rather, the increased mechanization and standardization of time in the public sphere was confronted in the cultural realm with a sustained exploration of the workings of time in human consciousness and memory, which was often envisioned as antithetical to the rationality of machine and clock time. Sigmund Freud's psychoanalysis,

[52] Renato Poggioli, *The Theory of the Avant-Garde*, trans. Gerald Fitzgerald (Cambridge, MA: Harvard University Press, 1968), 52–56. Even as moderate a vanguardist as Virginia Woolf, for example, made claims such as that "on or about December, 1910, human character changed" ("Mr. Bennett and Mrs. Brown," *The Captain's Death Bed and Other Essays* [San Diego: Harcourt Brace Jovanovich, 1950], 96).

William James' reflections on time and consciousness, and Henri Bergson's philosophy of *durée* all showed the ways in which psychological or "organic" temporality deviates from the linearity of mechanical and industrial time. The experience of time remained one of the dominant issues of philosophy in Europe up until the 1940s, although it was not always analyzed in psychological terms. But in its association with such notions as *consciousness*, *being* or *existence*, philosophical reflection on time tended to continue to focus on the realm of the pre-social or non-social. Edmund Husserl's explorations of internal time-consciousness (culminating in the *Vorlesungen zur Phänomenologie des inneren Zeitbewußtseins*, 1928) (Lectures on the Phenomenology of Internal Time-Consciousness), for example, proceeded by way of a phenomenological reduction that systematically excluded from consideration any empirical factors, and hence any influences from the social and historical domain to which the perception of time might be subject. Heidegger's *Sein und Zeit* (1927) (Being and Time) focused the analysis of time on the problem of mortality, and thereby on a factor that crucially shapes the time experience of the individual, but not necessarily that of an entire society or culture. Heidegger's claim that authenticity of being can only be attained through conscious confrontation with the fact of death was echoed later in Sartre's concern over the "bad faith" of any existence that does not recognize the absurdity of its being condemned to death (*L'être et le néant*, 1943) (Being and Nothingness). If the mechanization and standardization of public time reached a historic peak in the first decades of the twentieth century, then, it was confronted in the cultural realm by an intense interest in the nature and working of private temporality.

This interest also characterizes many of the major works of art and literature of the period. In the modernist novel, the temporal operations of the human mind and its potential conflicts with the linearity of public time became one of the most persistently recurring topics, as the novels of Proust, Mann, Joyce, Svevo, Woolf, Faulkner, Stein and many others testify. Similarly, the cyclical or spiral patterns of history and the recurrence of archetypes that many modernist texts foreground are designed to resist the linearity and mechanicity of standardized time. But the opposition to mechanical temporality found its perhaps most striking representation in the soft clocks that frequently appear in the paintings of Salvador Dalí. Apparently consisting of a viscous material of uncertain nature, Dalí's clocks melt over branches and edges of furniture into improbable oblong and three-dimensionally curved shapes that make any regular movement of the hands inconceivable. Paintings such as *The Persistence of Memory*, *Catalan Bread* and *Surrealist Poster* all feature these warped clock faces that symbolize the distortion of mechanic temporality in the workings of human consciousness and memory. Dalí's clocks cannot operate independently of their surroundings, as normal clocks are expected to do; they seem elastic, malleable, and adapt to the shape of the objects that they come in contact with: nothing could make clearer that there is no inflexible, universal standard of time in Dalí's universe. In some paintings, ants gather on the metallic hulls of old-fashioned pocket-watches as if they were decaying residues of organic matter, in yet another visual hint that the apparent solidity of time is susceptible to organic assimilation and corruption. The surprising combination of a mechanical device made out of durable materials with signs of viscosity and decay have justifiably made Dalí's clocks the most prominent icons of the pervasive high-modernist confrontation of mechanized, standardized public time with the unpredictable, non-linear meanderings of private temporality.

This conflict arguably no longer occupies center stage in contemporary time awareness. Postmodernist culture and technology have systematically problematized the distinction between the public and the private not only through the emergence of new media and social realms such as television and the Internet, but also through sustained analyses of how this distinction can work not to separate factually different social domains, but to perpetuate specific ideologies.[53] Public time no longer seems so much threatening as threatened, a parameter that can no longer be envisioned without difficulty. If one traces the development from the high-modernist to the postmodernist culture of time, therefore, one finds that two central issues are envisioned in fundamentally different ways: although both mod-

---

[53] Catherine Gallagher illustrates this when she describes how feminist concerns were initially rejected even within leftist movements because they supposedly belonged to the realm of the personal and not the political ("Marxism and the New Historicism," *The New Historicism*, ed. H. Aram Veeser [New York: Routledge, 1989], 42).

ernism and postmodernism foreground breaks or schisms in time, high modernism questions mainly the relevance and accessibility of the past, whereas postmodernism challenges the notion of time as such; and high modernism emphasizes the difference between private and public temporality, whereas both become precarious categories in postmodernist awareness.

3. From the Big Bang to nanoseconds: time scales and narrative coherence

If the conflict between mechanic and organic, public and private temporality constitutes one of the major concerns of culture and art in the first decades of the twentieth century, the modernist reflection on time can nevertheless not simply be reduced to this conflict. Other complications emerge when one considers the contribution of the natural sciences to the reconceptualization of time in the modernist period. Already in the nineteenth century, geology and evolution theory opened up the prospect that our planet and organic life had existed for time periods that lie beyond human experienceability and existential if not intellectual comprehension, a discovery which was not accepted without great resistance and intense debate even among scientists. Following the discovery of radioactivity in the early twentieth century, the age of the planet rose to hundreds of millions of years in scientists' estimation.[54] And in the late 1920s, Hubble's discovery of a universal redshift in the color spectrum of all observable galaxies first suggested that the universe itself is continuously expanding, and that it might be possible to estimate its age through the observation of this expansion. All of these discoveries began to introduce a time dimension into modernist cultural awareness that extended far beyond human history in its entirety.

If high-modernist society began to think in terms of time scales large beyond the reach of common-sense comprehension, the time of the unimaginably small equally came to form part of its understanding of the world. The discovery of subatomic particles and the laws of quantum mechanics not only brought about the recognition that substances which appear solid to human percep-

[54] Kern, *Culture*, 37–38.

tion are in reality made up of combinations of inconceivably small particles moving at great speeds, they also revealed that the very mechanisms of observation and measurement which function at the human scale do not apply in the same way to the subatomic world of electrons, protons and neutrons. The idea that at a certain level of scale, physical laws of cause and effect give way to statistical probabilities is one that has a profoundly destabilizing impact on the understanding of time. Quantum mechanics imposes strict limits on what "common-sense reasoning" can explain even in the supposedly "rational" world of physics: if we cannot simultaneously determine the position and the acceleration of an electron with accuracy, our possibilities for analyzing its movement over time are severely constrained. This constraint, however, does not apply to objects and movements at a naturally perceptible, everyday scale. Time, therefore, does not operate independently of the scale of the observed events, and this makes it impossible to think of it as a unified, homogeneous and neutral medium.

Although it is quite true that scientific advances such as relativity theory and quantum mechanics were much less accessible to the general population than technological inventions such as the automobile and the telephone, they nevertheless gained enough of a non-specialist audience that their impact on the cultural imagination should form part of an assessment of modernist temporal awareness. In view of these advances, the central problem for the modernist time sense is not just the confrontation of standardized public time with the unpredictabilities of personal, organic time, but more generally the realization that there is no single concept of time by means of which one can adequately account for the different layers of reality that make up the world. Neither the metaphor of the machine nor that of organic growth suffices any longer to unify the flow of time. The rift between the time of public institutions and that of the individual psyche forms part of this problem, but also the discovery that parts of the physical world operate according to temporal laws that run counter to what we intuit as "embodied" beings, as well as the apparent contradiction between the universality of entropic decay and the growing complexity of biological forms.

This beginning break-up of the common-sense unity of time

foreshadows to some extent the more radical "chronoschisms" we find in the postmodern era. But the changes which occurred in the modernist period nevertheless differ qualitatively from those we have witnessed in the last three or four decades. Although they prompt the investigation and redefinition of human time, they by no means invalidate it as the standard of perception and measurement. The functioning of the telephone or the radio may be difficult to understand for the lay person, but these devices at least seem to operate at human speed and to transmit human voices. Entropy and evolution may involve unimaginably large time scales where the development of the universe or the current constellation of species is concerned, but as principles they can be verified by bare-eye observation: the dissolution of milk in a cup of coffee, for example, or the study of morphological deviations in animal and plant species in geographically isolated habitats. Rather than devaluing the human scale of observation, then, the modernist culture of technology and science encourages the investigation of how human perceptive abilities and temporal sensibility relate to these alternative, newly discovered time dimensions. This may be one of the cultural reasons for the obsessive interest of a considerable number of high-modernist artists and writers in the individual's experience of time.

In the last three or four decades, however, the sense of the incommensurability of different time scales has been exacerbated to the point where human time seems dwarfed in importance compared to the realm of the very large and the extremely small. Nowadays, in graphical representations of the age of the Earth, human life as a species typically occupies the last minute on a twelve-hour clock face or the last fraction of an inch on a chronological meter: we have learned to accept as routine the idea that human life and consciousness are an extremely recent development at a planetary, let alone at a cosmic scale. In the meantime, the planetary and cosmic time scales themselves have extended to dimensions far beyond what was assumed earlier in the century, due to research in physical cosmology, which has become established as a serious branch of research in physics only in the last thirty years. After its beginnings in the late 1920s, the theory of the gradual expansion of the universe was elaborated theoretically in the 1940s by George Gamow, Ralph Alpher and Robert Herman, who first suggested a "big-bang" beginning of the universe. But during those years, research into the early stages of the universe was still considered a somewhat disreputable occupation for a physicist.[55] The impulse for its integration into the mainstream of the physical sciences did not come until the mid-1960s, with the discovery of the uniform microwave radiation background by Penzias and Wilson. This discovery gave empirical support to the theory of an initial "big bang" and led to the formulation of current theories of cosmological evolution. Not only do these theories take for granted the idea – quite innovative in the history of Western science – that the universe we live in is itself an object that evolves over time; they also indicate that this universe is approximately fifteen to twenty billion years old, a figure that far exceeds any previous estimates.

These discoveries might have remained a matter of specialization in a rather arcane branch of science. But particularly in the last ten to fifteen years, the opposite has been the case: popular scientific accounts of the origin of the universe have flooded the book market, from Steven Weinberg's *The First Three Minutes* (1977), Barrow and Silk's *The Left Hand of Creation* (1983), Heinz Pagels' *Perfect Symmetry* (1985), John Gribbin's *In Search of the Big Bang* (1986) to Stephen Hawking's best-selling *A Brief History of Time* (1988) and David Layzer's *Cosmogenesis* (1990). New discoveries in the field such as photographs of starlight which has traveled for about fifteen to twenty billion years and hence comes to human observation quite literally from the "beginning of time" are being reported and commented on in detail in newspapers and the daily news shows of all major American TV channels. But maybe not even televised discussions among scientists on our cosmological origins and future are as revealing as a scene from Woody Allen's popular film comedy *Annie Hall*. In a flashback which shows the adult protagonist as a neurotic eight- or nine-year-old, the boy is asked by a doctor for the reason of his depression; in a blank, toneless voice the child answers, "The universe is expanding!" Justly one of the most famous moments of the movie, this scene indicates how much a basic knowledge of

---

[55] Steven Weinberg, *The First Three Minutes: A Modern View of the Origin of the Universe*, updated edn (n.p.: Basic, 1988), 4, 122–32.

cosmological theories has come to form part of the common awareness if not of children, at least of the average film audience.

But of course, the joke lies not mainly in the fact that a nine-year-old boy would know about such theories; rather, it relies on the conceptual collapse of two radically incompatible time scales, the human and the cosmological. A process such as the expansion of the universe, which extends over tens of billions of years, could have no conceivable immediate effect on the history of humanity, let alone on that of a single individual and least of all on that of a young boy. That a nine-year-old would have anxiety attacks over it is comical and yet reveals precisely the crack of synchronicity in the postmodern time consciousness: our image of the world now routinely includes a time scale that lies so far above human experience and all but mathematical manipulation that our time sense quite literally "falls apart" into different temporal scales which have a simultaneous reality and yet cannot be contemplated simultaneously. The point here lies not so much in the fact that scientific developments have made this insight possible – science has for a long time explored realities that are not intuitively compatible with everyday experience – but that these scientific findings have attained such broad dissemination in Western societies that they affect cultural awareness far beyond the domain of scientific research and teaching.

Subatomic physics continues to be less accessible to a general audience, and seems on the whole to have met with less public interest. Nevertheless, research in this area also has boomed since the 1960s with the discovery of an ever-increasing number of subatomic particles: quarks, mesons, hadrons, bosons and a whole series of other elements that make up the "subatomic zoo." Some such particles can only be scientifically observed inside supercolliders which generate elements with life spans of 10^{-6} or 10^{-8} seconds[56] – time spans so small that only mathematical operations can give them meaning. In biology, the sharp increase in genetic research in recent years in particular has

---

[56] Frank Wilczek and Betsy Devine, *Longing for the Harmonies: Themes and Variations from Modern Physics* (New York: Norton, 1987), 190; Cindy Schwarz, *A Tour of the Subatomic Zoo: A Guide to Particle Physics* (New York: American Institute of Physics, 1992), 40; Steven Weinberg, *The Discovery of Subatomic Particles* (New York: Freeman, 1983), 163–64.

fuelled popular interest in the potential impact of the smallest components of organic life on everyday human existence.[57]

John Barth has poignantly and concisely characterized this sense of disparate scales of time and causation which affect human life and yet are beyond its grasp in the first of his "Two Meditations," entitled "Niagara Falls," a phrase which should perhaps be understood to consist of a noun and a verb rather than two nouns:

She paused amid the kitchen to drink a glass of water; at that instant, losing a grip of fifty years, the next-room-ceiling-plaster crashed. Or he merely sat in an empty study, in March-day glare, listening to the universe rustle in his head, when suddenly the five-foot shelf let go. For ages the fault creeps secret through the rock; in a second, ledge and railings, tourists and turbines all thunder over Niagara. Which snowflake triggers the avalanche? A house explodes; a star. In your spouse, so apparently resigned, murder twitches like a fetus. At some trifling new assessment, all the colonies rebel.[58]

As Claude Richard has pointed out, the juxtaposition of "ages" and "a second," of a supernova and domestic disaster in this passage forcefully points up the intrusion of geological and cosmological time scales into everyday perception, just as the question "Which snowflake triggers the avalanche?" foregrounds the impossibility of applying everyday notions of causality to the realm of the microscopically small.[59] The temporal rhythms of events at different scales of magnitude and, therefore, causes and effects, have been pulled apart so radically in the world Barth's vignette sketches that everything has become surprising, pointless and accidental. No scheme or method of explanation seems applicable to a universe whose temporal and causal structures we have no access to, and hence even psychological and political processes appear unpredictable – disproportionate effects of invisible causes.

But without question, the most consequential irruption of

[57] Since this research is less relevant for the understanding of time, however, I will not discuss it here in greater detail.

[58] John Barth, *Lost in the Funhouse: Fiction for Print, Tape, Live Voice* (New York: Bantam, 1969), 101.

[59] Claude Richard, "Causality and Mimesis in Contemporary Fiction," *SubStance* 40 (1983): 89–92. I am grateful to David Damrosch for pointing out to me that the preposition "amid" in the first sentence signals a dislocation of spatial as well as temporal perception, since it seems to indicate a space that is either divided and multiple or in motion.

temporal microstructures into Western (and increasingly, non-Western) societies has been brought about by the spread of computer technology, generating a completely new social environment that has come to be called the "nanosecond culture." A nanosecond (a billionth of a second) is the normal rhythm at which a device in the computer's microprocessor sends the electronic pulses that time and synchronize the execution of instructions throughout the system. Although this device is commonly referred to as a "clock," it is obviously quite different from the mechanical clock we have traditionally associated with the industrial age and its machines. Its functioning is no longer based on an abstraction and regularization of natural temporal cycles such as the day, as is the case with conventional twelve- or twenty-four-hour clocks, but an electronic pulsation unrelated to any naturally occurring processes.[60] The mechanical clock already presided over an age that increasingly alienated humans from natural temporal cycles and imposed a time frame shaped by the necessity of machines, production and consumption; nevertheless, this mechanical temporality is perceptible and experienceable in human awareness. Electronic time is not: events in a computer system take place far below the threshold of human temporal perception and consciousness.[61] In a passage frequently mentioned in discussions of the emerging computer culture, Tracy Kidder quotes the words of an engineer whose awareness has adapted to this new time frame:

The analyzers could . . . take several different kinds of snapshots, as it were, of the signals coming and going. . . . When the clock inside [the computers] ticked, every 220 nanoseconds – every 220 billionths of a second, that is – the analyzer would take a picture. . .

"It's funny," [the engineer] said, "I feel very comfortable talking in nanoseconds. I sit at one of these analyzers and nanoseconds are *wide*. I mean, you can see them go by. 'Jesus,' I say, 'that signal takes twelve nanoseconds to get from there to there.' Those are real big things to me when I'm building a computer. Yet when I think about it, how much longer it takes to snap your fingers, I've lost track of what a nanosecond really means . . ."[62]

---

[60] Bolter, *Turing's Man*, 101–03.
[61] *Ibid.*, 103–05.
[62] Tracy Kidder, *The Soul of a New Machine* (New York: Avon, 1981), 137; original emphasis (also quoted in Bolter, *Turing's Man*, 103).

The proverbial snapping of the fingers the engineer mentions corresponds to half a second – just barely perceptible in human time, but five hundred million nanoseconds in computer time.[63] With the introduction and spread of computer technology in Western culture, therefore, the very notion of the "instant" and "instantaneity" has changed its meaning quite radically from what it still meant at the time Toffler published *Future Shock* a mere two decades ago.[64] Certainly, one might argue that so far only a small elite of experts directly involved in the design and construction of computers is in any significant sense aware of this new temporal dimension. But already now, customers routinely ask for access and throughput times measured in milli- and microseconds when comparing the features of different computer models. More importantly, however, quite non-technical computer users experience the alternate temporality of the new medium when they work or play games on computers. First studies have shown that such users tend to underestimate grossly the time they spend during their games, estimating it in quarters of hours when they are hours in "real time."[65] William Gibson fictionalizes this time distortion in his novel *Neuromancer*, in which one of the so-called "console cowboys," who interface with the "cyberspace" of the computer directly through their neural systems, lives three days and nights in what one analogously might call "cybertime" while in "normal" time he lies on the floor, clinically brain-dead, for only approximately five minutes. This episode hyperbolically illustrates the tendency of

---

[63] Bolter, *Turing's Man*, 103.

[64] See Hayles, *Chaos Bound*, 280.

[65] These studies and their results are described in D. J. Bobko and M. A. Davis, "Effects of Visual Display Scale on Duration Estimates," *Human Factors* 28 (1986): 153–58, and B. S. Brown, K. Dismukes, and E. J. Rinalducci, "Video Display Terminals and Vision of Workers: Summary and Overview of a Symposium," *Behavior and Information Technology* 1 (1982): 121–40. A good deal more psychological research, though, will be necessary to put these findings on a firm empirical basis; one small-scale study of short-term tasks performed successively on paper and on a computer revealed no significant difference in time estimates, as shown in Ralph Juhnke and Jonathan N. Scott, "Psychology of Computer Use: V. Computer Use and the Experience of Time," *Perceptual and Motor Skills* 67 (1988): 868–69. For an interesting case study of "computer addiction" and the ensuing time experience in the life of a German entrepreneur, see Henri Bents, "Computerarbeit und Lebenszeit," *Zerstörung und Wiederaneignung von Zeit*, ed. Rainer Zoll (Frankfurt: Suhrkamp, 1988), 293–303.

computer use to expand the experience of the present at the expense of past and future.

The integration of inconceivably large and "slow" and unimaginably small and "fast" time scales into everyday awareness has two cultural consequences.[66] Even more than in the high-modernist period, it has become impossible to conceive of the world as structured according to a common temporality. Clearly, however, it would be insufficient simply to envision different physical time scales as parallel, unrelated strata, since the molecules swirling in a cup of coffee or the microprocesses inside a computer do ultimately form part of the large-scale evolution of the universe. The question of how one can relate events that occur at different time scales has not only been important for the development of recent scientific approaches such as chaos theory, it is also crucial for narrative, whose coherence depends on the reader's ability to connect the narrated events in a common temporal medium. Human time has traditionally provided such a medium, but as we will see, this standard is no longer unproblematical for postmodernist narrators. Postmodern culture exposes human time as just one among a multiplicity of temporal scales, one that can no longer be considered the measure and standard of continuity: we are now aware that events which may be perfectly continuous and coherent at one time scale may not appear so at ours. Hence the multiplication of time scales available to the postmodern imagination contributes to the experience of temporal discontinuity in the individual and social domains, and to the uncertainty regarding any relevant description of past and future.[67] To use a perhaps rather modernist metaphor, the postmodern subject cannot but be aware of the very large and the very small flywheels besides the "medium-sized" ones in the transmission that makes the temporal vehicle go forward; but just how these different "gears" engage and interact is inaccessible to human perception and experience. The paradox in the postmodern sense of time scale, then, is that although we know more about the overall functioning of time in our universe than ever before, our own operation within it has become more uncertain, so that temporal coherence increasingly eludes us.

---

[66] For discussions of the co-existence of widely divergent time-scales in contemporary culture, see also Adam, *Timewatch*, 118, and Toffler, *The Third Wave*, 296–98.

[67] See Adam, "Modern Times," 184.

4. Temporal experience and narrative form

Theorists of narrative generally agree that time is one of the most fundamental parameters through which narrative as a genre is organized and understood.[68] Indeed, some theorists have specifically characterized it as the mode by which we mediate and negotiate human temporality. Paul Ricoeur, for example, claims that "between the activity of narrating a story and the temporal character of human experience there exists a correlation that is not merely accidental but that presents a transcultural form of necessity. To put it another way, *time becomes human to the extent that it is articulated through a narrative mode, and narrative attains its full meaning when it becomes a condition of temporal existence.*"[69] Peter Brooks points out that "[n]arrative is one of the large categories or systems of understanding that we use in our negotiations with reality, specifically . . . with the problem of temporality: man's time-boundedness, his consciousness of existence within the limits of mortality. And plot is the principal ordering force of those meanings that we try to wrest from human temporality."[70] Similarly, Frank Kermode, in his classic study *The Sense of an Ending*, claims that narrative endings reflect the human need for a temporality shaped by the ordering force of the ending.[71] And Walter Benjamin already showed in his no less famous essay, "Der Erzähler" (The Storyteller), that the narrator attains the highest degree of authority at the moment of

[68] For classical studies on the relationship between time and narrative, see M. M. Bakhtin, "Forms of Time and of the Chronotope in the Novel," *The Dialogic Imagination: Four Essays*, trans. Caryl Emerson and Michael Holquist, ed. Michael Holquist (Austin: University of Texas Press, 1981), 84–258; E. M. Forster, *Aspects of the Novel* (San Diego: Harcourt Brace Jovanovich, 1985), 83–103; Eleanor N. Hutchens, "The Novel as Chronomorph," *Novel* 5 (1972): 215–24; A. A. Mendilow, *Time and the Novel* (New York: Humanities Press, 1972); Hans Meyerhoff, *Time in Literature* (Berkeley: University of California Press, 1955); Jean Pouillon, *Temps et roman* (Paris: Gallimard, 1946); Georges Poulet, *Etudes sur le temps humain* (Paris: Rocher, 1976). A fully articulated structuralist theory of narrative time is presented in Gérard Genette, *Narrative Discourse: An Essay in Method*, trans. Jane E. Lewin (Ithaca: Cornell University Press, 1980).

[69] Paul Ricoeur, *Time and Narrative*, vol. 1, trans. Kathleen McLaughlin and David Pellauer (Chicago: University of Chicago Press, 1984), 52; original emphasis.

[70] Peter Brooks, *Reading for the Plot: Design and Intention in Narrative* (New York: Random House, 1985), xi.

[71] Frank Kermode, *The Sense of an Ending* (London: Oxford University Press, 1967), 3–31.

death.[72] Benjamin, Kermode and Brooks all see human time as crucially shaped by mortality. Narrative time, in their view, is a way of confronting death through the movement toward the ending, understood as a moment of closure that retrospectively bestows meaning on the plot. Through the experience of reading, the readers live through the one moment in time that they cannot experience in their own lives: the moment just beyond death, which reveals life's final pattern. Narrative, then, is a means of bestowing meaning on one's life because it provides the possibility of looking back at life from beyond the ending.

What makes this type of narrative theory so seductive is that it bases itself on the universal human fact of death, as did the time philosophies of Freud, Heidegger and Sartre. But this universality is problematic in so far as it leads to the assumption that narrative as a genre is fundamentally invariant across cultures and historical periods; although its forms of appearance might change, its function for human temporal experience remains constant, and therefore narrative always retains an underlying temporal structure that defines the genre. None of these theories allows for the possibility that the human experience of time depends on cultural contexts that are themselves subject to change. Recent cultural theory has made us acutely aware that biological fact only becomes "natural" or "universal" through the operation of culture; in light of this insight, a theory of narrative that is based on an allegedly transhistorical experience of time appears questionable: the fact that mortality is a physical necessity for the individual by no means proves its universal cultural relevance. Obviously, Kermode and Brooks' theories are not therefore "wrong," but their historical scope may be much more limited than the theorists claim.

Even in studies of the nineteenth-century novel, where the structural pre-eminence of the ending has generally been taken for granted, the theoretical focus on teleological form and its relation to death has come under attack. D. A. Miller, for example, points to a questioning of narrative and its conditions of

---

[72] Walter Benjamin, "Der Erzähler," *Illuminationen: Ausgewählte Schriften*, ed. Siegfried Unseld (Frankfurt: Suhrkamp, 1961), 409–36. See also Garrett Stewart's study, *Death Sentences: Styles of Dying in British Fiction* (Cambridge, MA: Harvard University Press, 1984), which explores the relationship between narrative and death in texts from Dickens to Beckett.

existence in novelists such as Austen, Eliot and Stendhal that accompanies and informs the narrative process even in its tele- ological orientation. Because of this doubt of narrative that is articulated even in the traditional novel, he argues, closure does not in fact have the "totalizing powers of organization" that twentieth-century narratologists have ascribed to it.[73] Dietrich Schwanitz, whose systems-theoretical approach focuses not so much on the form as on the historical function of teleological narrative, arrives at a similar conclusion. He argues that the function of narrative changes with the gradual modernization of society in the seventeenth and eighteenth centuries and the altered time sense that comes with modernity. When innovation becomes a basic principle of social and economic processes, the future can no longer be mapped out on the basis of the past, but becomes unpredictable and contingent: historical time becomes asymmetrical. In this cultural framework, the novel arises as a new literary form that mediates between the past and future through the imposition of endings that give time a meaningful form but also open out onto what is to come.[74] Like D. A. Miller, then, Schwanitz implicitly questions the terminal, totalizing func- tion that other theorists attribute to narrative endings. The contrast of his approach with more conventional narratology could not be more pronounced: whereas Benjamin, Kermode and Brooks interpret closure as a narrative reflection of the indivi- dual's biologically closed future, Schwanitz reads it as a proce- dure designed to make time tellable in the face of a historical future too open and contingent to lend itself to narrative phrasing.

If the assumption that narrative form is primarily shaped by

[73] D. A. Miller, *Narrative and Its Discontents: Problems of Closure in the Traditional Novel* (Princeton: Princeton University Press, 1981), xiii–xiv.
[74] Dietrich Schwanitz, *Systemtheorie und Literatur: Ein neues Paradigma* (Opladen: Westdeutscher Verlag, 1990), 152–68. Schwanitz' paradigm for such endings is the love story, which ends when the hero and heroine are about to get married: the story of their mutual discovery comes to a meaningful end at the same time that the story opens out onto the prospect of their future life together (168–88). On the relation of modernization processes and the changed vision of the future they bring about, see also Niklas Luhmann, "The Future Cannot Begin: Temporal Structures in Modern Society," *Social Research* 43 (1976): 130–52; Giddens, *Consequences of Modernity*, 50–51; and Reinhart Koselleck, *Vergangene Zukunft: Zur Semantik geschichtlicher Zeiten*, 2nd edn (Frankfurt: Suhrkamp, 1992).

the ending does not do justice to the complexities of the conventional novel, it becomes even more problematic in twentieth-century fiction, which, as both Kermode and Brooks note, has become much more wary of teleological form and the imposition of endings.[75] Even in the high-modernist novel of the early twentieth century, endings no longer play the decisive structural role that narratology postulates. Whereas temporal succession was the principal medium of narrative meaning in the nineteenth-century novel, modernist novels tend to foreground simultaneity in their temporal organization. This emphasis on simultaneity is particularly striking in those texts that retell the same events several times from the perspective of different narrators (for example, *The Sound and the Fury* or *Absalom, Absalom!*) or that present the meandering consciousness of various characters as they confront an at least partially shared outer reality (for example, *Ulysses* or *Mrs. Dalloway*). But it also informs novels whose intense concern with the past would at first sight seem to call for a more conventionally chronological approach: in some texts, the narrator's piecemeal remembrance or retelling of past events, sometimes intermingled with perceptions from the present, turns the exploration of private memory into an exercise in narrative simultaneity (as in Proust's *A la recherche du temps perdu* or Ford's *The Good Soldier*), and in others, a sequence of events is gradually reconstructed from the accounts of a variety of narrators in such a way that eye-witness accounts of quite different moments in time are juxtaposed (as in Conrad's *Lord Jim*). Such strategies emphasize the importance of the voices or perspectives of the individual narrators or focal characters in their relations to each other over temporal sequence as a means of organizing narrative. But it is important to note that temporal succession, and more generally a coherent external reality, does in the end emerge from this juxtaposition in simultaneity: far from excluding or invalidating each other, the differing and sometimes unreliable accounts in the novels mentioned do in the end allow the reader to infer a fairly consistent story, whether it be the family history of the Compsons or the Sutpens, the events on the day of Clarissa Dalloway's party as well as those of the summer in Bourton thirty years earlier, or the fate of Jim from his

[75] Kermode, *Sense*, 4; Brooks, *Reading*, 313–14.

50

abandonment of the *Patna* to his death. Different versions of events, in other words, turn out to be complementary rather than mutually exclusive.[76]

This emphasis on the simultaneity of different perspectives and moments in time as an organizational device, and the diminished importance of temporal succession as a medium of narrative meaning, closely relates to some of the problems and conflicts in the modernist conceptualization of time that I discussed in connection with Dalí's soft clocks. Clearly, many modernist novels, with their emphasis on individual psychological time, register suspicion of and resistance to the increasing standardization and mechanization of time in the public sphere. But it is misleading to claim that the major concern of modernist "time novels" is to provide a record of individual temporal experience in its opposition to public time, since many modernist novels in fact do not focus on one individual mind, but juxtapose the memories and perceptions of several different characters (for example, any of the novels of Virginia Woolf or William Faulkner, as well as *Ulysses* or *Der Mann ohne Eigenschaften*). Through these juxtapositions, modernist novels generate a temporality that transcends the individual without obliterating it; they foreground the uniqueness of each psychological time world, but in the process also open up a time beyond individual perception by allowing the readers to experience subjective temporalities other than their own and to perceive events as they appear in these different frameworks. Even though the authors may not always have intended it, the multiplicity of private temporalities that combine in the modernist novel adds up to an alternative social time, a time beyond the individual that is less alienating and impersonal than the globally standardized one of the Greenwich mean. The narrative structure of the modernist novel, then, can be quite literally understood to create a social "soft-clock" temporality against the "hard" clocks that divide public from private and scientific from common-sense temporality.

This narrative organization typically brings with it a drastic reduction in the scope of narrated time as compared to the

[76] This is also Brian McHale's understanding of perspectivism in modernist fiction; see "Modernist Reading, Postmodern Text: The Case of 'Gravity's Rainbow'," *Constructing Postmodernism* (London: Routledge, 1992), 64–66.

nineteenth-century novel. Texts from Balzac to Dickens and Tolstoy had usually told stories that extended over many years, encompassing the entire life span of a character or even the life of several successive generations. Modernist novels tend to concentrate on much shorter time intervals: *The Good Soldier* narrates eleven years, Faulkner's *As I Lay Dying* a few days, *Ulysses* and *Mrs. Dalloway* one day only. Novels that do still cover a number of years tend to concentrate on a very few select scenes from this period: for example, Woolf's *To the Lighthouse*, Faulkner's *The Sound and the Fury*, or Malcolm Lowry's *Under the Volcano*. Others resort to a radical fragmentation of longer time periods into tiny facets of a few hours, such as Anderson's *Winesburg, Ohio* or Dos Passos' *Manhattan Transfer*.[77] This condensation parallels the general cultural interest in speed and short time spans; but perhaps more importantly, it follows from novelists' attempt to explore the simultaneous rather than the sequential structure of time as a means of organizing narrative.

Novels from the 1950s and 60s continue and intensify the temporal reduction characteristic of modernist narrative: Butor's *L'emploi du temps* spans twelve months; Robbe-Grillet's *Le voyeur* three days, *Les gommes* twenty-four-hours; Marguerite Duras' *L'après-midi de Monsieur Andesmas* and B. S. Johnson's *The Unfortunates* describe one afternoon; Claude Mauriac's *La marquise sortit à cinq heures* one hour; Duras' *Le square* one conversation; García Márquez' *La hojarasca* thirty minutes; Mauriac's *L'agrandissement* five minutes. Most of these novels would probably be more appropriately described as "late modernist" than as "postmodernist" since they pursue goals very similar to those of modernist texts, although with more radical means: García Márquez' *La hojarasca*, for example, clearly modeled on Faulkner's narrative procedures, explores the parallel perceptions and reactions of three individuals to a single chain of events; Mauriac's *La marquise* presents the multifarious intersecting processes of thought and perception that occur around a modern city square not unlike the cityscapes of *Manhattan Transfer*, *Ulysses* or *Mrs. Dalloway*; and B. S. Johnson's *The Unfortunates* is an exploration of

---

[77] Darío Villanueva describes "temporal reduction" as one of the hallmarks of twentieth-century fiction and gives a detailed classification of its different types as well as an abundance of examples in *Estructura y tiempo reducido en la novela* (Valencia: Bello, 1977).

human memory not in principle unlike Proust's, although Johnson uses the innovative device of the loose-leaf novel to represent physically the arbitrariness of associations as they occur in the human mind. In spite of this device, the story that emerges, no matter what page ordering is chosen, remains quite unambiguous: the narrator's memory of a close friend dying gradually of cancer. The point of the temporal experiment in these novels remains mainly psychological or, in Brian McHale's term, epistemological:[78] the narrator's goal is to explore how human perception and memory shape or distort time, and how individual temporalities are related to each other and to "objective" time.

Postmodernist novels properly speaking take a very different approach to time. They too present different versions of the events they describe, or piece a story together from flashbacks. But the narrative technique differs from that of high-modernist and late-modernist novels in two fundamental respects: the differing accounts or flashbacks are not linked to the voice or mind of any narrator or character configured with a view toward psychological realism, and they tell event sequences in contradictory and mutually exclusive versions that do not allow the reader to infer a coherent story and reality. In Clarence Major's *Reflex and Bone Structure*, for example, one of the protagonists, a woman named Cora, has apparently been murdered in her apartment. But repeated descriptions of her apartment and body are juxtaposed with other scenes in which Cora is not only alive and well, but has affairs with various men, starts a career as a singer, and flies to foreign countries; these episodes at first sight appear to be flashbacks to earlier moments of Cora's life, until we are told that Cora dies in a plane crash on her way to Russia. Clearly, this is no longer the kind of variation that could be explained on the basis of a mingling of past and present or differing psychological realities. The reader cannot determine with certainty if any of the scenes are supposed to form part of the narrated reality, or whether they are to be understood as figments of the narrator's imagination or simple exercises of style.

The philosophy of time that underlies this type of narrative organization is prefigured most clearly in one of the most important models for postmodernist fiction, Jorge Luis Borges'

---

[78] Brian McHale, *Postmodernist Fiction*, 9–11.

short story "El jardín de senderos que se bifurcan" (The Garden
of Forking Paths) from 1941. In the climactic scene of this story,
the protagonist, Yu Tsun, visits the sinologist Stephen Albert and
discovers that the latter has solved an enigma regarding the work
of Yu Tsun's ancestor Ts'ui Pên. Albert explains to his visitor:

"A diferencia de Newton y de Schopenhauer, su antepasado no creía en
un tiempo uniforme, absoluto. Creía en infinitas series de tiempos, en
una red creciente y vertiginosa de tiempos divergentes, convergentes y
paralelos. Esa trama de tiempos que se aproximan, se bifurcan, se cortan
o que secularmente se ignoran, abarca *todas* las posibilidades. No
existimos en la mayoría de esos tiempos; en algunos existe usted y no yo;
en otros, yo, no usted; en otros, los dos. En éste, que un favorable azar
me depara, usted ha llegado a mi casa; en otro, usted, al atravesar el
jardín, me ha encontrado muerto; en otro, yo digo estas mismas palabras,
pero soy un error, un fantasma. . . . El tiempo se bifurca perpetuamente
hacia innumerables futuros."[79]

(As opposed to Newton and Schopenhauer, your ancestor did not
believe in a uniform, absolute time. He believed in infinite series of times,
in a growing and vertiginous network of divergent, convergent and
parallel times. This web of times that approach each other, bifurcate,
cross or ignore each other for centuries, includes *all* possibilities. We do
not exist in the majority of those times; in some, you exist and not I; in
others, I, not you; in [yet] others, both of us. In this one, which a fortunate
coincidence has afforded me, you have come to my house; in another,
crossing the garden, you have found me dead; in [yet] another, I say
these same words, but I am an error, a ghost. . . . Time bifurcates
incessantly toward innumerable futures.)

When Albert explains how this philosophy relates to the incomprehensible novel Ts'ui Pên left to posterity, Yu Tsun dimly
begins to perceive the existence of other temporalities that
surround him and his host. "Desde ese instante, sentí a mi
alrededor y en mi oscuro cuerpo una invisible, intangible pulula-
ción," he notes at first[80] (From that moment on, I felt around me
and in my dark body an invisible, intangible swarming). Later,
this sensation becomes more concrete: "Volví a sentir esa pulula-
ción de que hablé. Me pareció que el húmedo jardín que rodeaba
la casa estaba saturado hasta lo infinito de invisibles personas.
Esas personas eran Albert y yo, secretos, atareados y multiformes

[79] "El jardín de senderos que se bifurcan," *Ficciones*, 12th edn (Madrid: Alianza,
1984), 114–15; original emphasis.
[80] *Ibid.*, 113.

en otras dimensiones de tiempo"[81] (I again felt that swarming I mentioned. It seemed to me that the humid garden surrounding the house was infinitely saturated with invisible persons. Those persons were Albert and I, hidden, busy and manifold in other time dimensions). The alternative time dimensions Yu Tsun here dimly perceives spell out other narrative lines, many of which are incompatible with the plot as it evolves in the short story itself.

Many postmodern novels have taken up the central metaphor of Borges' seminal short story and exploited it in their narrative structure. Quite literally, it informs texts such as John Barth's short story "Lost in the Funhouse," in which every bifurcation inside the funhouse leads into a different future. But many other texts that abandon the spatial metaphor of the maze nevertheless develop story lines that exclude and invalidate each other, leaving the reader with a spectrum of possible developments rather than a single plot line. Postmodernist novels thereby project into the narrative present and past an experience of time which normally is only available for the future: time dividing and subdividing, bifurcating and branching off continuously into multiple possibilities and alternatives. It forms part of the inherent asymmetry of time that in everyday experience we envision what is to come as open and indeterminate with regard to a multiplicity of possibilities, whereas the past and present are continuously narrowed down to one temporal strand from amongst these possibilities. In the universes of postmodern novels, however, we cannot be sure even retrospectively which one of several possible developments turned from possibility to reality, let alone do we know which one is being realized in the narrative present. Through this narrative strategy, the reader is made to live in a constant retrojection of the time experience of the future; as a consequence, time in these texts appears labyrinthine in all its dimensions.

This type of textual organization is created by means of three major narrative strategies used by themselves or in combination: repetition, metalepsis and experimental typographies. Repetition is, of course, so general a feature of literary texts that one must be cautious about claiming it as characteristic of any particular

[81] *Ibid.*, 115.

period or genre.[82] But whereas the repetition of certain plot elements and tropes occurs in all kinds of narrative from the folktale to the classical novel, many postmodern texts stand out through the insistent reiteration of identical scenes, presented in almost literally the same words every time. Only slight variations distinguish one description or account from the other, although these gradual alterations of wording or narrated elements can lead to quite disparate and even contradictory versions of what the reader must take to be the same scene or incident.

As I already indicated, the crucial difference between these almost literal repetitions and the kind of retelling one finds in the modernist novel is that in modernism, repetition and variation of the same events are motivated by the differing perspectives of the narrators or focal characters whose views they reflect. The readers may not be able to decide which versions (if any) "really" correspond to the events as they happened in the story, but based on what they find out about the focal characters, they can at least make an assessment as to what kinds of distortions are likely to have occurred in a particular retelling. Furthermore, the comparison of different narrators' accounts in a modernist novel usually allows one to form a fairly consistent picture of the events that lie behind them.[83] No such motivation, however, is normally given for postmodernist repetitions. As a consequence, it is also impossible for the reader to infer a coherent image of the actions that underlie the repetitions, since there is no criterion for evaluating the reality of any version the text happens to present. A few more examples may make this clear. Robert Coover's short story "The Elevator," for instance, consists of nothing but a series of scenes of a character taking the elevator in his office building: sometimes up, sometimes down, sometimes in the morning, sometimes in the evening, sometimes alone, sometimes in the company of colleagues, sometimes accompanied by a woman, sometimes silent, sometimes engaged in conversations with varying outcomes, or sometimes even in sex. Some of these scenes might succeed each other at different moments in time, but others are clearly mutually exclusive versions of the same elevator ride. At the end, we cannot be sure if any of the scenes even took place, or

---

[82] Brooks, *Reading*, 99; see also J. Hillis Miller, *Fiction and Repetition: Seven English Novels* (Cambridge, MA: Harvard University Press, 1982), 2–3 and 5–6.

[83] Brian McHale, "Modernist Reading," 64–66.

whether they were fantasies of the protagonist's or narratorial games with language. Similarly, Christine Brooke-Rose's novel *Out*, as we will see in detail in Chapter 6, returns over and over again to a scene in which, in a futuristic world in which Africans form the uppermost social class, an elderly white man goes to ask for a job as a gardener at an African lady's manor house. In some versions of the scene, he is received by the head gardener, who is sometimes white and sometimes colored; other versions indicate that it is the gardener's wife who greets him. Sometimes the gardener is affable and shows him around the estate, but does not admit him for a job until a later season; sometimes the two get into a fight concerning their differing national and racial pasts; sometimes the gardener simply denies that the manor needs an additional employee. Along with the dialogue, descriptions of the scenery, the season, the watering of the plants and other elements vary to such an extent that the same general setting is still recognizable, but none of the details can be held on to. The readers are left with the general impression that they are reading the same scene over and over again, but few consistent details can be relied on to prove this.

The interest of these diegetic experiments no longer lies in the exploration of what distortions or refigurations a certain sequence of events undergoes in the perception or memory of different characters. Rather, the text explores the temporal micro-texture of crucial scenes in such detail that the reader is alerted to the most minute element of change. As Roland Barthes observes with regard to the works of Robbe-Grillet, time is constituted as a series of slices which *almost* exactly correspond to each other, and their temporality lies precisely in this "almost."[84] Due to this focus on the microstructure of time, what we learn is not so much how one event leads to another; in fact, the reader can never be certain whether one thing leads to another at all. Instead, the focus is on the constitution of the moment itself. Time "passes," in other words, but not in the way in which we usually understand this phrase: it does not set up any irreversible directionality but reconfigures the elements of the individual moment just enough for change to be perceptible. Instead of bridging the gap from one instant to the next, it introduces difference into the

---

[84] Roland Barthes, "Littérature objective," *Essais critiques* (Paris: Seuil, 1964), 36.

instant itself, splitting it into multiple bifurcations and virtualities.[85]

Inevitably, the insistent play on the almost same without any psychological motivation introduces a strong element of contingency into narrative. But this is no longer the kind of contingency which turned the Proustian madeleine into a vehicle of involuntary memory and heightened awareness. On the contrary, postmodernist repetition strategies seem designed precisely to preclude moments of epiphany and privileged insight, since each instant is submerged in a series of alternative versions none of which can claim priority over the others. The present is trapped in its own mutations, without any possibility of linkage to past or future, and with at best a promise of meaning that is never fulfilled. As opposed to modernist texts, then, where contingency is a force that overcomes chronoschisms and gathers temporality together, it disseminates and divides time in postmodernist novels.

This dissemination persists even when there is in fact a textual or formal principle that governs the repetition. Robbe-Grillet's *Topologie d'une cité fantôme*, as Chapter 3 will show, revolves around a series of variations on the theme of the raped virgin. Many of these variations are motivated linguistically by the combination and recombination of a very limited number of phonetic elements that appear in such words as *vierge, vagin, vigie, navire, divin, divan, David, gravide, Diana* and *Vanadium*. But the reason why this particular phonological set (mainly /v/, /g/, /d/, /a/ and /i/) was chosen is a purely formal one: it consists of the letters of the name *Gradiva*, which is the title of one of Robbe-Grillet's intertextual sources, as well as an anagram of the Latin word for "pregnant" that points to the text's self-generation. This matrix word could be easily replaced by any number of others; neither does there seem to be any logical necessity to any

---

[85] The critique of the present and the self-identical now that is articulated through these narrative strategies is comparable in some of its aspects to the one carried out by Jacques Derrida in his critique of Husserl's time philosophy: see "*Ousia* and Gramme: Note on a Note from *Being and Time*," *Margins of Philosophy*, trans. Alan Bass (Chicago: University of Chicago Press, 1982), 29–67, and *Speech and Phenomena: And Other Essays on Husserl's Theory of Signs*, trans. David B. Allison (Evanston: Northwestern University Press, 1973). For a close analysis and critique of Derrida's argument concerning Husserl and Heidegger, see David Wood's *The Deconstruction of Time* (Atlantic Highlands: Humanities Press International, 1989), 111–33, 251–64 and 267–77.

of the specific combinations the text chooses to explore, or to the sequence in which they appear. In other novels, repetition may be textually motivated by a formal principle that is either inaccessible or very difficult to guess for the reader. Brooke-Rose's *Between*, for example, systematically avoids all forms of the verb *to be*, and a fair number of repetitious scenes can be "explained" in terms of this omission – but no critic ever noticed this principle until the author herself pointed it out.[86] In either case, the order of specific scenes is not predicted even by the formal matrix, and hence the temporal development of the text remains contingent at least as far as the reader is concerned. What postmodernist repetition creates, then, is not a temporality ruled by cause and effect, a medium of stability and continuity, but an agent of contingency and dispersion.

If certain forms of repetition disrupt the causality that was traditionally associated with temporal sequence in the novel, systematic violations of the boundary between frame narrative and embedded story destabilize another kind of conventional narrative causality: the narrator's control of the story. The nesting of diegetic levels or *recursion* is, of course, not specific to postmodernist novels, or indeed to the novel at all. In its technical mathematical sense, *recursion* refers to the repeated application of a rule or routine to the variable values of a function. But as a structural pattern, it can be found in a much wider variety of information practices and sign systems, such as the embedding of sentences in natural languages or the modulation of a tune across different keys in music.[87] In literature, the embedding of stories within stories and of plays within plays is the most obvious corresponding form. This type of pattern in itself does not necessarily cause any disruption of linear time; instead, time simply seems to be suspended at one level while it proceeds at another. But certain strategies of recursion can nevertheless blur or block temporal progression: for example, switches of level may occur so frequently that it becomes difficult for the reader to

---

[86] Christine Brooke-Rose, "Illicitations," *Review of Contemporary Fiction* 9.3 (1989): 102–03; see also "Conversation with Christine Brooke-Rose," with Ellen G. Friedman and Miriam Fuchs, *Utterly Other Discourse: The Texts of Christine Brooke-Rose*, ed. Ellen G. Friedman and Richard Martin (Normal: Dalkey Archive Press, 1995), 32–33.

[87] Douglas R. Hofstadter, *Gödel, Escher, Bach: An Eternal Golden Braid* (New York: Vintage, 1980), 127–52.

remember and piece together the fragmented pieces of each story line.[88] We will see an example of such disruption in the second reading itinerary of Cortázar's *Rayuela* in Chapter 2. A similar blurring of the time sense sets in when different levels of the nested structure resemble each other closely enough that at least a temporary confusion becomes possible; in other words, when some form of *mise en abyme* is involved.[89] And linear temporality may collapse completely when, as is frequently the case in postmodern fiction, the boundaries between nesting and nested text are crossed by characters or other textual elements that "migrate" from the embedded story and participate in the framing events, in a process which Gérard Genette has called "metalepsis."[90] A concise example of this is Julio Cortázar's short story "Continuidad de los parques," in which a man sits down in a green velvet armchair to read the story of a married woman and her lover who are planning to murder the woman's husband. As they penetrate into the house to carry out their plan, they open a door and find the husband reading in a green velvet armchair: the reader in the frame narrative is suddenly no longer outside the story he reads, but involved in it; he literally becomes its victim.

Recursion and metalepsis crucially shape a great number of postmodern novels – Fowles' *The French Lieutenant's Woman*, Federman's *Double or Nothing*, B. S. Johnson's *Christie Malry's Own Double-Entry*, Brooke-Rose's *Thru*, Calvino's *If on a Winter's Night a Traveler*, Barth's "Menelaiad" and the stories in *Chimera*, Robbe-Grillet's *La maison de rendez-vous* and *Topologie d'une cité fantôme* and many others play – with the multiplication of diegetic levels and their transgression.[91] To see how this splitting of the narrative thread into a multiplicity of levels affects time, we must return to our earlier observation that the experience of temporal continuity depends on our ability to construct events in succession at a similar scale or a similar level of

[88] McHale, *Postmodernist Fiction*, 113.
[89] Hofstadter, *Gödel, Escher, Bach*, 128. The classical study of *mise en abyme* is Lucien Dällenbach's *Le récit spéculaire: Essai sur la mise en abyme* (Paris: Seuil, 1977); see also Jean Ricardou, *Problèmes du nouveau roman* (Paris: Seuil, 1967), 171–90.
[90] Gérard Genette, *Narrative Discourse: An Essay in Method*, trans. Jane E. Lewin (Ithaca: Cornell University Press, 1980), 234–37.
[91] For a more detailed discussion see McHale, *Postmodernist Fiction*, 112–30.

abstraction.[92] Narrative leaps between diegetic levels prevent exactly that, since framed and framing story cannot normally be construed as pertaining to the same time sequence: while events proceed at one level, they are suspended at the other levels until the narrative focus returns to them. But to say this is to simplify the temporal processes that occur during the reading of framed stories. For the reader, the embedded narrative is intercalated between two moments of the main story and serves to dilate that instant "in between." This fact can sometimes be foregrounded in the story itself: the most famous example is the series of stories Scheherazade tells in the *Arabian Nights* to extend the duration of her life, which is to end along with her storytelling. Recursion, in other words, is a means of articulating a temporal interval through a narrative that is not its own, but that of another moment in time: that is, of giving it a structure of meaning while "at the same time" leaving it semantically empty as an interval of pure chronology, since nothing can happen in the frame narrative while the framed story is being told. Recursion figures the moment as what it is not, replacing it by the story of another moment; somewhat paradoxically, it becomes narrative by not being narrated.

If recursive processes are carried far enough, they can produce texts in which there are still distinct nesting levels, but no single "monitoring level" at which the nesting "bottoms out": a visual example of such a "heterarchy" without the oriented layering characteristic of a hierarchy is M. C. Escher's painting of two hands which draw each other, since neither one can unambiguously be claimed for the status of "picture within the picture."[93] In narrative, an analogous structure would be that of Coleman Dowell's novel *Island People*, in which one of the characters not only emerges from an embedded story to converse with the narrator, but even takes over the writing of the latter's journals and narratives; some of these revolve around a character bearing the same name as the narrator, so that in the end it becomes practically impossible to decide who has invented whom.[94] In

---

[92] See Wolf-Dieter Stempel, "Möglichkeiten einer Darstellung der Diachronie in narrativen Texten," *Zeitgestaltung in der Erzählkunst*, ed. Alexander Ritter (Darmstadt: Wissenschaftliche Buchgesellschaft, 1978), 303.

[93] Hofstadter, *Gödel, Escher, Bach*, 133–34.

[94] For a more detailed analysis of *Island People*'s metaleptic structure, see my

such inversions of cause and effect, the directionality of time comes into question along with the authority of the narrator. However, as Douglas Hofstadter points out, there is an inherent limit to this type of experiment, since it always ends up reconfirming the authority of one narrator who *does* remain at a so-called "inviolate level" outside the heterarchy. The reader knows that characters can only emerge from stories and talk back to narrators *in stories*, and so the questioning of narratorial authority within the story ultimately confirms the existence of such authority outside it.[95] But knowing this does not help the reader untangle the text's temporal loops, although it does foreground their textual nature.

In literary narrative, repetitions and recursions are articulated by means of written language. Print typography and the book format place a number of "natural" constraints on how temporality can be presented, and some postmodern texts foreground and exploit these particular constraints in ways that were common in avant-garde poetry of the early twentieth century, but did not make their way into fiction until the 1960s. Written language, especially when configured in narrative structures, is forced to present time in a medium that operates on the basis of discrete, digital units: words. Punctuation, articulation in sentences, and the division of longer texts into numbered pages impose further boundaries and discontinuities on what Bergson and many modernist writers conceived of as the uninterrupted flow of *durée*. When postmodernist texts do away with punctuation, they tend to replace it with typographic devices that foreground linguistic discontinuity even more dramatically: Beckett's *How It Is*, for example, as we will see in Chapter 4, suspends punctuation and capitalization only to divide each of its pages into approximately equal blocks of text and blank space. Raymond Federman's *Double or Nothing* goes even further by configuring the typography of every single one of its almost two hundred pages differently, breaking down paragraphs and sentences into other, visually motivated units. Brooke-Rose's *Thru* contains pages which are configured in crossword-puzzle fashion, so that the reader is forced not only to take in every

article "Time Frames: Temporality and Narration in Coleman Dowell's *Island People*," *Journal of Narrative Technique* 21 (1991): 274–88.
[95] Hofstadter, *Gödel, Escher, Bach*, 688–89.

word individually, but even to break it down into its constituent letters, which form part of several differently oriented words at the same time. William Gass' *Willie Masters' Lonesome Wife* incorporates photographs and the "accidental" ring-shaped marks of glasses into its print configuration, and divides some pages into two or three typographically distinct areas, each of which follows a different narrative strand. The reader must choose which story line to follow, and then is forced to flip back and forth through the text to catch up on the other strands. These experiments put postmodern fiction at the opposite extreme of texts such as Molly Bloom's monologue at the end of *Ulysses*, which in its suspension of syntax and punctuation attempts to come as close as possible to representing the uninterrupted flow of time and mind. Contemporary texts, on the contrary, disarticulate time into moments through their non-linear typography, and suggest that every page can be read following a variety of itineraries.

Such strategies of "concrete prose"[96] transform temporal processes into visual and spatial objects, and in this respect it makes sense to speak of a postmodern tendency toward the spatialization of time that is quite unlike the metaphoric spatialization Joseph Frank claimed was characteristic of high-modernist poetry and novels.[97] These typographical structures remain strictly local, however, since principles of printed configuration can, in most cases, be formulated only for very restricted passages, not for the text as a whole. In the reading process, the foregrounded spatiality of print is thereby itself subjected to the discontinuity of change, and to a contingency that makes it impossible for the reader even to predict what the next page will look like, let alone the text in its entirety. The typographical configuration of some postmodern novels, then, contributes to the fracturing of narrative time into alternative temporal universes.

The three narrative strategies I have discussed – repetition, metalepsis and "concrete" typography – do not always occur together, and they are often complemented by other, more author-specific techniques, some of which I will analyze in later chapters. But all of them crucially contribute to a specifically postmodernist

---

[96] See McHale, *Postmodernist Fiction*, 184–87.
[97] Joseph Frank, "Spatial Form in Modern Literature," *The Idea of Spatial Form* (New Brunswick: Rutgers University Press, 1991), 3–66.

articulation of narrative time. Four general characteristics define this time sense. First, postmodernist novels focus on the moment or the narrative present at the expense of larger temporal developments, not unlike modernist novels. Second, the moment is not envisioned as a self-identical instant of presence, but as partaking of or leading to an indefinite number of different, alternative, and sometimes mutually exclusive temporalities which, as I suggested, can be understood as a projection of the temporal mode of the future into the past and present. Third, the juxtaposition of alternative plot developments and the metaleptic crossing of boundaries between diegetic levels leads to a double symmetrization of time and causation: on one hand, the temporal ordering of events becomes considerably less important than it was in the conventional and the high-modernist novel; and on the other, the hierarchical logic of the relationship between narrator and narrated material becomes susceptible to inversion, so that characters gain access to and alter the world of the narrator just as the latter shapes that of the characters. Fourth, none of these infractions of classical narrative logic are justified in terms of the psychology of the human mind, as they were, for the most part, in the modernist novel; postmodernist narrative time is detached from any specific human observer, and in some cases is not meant to represent any temporality other than that of the text at all.

Clearly, the reduction of temporal scope in the postmodernist novel forms part of a more general culture of time that has become wary of hypostatizing long-term historical patterns and developments. The focus on the present, the moment now at hand, also seems to link metafiction firmly to contemporary media and consumer culture with its relentless emphasis on the present as the only time phase available for gratification, planification and control. But in this context, differences in temporal philosophy also emerge very strikingly. Even a first reading of Beckett, Perec, Robbe-Grillet, Arno Schmidt or Luisa Valenzuela reveals that their novels resist easy consumption and immediate gratification in a way that distinguishes them sharply from the kinds of narrative that typically occur in magazine, film, television, video and advertising production; the difficulty and sometimes even the tedium of such a first reading bears witness to a narrative organization that does not lend itself to fast assimilation and easy retelling. This difficulty does not provide a basis for judging the aesthetic value of such fiction in comparison to other forms of contemporary narrative; but it does point to a different type of time structure that does not put the present at the reader's disposal. On the contrary, the moment becomes increasingly difficult to grasp as it is split into multiple versions of itself, embedded in intricate and sometimes logically impossible recursion structures, and fractured into experimental typographical configurations. Similarly, this kind of temporality does not allow for privileged instants of epiphany, visions of coherence, or unmediated access to the past as one finds them in many modernist novels; the narrative organization systematically prevents any such privileging, since any epiphany attained in a specific episode might be cancelled out by a subsequent, different version of the same episode. By refusing to compensate the absence of long-term narrative developments with the self-presence of the individual moment, postmodernist narrative form resists the cultural fixation on the now.

Whether the labyrinthine vision of multiple temporalities that many postmodern novels offer presents any genuine alternative to this fixation, however, is more difficult to say. Very strikingly, the multiplicity of temporal universes in these novels does not seem to lead to a wider spectrum of plot possibilities and a vastly enriched narrative repertoire, but on the contrary to the almost obsessive repetition of a relatively restricted inventory of scenes and, even in texts with wildly proliferating plots such as those of Thomas Pynchon, to a pervasive sense of paranoia and control. Perhaps with such restrictions in mind, Gary Saul Morson accuses the Borgesian time concept of being even more ferociously determinist than the conventional linear one, since the individual in Borges encounters the multiplicity of temporal universes without having any part in shaping them through his intentionality and agency.[98] Certainly, postmodernist novels do not generally make any attempt to celebrate the freedom of the individual either in their content or their organization; their protagonists tend to appear as victims rather than as beneficiaries of multiplicity and ambiguity. But these postmodernist characters are not conceived mimetically as "realist," self-possessed indivi-

---

[98] Gary Saul Morson, *Narrative and Freedom* (New Haven: Yale University Press, 1994), 227–33.

duals with the ability to intend and act in the first place; frequently, they appear as partly human and partly linguistic constructs, and sometimes have the paradoxical capability of recognizing themselves as textual entities: the protagonist of Ronald Sukenick's *Out*, for example, changes names and identity in almost every chapter, the I-narrators of some of Robbe-Grillet's later novels switch name and gender repeatedly, and B. S. Johnson's Christie Malry talks back to his creator knowing full well that he is a character in a novel. But even if we assumed with Morson that metafictional novels relied on rationally and realistically conceived characters who find themselves in a deterministic universe, the question remains whether the text as such could be considered determinist if it juxtaposes several universes that take the same events to different outcomes, and gives none of them ontological priority over the others. It is precisely this kind of juxtaposition that opens up interpretive possibilities for the reader and manifold layers of textual self-referentiality that cannot appropriately be called determinist.

It would be more accurate to say that novels with titles such as *In Transit*, *Between* or *How It Is*, in analyzing the constant emergence of the moment out of different histories, languages, voices, images or identities, explore the temporal interplay between determinism and indeterminacy, or between causality and contingency. This exploratory intent shapes narrative procedures which treat episodes that already form part of the narrated past as if they were still part of the indeterminate possibilities and hypothetical alternatives of the future: the determinacy of the material of the past is subjected to the indeterminacy of the future mode in such a way that a finite narrative repertoire can be deployed in infinite variations. The same intent also underlies other strategies that characterize not only the novel but other art forms: intertextual appropriation of previous art works and aesthetic forms that is turned into a procedure of innovation, pastiche and the deliberate cultivation of plagiarism obey the same temporal principle.[99] The difficulty of envisioning the

---

[99] Jameson, *Postmodernism*, 17–18, 286. See also Raymond Federman, "Imagination as Plagiarism," *New Literary History* 7 (1975–76): 563–78, and Douglas Crimp, "Appropriating Appropriation," *Image Scavengers: Photography*, ed. Paula Marincola (Institute of Contemporary Art/University of Pennsylvania Press, 1982), 27–34.

future that characterizes the historical imagination as well as the invention of literary narrative is, in the realm of art at least, transformed into a new way of articulating the past and present not in terms of sequentiality, but of an often deliberately paradoxical and self-contradictory simultaneity.

The temporal structure of the postmodernist novel, then, is a way of dealing aesthetically with an altered culture of time in which access to the past and especially to the future appears more limited than before in cultural self-awareness. If the teleological form of the nineteenth-century novel mediated the relationship between past and future in an era in which the future had become unpredictable on the basis of past social patterns, the postmodernist novel confronts the more radically contingent future of Western societies in the late twentieth century by projecting the temporal mode of the future into the narrative present and past. Narrative, in other words, takes on the temporal structure of a future that can no longer be envisioned without great difficulty, so that the time experience of the future is displaced into the reading experience. The novels of Thomas Pynchon and Christine Brooke-Rose that I will discuss, *Gravity's Rainbow* and *Out*, show this very clearly, since their protagonists' loss of a vision for the future is accompanied by a narrative present constantly splitting into alternative and incompatible versions of itself. Brooke-Rose's *Out* and Bruce Sterling's *Schismatrix*, which I will briefly analyze in the epilogue, are in fact science-fiction novels that quite literally propose a version of the future: but in this case, a version of the future that is highly aware of the difficulties of articulating any such version, and that incorporates these difficulties into the novel's narrative organization (in Brooke-Rose's case) or into its thematic frame of reference (in Sterling's case). Contingency is made narratable not by its conversion into teleological form, as in the nineteenth-century novel, or by its recuperation through the human mind, as in the high-modernist novel, but through its displacement from the future to the present and past.

One might argue that this displacement is in essence an escapist strategy designed to help narrative literature avoid the more difficult task of projecting avenues into the future at least in the imaginative realm. This critique is, in my view, justified, and perhaps helps to explain why authors who assign to their fictions the task of overt social and political intervention have tended to rely less on metafictional strategies than some of those authors whose main goal is aesthetic innovation, although the boundary between the two groups is by no means clear-cut. I would hold against this critique, however, that if metafictional texts are escapist in this particular sense, they in no way offer an easy escape. The difficulties that many postmodernist texts cause in the reading are not just self-serving intricacies, but provide a basis for reflecting on the interplay of determinism and indeterminacy, or causality and contingency in our temporal experience. In this sense, their project parallels that of theories of complexity and non-linear dynamics that have emerged in the natural sciences in the last twenty years, which equally aim to explore the relationship between the predictable and the unpredictable in the evolution of systems over time. Texts such as Sterling's *Schismatrix* make this parallel explicit by incorporating some of these scientific theories into the narrative plot; but even the great majority of postmodernist texts that make no direct reference to such theories participate in their project through their specific type of narrative organization. Viewed from this perspective, what appears to be a lack of social or political project is quite possibly due to a higher level of abstraction in the approach postmodernist novels take to the problem of contemporary history.

5. Historicizing posthistory

Somewhat simplistically, one could say that postmodernist texts take to the extreme a narrative technique that was typical of high-modernist novels, the juxtaposed accounts of identical events by different characters, but strip it of the element of human observation: what is left are contradictory accounts without any overarching psychological motivation.[100] The preceding analysis of the organization of narrative time indicates the reasons for this

[100] Brian McHale makes a related point in "Modernist Reading" when he analyzes the ways in which, in *Gravity's Rainbow*, events and phenomena that characters perceive are later invalidated by the narrator, other events, or by their belated attribution to a character's dreams, fantasies or hallucinations: in either case, it becomes impossible to construct a coherent fictional universe through the thoughts and perceptions of the characters, whereas this construction is possible in most modernist novels (64–73).

development. On one hand, in novels that are concerned with the way in which events at widely diverging time scales relate to each other, the human time dimension may lose its pre-eminence because humans have only mediated access to developments at other time scales. On the other hand, if the peculiar time structures of postmodernist novels should be understood as projections of the future mode into the present and past, as I have argued, this precludes a consistent observer position, since by definition the future cannot be accessed and observed directly. These two points may become clearer when we look at an example, John Barth's short story "Menelaiad" from *Lost in the Funhouse*.

At first sight, the "Menelaiad," a postmodernist retelling of Menelaus' unhappy marriage to Helen and its consequences, displays a very tidy symmetrical organization: it consists of fourteen numbered sections divided in two sets. The first set of sections, numbered 1 to 7, leads the reader backwards in time from the period after the Trojan war, when Menelaus has long been reunited with Helen, to the first days of their marriage; every time Menelaus tells a part of his story, he is asked by his listener(s) first to narrate a previous episode, so that each section is also embedded in the previous one. In the story, this progressive embedding is signalled by an additional pair of quotation marks for every level. The second set, numbered 7 to 1, takes the reader forward in time again to the narrative present, and progressively out of the nested narrative frames. But in fact, this perfect numerical order only camouflages a temporal and causal chaos in which neither time references nor diegetic levels can be identified at all.[101] To begin with, the reader does not know and never finds out what moment of his long story Menelaus' voice really speaks from. In the first embedded text, Menelaus observes:

"One evening, embracing in our bed, I dreamed I was back in the

---

[101] Aleid Fokkema analyzes structures of recursion in *Lost in the Funhouse* and discusses how in the "Menelaiad," the intervention of certain characters at narrative levels other than their own leads to chronological paradoxes ("Gödel, Escher, Barth: Variations on a Triangle," *Delta* 21 [1985]: 65–78). See also Beth A. Boehm's analysis of the relationship between storyteller and audience in the "Menelaiad" ("Educating Readers: Creating New Expectations in *Lost in the Funhouse*," *Reading Narrative: Form, Ethics, Ideology*, ed. James Phelan [Columbus: Ohio State University Press, 1989], 109–13).

wooden horse, waiting for midnight. Laocoön's spear still stuck in our
flank . . . But in the horse, while smart Odysseus held shut our mouths, I
dreamed I was home in bed before Paris and the war, our wedding night
. . . Now I wonder which dream dreamed which, which Menelaus never
woke and now dreams both.

"And when I was on the beach at Pharos, seven years lost en route from
Troy, clinging miserably to Proteus for direction, he prophesied a day
when I'd sit in my house at last, drink wine with the sons of dead
comrades, and tell their dads' tales; my good wife would . . . dutifully
pour the wine. That scene glowed so in my heart . . . and the Nile-murk
on my tongue turned sweet. But then it seems to me I'm home in Sparta,
talking to Nestor's boy or Odysseus's; Helen's put something in the wine
again . . . and the tale I tell so grips me, I'm back in the cave once more
with the Old Man of the Sea."[102]

This introductory passage makes it impossible for the reader to
decide which of the scenes whose chronological order seems so
transparent in the successive embeddings actually lies in the past,
and which still in the future for the narrating voice. The present
eludes the reader's grasp because what we take to be the present
at one moment may be a memory that Menelaus looks back on
from a later stage, or an image of the future he creates out of
Proteus' prediction. Menelaus, whose history is reconstructed in
this elaborate textual and temporal structure, really turns out to
be a paradigmatically "posthistorical" figure whose past, present
and future all appear in some sense simultaneous and therefore
cannot be apprehended historically.

   The only meaning the notion of "present" still has in these
circumstances is that it is the attempt to grasp the present; this
insight emerges from the double vertigo that overcomes Menelaus during his drawn-out struggle with Proteus on the beach at
Pharos. His first realization in this fight, during which Proteus
successively turns into different kinds of animals, into salt-water,
into a tree, and finally into an old man, is a properly temporal
one. It occurs to him that Proteus, not bound by the same time
scale as Menelaus, might remain in one shape for longer than
Menelaus can hold on: " " " "My problem was, I'd leisure to think.
My time was mortal, Proteus's im-; what if he merely treed it a
season or two till I let go?" ' " " "[103] Reflected in Menelaus' dealings

[102] Barth, "Menelaiad," *Lost in the Funhouse*, 127–28.
[103] *Ibid.*, 138.

with gods and demi-gods, we here encounter precisely the problem of disparate time scales we earlier discussed as part of the postmodern scientific *Weltbild*, the idea that present events might be taking place at a time scale that is simply inaccessible to human perception and manipulation. This consideration ultimately renders even human time incomprehensible to Menelaus:

> " ' "What was it anyhow I held? If Proteus once was Old Man of the Sea and now Proteus was a tree, then Proteus was neither, only Proteus; what I held were dreams. But if a real Old Man of the Sea had really been succeeded by real water and the rest, then the dream was Proteus. And Menelaus! For I changed too as the long day passed: changed my mind, replaced myself, grew older. How hold on until the 'old' (which is to say the young) Menelaus rebecame himself?" ' "[104]

Proteus' successive metamorphoses become, for Menelaus, metaphors of human change through time; and yet they are ironic metaphors, since they imply a reversibility that human temporality lacks. But both the metamorphoses and human aging disperse identity over time, and this process continues even when Proteus finally returns to his shape as an old man and asks Menelaus to let him go. As Menelaus refuses, Proteus angrily points out to him that nothing proves that Menelaus is in fact holding Proteus at that very moment at all, since Proteus himself might well have turned into Menelaus, and indeed into Menelaus holding Proteus. This is the second moment of vertigo in the struggle: under Menelaus' very eyes, the present splits into two different versions of itself, and he has no way of deciding which is the "real" one. As a consequence, he becomes unable to affirm anything at all about the present moment, except that it is the instant in which he attempts to grasp the present, and Proteus becomes the figure for the multiple temporalities in which Menelaus loses himself.

He loses himself not only in the sense of being deprived of a clear sense of his own identity; he also, quite literally, turns from a human being into a voice that may be no more than a tape-recording. This voice, finally without quotation marks, narrates the beginning and ending of the short story, referring to Menelaus sometimes in the first and sometimes in the third person. "No matter; this isn't the voice of Menelaus; this voice *is*

---

[104] *Ibid.,* 138.

Menelaus, all there is of him," this speech without speaker affirms at the beginning.[105] And at the end it explains: "When I understood that Proteus somewhere on the beach became Menelaus holding the Old Man of the Sea, Menelaus ceased. Then I understood further how Proteus thus also was as such no more, being as possibly Menelaus's attempt to hold him, the tale of that vain attempt, the voice that tells it."[106] The "I" by this time has become an unidentifiable amalgam of Proteus and Menelaus, a voice detached from either character that refers to both of them in the third person. The "history" of Menelaus, then, in a movement that emerges from and repeats the moment in which Proteus turns into Menelaus holding Proteus, has here generated the voice that tells it. This voice, however, has more affinities with a pre-recorded program than a human story-teller; at the very beginning, it declares, "When I'm switched on I tell my tale, the one I know, How Menelaus Became Immortal, but I don't know it," a phrasing which suggests a radio or a tape-recorder.[107] Menelaus' immortality depends on the elimination of his identity as a human being: the story can only be told because Menelaus' and Proteus' identities have disappeared, but this disappearance is also what the story is about and aims to achieve.

Barth's short story makes explicit what is implied in other texts with similar organizational patterns. Proteus, the figure who has privileged access to the future, prophesies to Menelaus what is to come; but far from clarifying Menelaus' future, these prophecies instead make his past and present indistinguishable from it, and fracture Menelaus' identity to the point where his text is all that remains of him, since he cannot retain a stable self in Protean time. The voice that is "switched on" is all that is left of the high-

---

[105] *Ibid.*, 127; original emphasis.
[106] *Ibid.*, 161.
[107] *Ibid.*, 127. In the "Author's Note" which precedes the short stories of *Lost in the Funhouse*, Barth footnotes several of the stories by saying that they were intended for a recorded voice: "'Menelaiad,' though suggestive of a recorded authorial monologue, depends for clarity on the reader's eye and may be said to have been composed for 'printed voice'" (ix). Walter Verschueren sees the "great accomplishment of the 'Menelaiad' . . . in the intermediate and ambivalent level of the tape discourse . . . its project can be described as the attempt by the voice of the tape discourse to recover, in a purity and uniqueness of context, the intentional consciousness of the original speech act" ("'Voice, Tape, Writing': Original Repetition in *Lost in the Funhouse* [Beyond Phenomenology: Barth's 'Menelaiad']," *Delta* 21 [1985]: 80).

modernist exploration of consciousness and memory. Where past and present are structured like the future, there is no room for human observers, who in the process of observation would be constantly fractured into multiple versions of themselves: hence the strangely inconsistent, self-contradictory or disintegrating narrators that characterize many postmodern novels. There is not, in other words, a perspective with the distance that would make it possible to transform this sort of time into conventional narrative or historical form.

If indeed the changes in narrative organization I have discussed are related to more general developments in the Western culture of time, these difficulties associated with the position of the narrator must lead one also to question the position of the critic who analyzes cultural and literary phenomena, and the temporal orientation that guides this analysis. Some theorists see something akin to paradox in the attempt to account historically for a culture that resists the concept of history. Katherine Hayles, for example, claims that "[a]nalyzing postmodernism . . . amounts to writing the history of no history. In an important sense, to write the history of postmodernism is to indulge in anachronism."[108] One might want to hold against this claim that a method of study is not obligated to replicate the structural features of the object of study: the post- or antihistorical dimensions of postmodern culture do not automatically force an analysis of this culture to proceed post- or antihistorically itself. As Andreas Huyssen notes, "the waning of historical consciousness is itself a historically explainable phenomenon."[109] Nevertheless, one must ask to what extent a literary or cultural analysis should insist on establishing historical coherence by outlining, for example, the transition from high-modernist to postmodernist art, when postmodernist artifacts stress the impossibility or irrelevance of such coherence.

A full answer to this question can probably not be given without a detailed examination of the theoretical foundations and procedures of literary history, a project which lies beyond the

---

[108] Hayles, *Chaos Bound*, 281. Niethammer circumvents this paradox by arguing that it will be up to others to judge "de[n] Reflex des Historikers, Posthistoire zu historisieren" (the reflex of the historian to historicize posthistory) (*Posthistoire*, 10).

[109] *Twilight Memories*, 9.

scope of this book. But it is worth noting that a concept such as that of posthistory, even as it declares the end of conventional temporality and indeed the end of ending, relies itself to some extent at least on the conventional narrative mechanism of closure to structure time: placing oneself at or after the end of history provides one with a vantage point from which past time becomes narratable because it is concluded, and hence allows the observer to contemplate it from the distance afforded by closure. One may regret this as a methodological anachronism, but clearly any historical approach requires some mechanism whereby the observer gains distance from the time period to be described, as Fredric Jameson points out: "Historicity is . . . neither a representation of the past nor a representation of the future (although its various forms *use* such representations): it can first and foremost be defined as a perception of the present as history; that is, as a relationship to the present which somehow defamiliarizes it and allows us that distance from immediacy which is at length characterized as a historical perspective."[110] The paradox of the multiple alternative temporalities that structure postmodern novels lies in the fact that they make conventional observer positions impossible, but precisely thereby do achieve the defamiliarization that creates a distance from the present. This kind of distancing certainly does not lead directly to anything like a historical perspective, but at the very least it allows one to reflect on the possibility of different and perhaps alternative histories to frame the present, which themselves have to be evaluated with critical distance. Whether the historicization of contemporary posthistory that has been proposed here does justice to its object can only be judged with such distance – among others, that of time.

[110] Jameson, *Postmodernism*, 284; original emphasis.

II

Time Forks and Time Loops

Time Fosts and Time Loops

2

❖❖

Number, chance and narrative: Julio Cortázar's *Rayuela*

❖❖

Julio Cortázar's *Rayuela*, first published in 1963, is one of the most famous experiments with narrative order in the novel after World War II. According to the author's instructions at the beginning of the text, this novel can be read following two different reading procedures; in the first of these, the novel is read in the normal order of its chapters and tells a fairly straightforward and linear story of a middle-aged Argentinean in Paris and Buenos Aires, but ends after about two-thirds of the text. The second one is a radically non-linear itinerary that begins with Chapter 73, leaps back and forth and ends with either Chapter 58 or 131, covering the entirety of the text. The reader is free to choose either itinerary. This textual organization is obviously quite different from earlier experiments with narrative chronology and causation undertaken by such high-modernist novelists as Joseph Conrad, Marcel Proust, Ford Madox Ford, Virginia Woolf or William Faulkner, who abandoned linear order so as to represent more accurately the intricate operations of human memory, the discontinuities typical of a "spontaneous" act of narration, or the piecemeal accumulation of evidence from different sources that finally leads to a coherent representation of past events. Their often highly innovative texts foregrounded the discrepancy between the order in which events are presented in the narration and the order in which the reader must infer them "really" to have occurred – in narratological terms, the distinction between discourse order and story order – but none of them included experimentation with the physical format of the printed book. *Rayuela*, by contrast, focuses on the diverging temporalities of the narrated story and the sequence of the pages on which it is printed.

Similar experiments have been attempted repeatedly by novelists over the last forty years, and *Rayuela* is not in principle the most radical among them. In the 1960s, several authors went further than Cortázar in questioning traditional book format by publishing loose-leaf novels, texts in which individual pages or short chapters were not bound and numbered, but stacked in a box, and could be picked up in any order by the reader. Nevertheless, loose-leaf texts such as B. S. Johnson's *The Unfortunates* or Marc Saporta's *Composition No.1* are ultimately less complex in their organization than *Rayuela*, since they either tell stories whose sequence can be easily reconstituted no matter what the order of the reading (as in the case of *The Unfortunates*), or the occasional indeterminacy of narrative order seems to matter little for the overall effect of the story (as in *Composition No.1*). *Rayuela*'s complexity, by contrast, derives from the way in which it deploys both modernist and postmodernist strategies of narrative: potentially postmodernist devices such as the two reading itineraries and the embedding of imaginary authors and their writings into the text, which in other novels lead to the emergence of alternative or paradoxical universes, are used for by and large modernist effects in Cortázar's text. But *Rayuela* does take a turn toward the postmodern in its continuous reflection on what distinguishes narrative order from mere cataloguing or numerical progression. In its self-reflexive play with lists and various kinds of classification systems, it explores the danger of narrative lapsing into enumeration, and examines how narrative time functions or fails to operate as a vehicle of meaning. This play ultimately leads the plot to a clearly postmodernist series of alternative endings none of which is more authoritative than any of the others. In its organization, therefore, *Rayuela* maps some of the transformations that take place in the transition from modernist to postmodernist narrative.

1. Itineraries

Rayuela's most conspicuous organizational feature is its division into the two different reading itineraries that are proposed on its very first page: "A su manera este libro es muchos libros, pero sobre todo es dos libros"[1] (In its own way, this book is many

---

[1] *Rayuela*, 3. All quotations from *Rayuela* refer to the critical edition by Julio Ortega and Saúl Yurkievich (n.p.: Colección Archivos, 1991). Translations are mine unless otherwise indicated.

books, but above all two books), the author or perhaps narrator explains in the "Tablero de dirección" (Table of Instructions). The two itineraries are then defined as follows:

El primer libro se deja leer en la forma corriente, y termina en el capítulo 56, al pie del cual hay tres vistosas estrellitas que equivalen a la palabra *Fin*. Por consiguiente, el lector prescindirá sin remordimientos de lo que sigue.

El segundo libro se deja leer empezando por el capítulo 73 y siguiendo luego en el orden que se indica al pie de cada capítulo. En caso de confusión u olvido, bastará consultar la lista siguiente: . . .

Con objeto de facilitar la rápida ubicación de los capítulos, la numeración se va repitiendo en lo alto de las páginas correspondientes a cada uno de ellos.

(The first can be read in the normal fashion and ends with Chapter 56, after which there are three gaudy little stars which stand for the words *The End*. Consequently, the reader may disregard what follows without remorse.

The second book can be read beginning with Chapter 73 and then following the sequence indicated at the end of each chapter. In case of confusion or forgetfulness, one need only consult the following list: . . .

To make it easy to locate the chapters quickly, the numbering is repeated at the top of each of their pages.)

This instruction for reading is striking in several ways. Most obviously, it suggests that the structure of *Rayuela* confronts two different types of textual organization with each other: the first narrative the reader is invited to follow proceeds in a linear fashion at least as far as the printed pages are concerned, leads to a clearly marked moment of closure, but covers only roughly two thirds of the novel's text. The second one, which takes the reader through all chapters but one (Ch. 55 is omitted in this itinerary), preserves the basic sequence of the first fifty-six chapters, but inserts ninety-nine others between them and forces the reader to leap back and forth between different sections of the text. This second narrative does not, strictly speaking, come to an end: Cortázar's listing of chapters closes with "88 – 72 – 77 – 131 – 58 – 131 – ," indicating that at the end of the novel, Chapters 131 and 58 simply alternate with each other in a potentially infinite sequence.

Since this instruction offers the reader at least two and possibly more ways of reading the novel, many of Cortázar's critics over the last three decades have hailed *Rayuela* as a prototype of what

Umberto Eco calls "opera aperta," the open work, and Roland Barthes "texte scriptible" or writerly text.[2] According to these critics, Cortázar calls for the active participation of the reader in the production of the text, especially since the second itinerary, which does not so much tell a progressively unfolding story as bring together fragments, images and partial narratives from a variety of discursive contexts, requires considerable effort from the reader if it is to coalesce in a coherent whole. This approach is confirmed by much of the novel's metafictional comment on itself. The protagonists frequently discuss literary theory and literary works, in the first section of *Rayuela* particularly the work of the novelist Morelli, whose philosophy of narrative often seems to describe precisely that of the novel he appears in: for example, he aims at disrupting the normal reading habits of his audience, at breaking away from the conventions of printed order, and at creating a text that goes beyond conventional character psychology toward a more impersonal structure (Chs. 99, 61). Along with its innovative structure, then, *Rayuela* supplies its readers with a fairly explicit theory of narrative that encourages them to think of themselves as the author's collaborators in their leaping progression through the text.

Although this view prevails in most critical approaches to *Rayuela*, it has not gone entirely unchallenged. The reasons for such a challenge emerge, to begin with, from the very same "Table of Instructions" that is usually read as an unconventional novelistic program daring the readers to abandon their usual passive role, to make their own choices and to articulate their own construction of the text. If indeed *Rayuela* consists of "many books" any of which may be selected by the reader, one might ask what justifies the existence of instructions at the beginning of the text? Clearly, the author does not seem to want the audience to approach the novel in any way it chooses, since he proposes two specific orders of reading it. This impression is confirmed by a sentence that does not appear in the first edition of *Rayuela* from 1963, but that Cortázar added subsequently: in the second edition

---

[2] This connection with Eco and Barthes is made by Scott Simpkins in "'The Infinite Game': Cortázar's *Hopscotch*," *Journal of the Midwest Modern Language Association* 23 (1990): 61. See Umberto Eco, *The Role of the Reader: Explorations in the Semiotics of Texts* (Bloomington: Indiana University Press, 1979), and Roland Barthes, *S/Z* (n.p.: Seuil, 1970).

from 1965, the initial suggestion in the "Table of Instructions" that *Rayuela* consists above all of two texts is followed by the observation, "El lector queda invitado *a elegir* una de las dos posibilidades siguientes" (The reader is invited *to select* one of the following two possibilities; original emphasis). This phrase suggests not only that there are really no more than two choices, but also that these choices are mutually exclusive.[3] Furthermore, the detailed list of chapter numbers which defines the second itinerary turns out to be quite unnecessary upon closer inspection, since each chapter in the text is immediately followed by the number of the one the reader should turn to next. As Scott Simpkins has pointed out, the chapter list is provided only because, as the author specifies, he does not want the reader to deviate from the prescribed route even by accident, "in case of confusion or forgetfulness," a concern that also informs the emphasis on ubiquitous chapter numbering in the last sentence of the "Table of Instructions."[4]

If none of these preliminaries bespeak an author eager to relinquish control of his text to the readers, some of the metafictional comments within the novel seem equally designed to restrict rather than expand the scope of choices available to the audience. As most critics of *Rayuela* have pointed out, both the novelist Morelli and the protagonists who read and comment on his work persistently revile "passive" readers or "lectores-hembra" (female-readers) who do not go beyond receiving what the author supplies them with, and rely on conventional sense-making procedures in their reading (see, for example, Ch. 99: 444 and 448).[5] What Morelli strives for are readers who become co-authors, "accomplices" in the act of producing the text. It is hard not to read the dichotomy of the "Table of Instructions" with this distinction in mind: Cortázar is surely turning ironically on the

---

[3] Robert Brody, *Julio Cortázar* (London: Grant & Cutler, 1976), 37; Simpkins, "'The Infinite Game,'" 72: n. 11.

[4] Simpkins, "'The Infinite Game,'" 63.

[5] Cortázar later apologized for the awkwardness of a terminology which systematically associates passivity and lack of engagement with femininity. This sexism is hardly an accidental shortfall, however, as Jean Franco has pointed out (*An Introduction to Spanish-American Literature*, 3rd edn [Cambridge: Cambridge University Press, 1994], 337–38): through the systematic association of some of the female protagonists with irrationality and intuition, it is hardwired into the basic configuration of the novel and not just a matter of an occasional metafictional comment.

passive readers when he suggests that they can stop reading at Chapter 56 and ignore the rest of the novel "without remorse." In terms of the reading strategies that the metafictional comments in the novel promote, this hardly appears as an acceptable choice; as a consequence, the only option that really remains open is that of the second itinerary. In the view of some critics, the authorial instructions turn *Rayuela* into a text that manipulates and controls its readers precisely by making them believe that the novel is open to any approach they might want to take. Simpkins, for example, who critically analyzes the marginalization of certain types of readers in the novel, concludes that what freedom there is in interpreting the novel is gained by resisting the thrust of the authorial instructions and metafictional comments, not by accepting its invitations. Ultimately, in this reading, the "Table of Instructions" should not be taken as the authoritative guide *to* the text, but as a ploy *in* the text that has no greater authority than any of its other parts.[6]

Interpretations of *Rayuela*, then, run the gamut between those that characterize it as a textual field wide open for the active engagement of the reader, and those which understand its deliberately foregrounded openness as a stratagem designed to ensure closer authorial control over the reading process. I would argue that this conflict cannot be satisfactorily resolved unless one takes into account the ways in which *Rayuela* takes up and transforms typically modernist strategies of narrative. Without any question, *Rayuela*'s second itinerary requires a much greater interpretive effort on the part of the reader than a conventional realist text; but the multitude of fragments and quotations by means of which Chapters 57 to 155 split up the more straightforward narrative of the first fifty-six chapters is not inherently more difficult to assimilate than the juxtaposition of radically different voices and discourses in such high-modernist novels as *Manhattan Transfer*, *Ulysses* or *Berlin Alexanderplatz*, or long poems such as William Carlos Williams' *Paterson*. In this respect, *Rayuela*

---

[6] Simpkins, "'The Infinite Game,'" 66 and 70–71. A related argument is proposed in Michael Hardin's "Non-Cooperative Game Theory and Female-Readers: How To Win the Game of *Hopscotch*," *Hispanófila* 11 (1994): 57–72, which makes the daring but implausible suggestion that taking the female-reader's route and stopping at Chapter 56 is the only way of gaining the upper-hand in the struggle of control between author and reader. This application of game theory to the novel, however, is a good deal less convincingly argued than Simpkins'.

is less innovative than it appears at first sight, since it really continues a type of literary experimentation that began in the 1920s, and it is no more and no less open to active reader engagement than many modernist texts that preceded it. What *is* different about Cortázar's novel, however, is that the issue of how the reader should establish narrative coherence in this kind of experimental structure is explicitly foregrounded and discussed in the text itself. Arguably, the fact that the text recommends certain reading strategies and discourages others does indeed restrict the audience's freedom to articulate its own approach, although it should also be emphasized that readers always have the freedom to reject those recommendations.

In the critical debate of how "open" or "writerly" a text *Rayuela* is, and whether author or reader exerts ultimate control over its shape, the actual narrative material whose control is at stake often takes second place after more theoretical considerations of the relationship between author and audience. But the question of how much control over the text author or reader could or should assume vitally depends on how this affects the story that is being told; in the case of *Rayuela*, we must ask what difference it makes whether we read the novel according to the first or the second itinerary (or, possibly, others). At least one critic has argued that the plot line does not fundamentally change, since the interpolation of additional narrative material into the novel's second reading itinerary does nothing to put the basic story in question or to undermine the "structure and stability of the fictional world." For him, this stability implies that *Rayuela* should be considered a late-modernist rather than a postmodernist text, since postmodernist narrative persistently questions the fictional universes it establishes.[7] Indeed, the second narrative itinerary complements but never contradicts the first one; there is no suggestion that any of the events in the first narrative did not take place, or that they did not occur as reported, although Cortázar's strategy of splitting the text into two narrative strands would easily have lent itself to such questioning. In other words, although the narrative structure opens up the possibility of alternative fictional universes, it is not

---

[7] Brian McHale, *Postmodernist Fiction* (New York: Methuen, 1987), 253: Note 26.

after all used to that effect: *Rayuela* deploys postmodernist narrative techniques for modernist purposes.

The actual text of *Rayuela*, however, is more complex than this description of the general narrative organization suggests. Precisely because McHale is, broadly speaking, right in arguing that *Rayuela* is a modernist text which uses certain postmodernist devices and strategies without exploiting them in the spirit of more typically postmodernist novels, it is worth analyzing in more detail just how these innovative strategies are applied, and what purposes they serve. A closer look at the two itineraries will begin to open up some of the text's organizational intricacies, and show that *Rayuela* is more of a hybrid text than McHale allows for.

The linear reading of *Rayuela* includes the two sections titled "Del lado de allá" ("From That Side"; Chapters 1–36) and "Del lado de acá" ("From This Side"; Chapters 37–56). The two "sides" refer to the geographical locations in which the chapters are set: Paris in the first section and Buenos Aires in the second. But they also point to the symmetry which shapes the two sections in relation to each other: many of the major characters and events that occur in Paris are mirrored, repeated and sometimes inverted in the Buenos Aires chapters. The link between the two parts is the novel's protagonist, Horacio Oliveira, who lives in Paris and later returns to Buenos Aires, his city of origin. While in Paris, much of Oliveira's life revolves around a group of international, mostly male Bohemians who call themselves the "Serpent Club," and in particular around his relationship with an Uruguayan, Lucía, nicknamed "la Maga." Lucía, with her lack of education and intuitive approach to life, is clearly somewhat of a misfit in the highly literate and intellectual club, and often struggles hard to follow the conversations among Oliveira's friends. Neither does her relationship with Oliveira run smoothly: after Lucía brings her sick baby boy Rocamadour to live with them in their shared apartment, tensions between the two increase; Oliveira starts seeing another woman, Pola, and accuses Lucía of having an affair with their mutual friend Gregorovius. Finally, the two decide to break off their relationship. On the very same day, Lucía's isolation comes to a head in a climactic scene in which Oliveira and the entire Serpent Club gather at her apartment for one of their usual discussions; the lights are turned off so as not to disturb Rocamadour. But when Oliveira approaches Rocamadour's bed in the dark, he realizes that the baby has died, and whispers the news to his friends, until everybody in the room except Lucía is aware of her son's death. In the darkness, a brilliant discussion about the foundations of knowledge develops even as the Club anxiously awaits the moment in which Lucía will turn to her son to give him his medicine. This scene marks the end of the Club: Oliveira disappears for a week without explanation, and when he returns, Lucía has vanished; whether she has left town to move somewhere else, returned to South America, or even drowned herself in the Seine, he is unable to find out with any certainty. The Club accuses him of insensitivity toward her, but he angrily rejects both the accusation and the Club as a whole; instead, he goes to spend a night with a clocharde in an act of deliberate self-abasement.

At the beginning of the second section, he has returned to Buenos Aires. But on "this side," things quickly begin to resemble those "on the other side." Although Oliveira now lives with a former lover of his, Gekrepten, his true affections seem to focus on Talita, the wife of his old friend and alter ego, Traveler. Talita had immediately reminded Oliveira of Lucía when he arrived in Buenos Aires, and from the beginning he is stricken with a sense of foreboding regarding the future of their relationship. But this does not keep him from moving into a hotel room across the street from the Travelers', or from accepting to work with them as staff in an asylum for the insane. In this ominous setting, Oliveira does end up mistaking Talita for Lucía one night while she is playing hopscotch in the garden; when they have to go down to the basement morgue later that night, he kisses her, and then immediately imagines that Traveler will kill him in revenge. He feverishly builds an intricate and absurd defense system in his room with the help of one of the inmates, which succeeds only in collapsing with a tremendous noise when Traveler does indeed enter his room – not, however, to harm him, but because he and Talita are extremely worried about their friend's state of mind. Both in fact vigorously defend him against the asylum director and the doctor, who after this incident believe that Oliveira himself must be in need of clinical attention. At the end, Oliveira leans out of his window and looks down on Talita and Traveler, who are standing in the garden with one foot each in the hopscotch diagram; in a moment of supreme harmony, he considers their exemplary loyalty to him and reflects at the same time that his best move would indeed be to take the leap.

The triangular relationship between Oliveira, Talita and Traveler mirrors the earlier one between Oliveira, Lucía and Pola, whereas Gekrepten occupies a position similar to that Gregorovius.[8] The ignorant remarks about literature and culture that the pensioners in Oliveira's hotel backyard exchange during their evening conversations ironically echo the Serpent Club's discussions of art and philosophy. Oliveira's descent to the morgue with Talita and his kiss, which really is meant for Lucía, re-enacts his one-night affair with the clocharde Emanuelle, whom he allowed to make love to him while fantasizing about Pola. And Oliveira's potential suicide, finally, corresponds to Lucía's alleged drowning in the Seine. In a sense, these doublings and repetitions are triggered by Lucía's unconfirmed death: Oliveira sees her in Talita because he cannot believe she is dead. And indeed, the evidence remains inconclusive: two Serpent Club members mention rumors about her suicide, but do not give any precise details; Emanuelle, the clocharde, refers to a woman found in the Seine, but does not know her identity; and a note in the newspaper about a drowned woman does not correspond to Lucía in its description. Oliveira, unconvinced that she is dead, searches for her in Montevideo on his way back to Argentina; he does not find her, but instead briefly mistakes a woman on the boat to Buenos Aires for her, and then discovers a resemblance to her in Talita – the resemblance which gives rise to a whole series of echoes, mirror-images and repetitions of events that had previously occurred in Paris.

In the narrative that emerges from the first reading itinerary in *Rayuela*, then, we find a bipartition that resembles the division proposed in the "Table of Instructions" in so far as it also offers two different fictional worlds to the reader. Once again, the confrontation of the two worlds could have easily been used to destabilize one or both in typically postmodernist fashion: in

---

[8] Steven Boldy, *The Novels of Julio Cortázar* (Cambridge: Cambridge University Press, 1980), 83; Ana María Barrenechea, "Los dobles en el proceso de escritura de *Rayuela*," *Revista iberoamericana* 125 (1983): 812–27; E. D. Carter Jr., "La sombra del perseguidor: El doble en *Rayuela*," *Explicación de textos literarios* 17 (1988–89): 67–99.

some of Jorge Luis Borges' short stories, for example, literal or metaphorical mirror-images take on precisely this function. But this is not the case in *Rayuela*: Oliveira and Traveler, Lucía and Talita, although they are doubles of each other, remain clearly distinct and, on the whole, realistically conceived characters. Events in Buenos Aires and in Paris give each other greater resonance and amplify each other's meaning, but they never enter into collision or contradiction. The fictional worlds on the "two sides" of the first sequence always remain compatible with each other in a temporal succession that never splits into alternative strands of narration.

This symmetrical structure, which hinges on Oliveira's move from Paris to Buenos Aires, becomes a good deal more complicated when we turn to *Rayuela's* second narrative sequence, which includes not only the story just surveyed, but also the text of the third section titled "De otros lados (*Capítulos prescindibles*)" (From Other Sides [*Expendable Chapters*]), an accumulation of additional scenes and anecdotes, quotations, footnotes, and a large body of theoretical reflections about novel-writing attributed to the novelist Morelli. These "expendable chapters" follow no discernible order in themselves; they are interpolated between the chapters of the first two sections, spacing them out without altering their basic sequence. The only exception is Chapter 55, which is omitted entirely in the second itinerary and "replaced" by Chapters 129 and 133, which contain the same text, but with substantial additions. The alternation between basic and "expendable" chapters obeys a fairly regular rhythm in that between one and three chapters of the main narrative are followed by one to three expendable chapters. The second itinerary, in opposition to the clear-cut, three-starred end of the first one, ends in two chapters which refer the reader to each other in a potentially interminable alternation: Chapters 58 and 131, pointing to each other, open the end of the book up onto a virtual infinitude of reading repetitions.

The intercalation of these ninety-nine additional chapters substantially alters the temporal organization of the basic sequence of fifty-six. Most obviously, they delay and space out the development of the plot, sometimes to the point of disrupting it completely: since Oliveira's story is not very tightly knit in the first place, the expendable chapters, which often have no well-defined temporal relation to the basic sequence, make it much more difficult to identify the progression of the narrative. In fact, a reader who first follows the second, more complicated itinerary is hard put to it even to recognize that there is any such basic plot. "This effect reverses that of realistic conventions, where what is widely dispersed proves to have a hidden connection; here what appears to be single, identifiable as 'the same,' becomes dispersed, multiplied."[9] The scene of Rocamadour's death, for example, is followed by a series of no less than twenty-two expendable chapters, so that by the time Oliveira returns to the apartment a week later in narrated time, the readers themselves come back from a digression so long that Rocamadour is all but forgotten. Since we are not told what actually happened during this period, the sheer length of narrative discourse here comes to stand in for the gap in story time – without, however, "filling" it in terms of content. Although the expendable chapters do not put in question the basic story line of *Rayuela*, then,[10] they do introduce a type of temporality that is completely different from the one suggested by a linear reading of the first fifty-six chapters.

If the symmetries and recurrences of the first reading itinerary suggest that Oliveira is trapped in a past that is never quite concluded and therefore keeps repeating itself, the dispersion of the second one indicates, by contrast, that neither past nor present can be held on to, scattered as they are in the midst of memories, quotations and self-reflections. If one reads Oliveira's story according to the second trajectory, it is not so much a story as a fragmented sequence of contingencies not substantially different from the anecdotes and *faits divers* from newspapers, almanacs and encyclopedias that surface again and again in the expendable chapters. These vignettes or aphorisms, often based on quite trivial, everyday occurrences, attain their striking literary resonance precisely because they are separated from their context and the causal connections they originally emerged from. Mixed into and read amongst this accumulation of often quite random

---

[9] Elizabeth Deeds Ermarth, *Sequel to History: Postmodernism and the Crisis of Representational Time* (Princeton: Princeton University Press, 1992), 125.

[10] "El propósito . . . no es desordenar la narrativa, sino de señalar la posibilidad de desorden," Alfred J. MacAdam observes in "*Rayuela*: La cuestión del lector," *Explicación de textos literarios* 17 (1988–89): 221 (The objective [of the second reading itinerary] . . . is not to put the narrative in disorder, but to signal the possibility of disorder).

incidents and meditations, the fundamental contingency of Oliveira's own life appears in stark relief. Himself a foreigner whose reasons for coming to Paris are never clarified in the novel, he associates with a set of international Bohemians as alienated from their original contexts as he is. During the beginning of his relationship with Lucía, the two never set up times or places to meet and never visit each other in their apartments, but rely on accidental encounters. In fact, the novel begins with Oliveira during one of those walks through Paris which just might lead him to his girlfriend:

¿Encontraría a la Maga? Tantas veces me había bastado asomarme . . . y acercarme a la Maga que sonreía sin sorpresa, convencida como yo de que un encuentro casual era lo menos casual en nuestras vidas, y que la gente que se da citas precisas es la misma que necesita papel rayado para escribirse o que aprieta desde abajo el tubo de dentífrico. . . . Andábamos sin buscarnos pero sabiendo que andábamos para encontrarnos.

(Ch. 1: 11)

(Would I find la Maga? So many times it had been enough for me just to show up . . . and approach la Maga, who smiled without surprise and was convinced, as I was, that an accidental encounter was the least accidental thing in our lives, and that the people who make precise appointments are the same as those who need ruled paper to write to each other and who squeeze the tube of toothpaste from the bottom. . . . We walked around without looking for each other but knew that we were walking to find each other.)

From the very first page of the novel, contingency is thereby turned into a principle of action, and attempts to avoid it derided. Connections, friendships and love originate from these itineraries of contingency, whereas order and plot are precisely the forces that undo such associations: "Y mirá que apenas nos conocíamos y ya la vida urdía lo necesario para desencontrarnos minuciosamente" (And look, we had barely come to know each other, and already life was plotting everything necessary to drive us thoroughly apart), Oliveira remembers (Ch. 1: 13). His acquaintance with Morelli similarly arises from sheer coincidence, his accidental presence at a car accident whose victim turns out to be the very man whose novels he has been reading and discussing for years.[11] Finally, Oliveira experiences moments of sudden insight

[11] Ermarth comments on the relation of these accidents to the surrealist *hasard objectif* in *Sequel to History*, 135–36. See also Rolf Kloepfer, "La libertad del autor

when an accidental detail of sight, sound or smell floods him with memories from his past in Argentina, sometimes to the point of assimilating the past and the present moment so completely that they become indistinguishable.[12] The temporality Oliveira lives in, then, is one in which meaning arises from contingency, whereas order and design are apt to destroy it. This experience of time is confirmed in the juxtaposition of the two reading itineraries: the linear one leads Oliveira to the brink of suicide, whereas the non-linear one, as we shall see, ends in an amalgamation of temporal moments from past and present that defies any sort of closure.

If even the first, relatively linear itinerary emphasizes the role of contingency in this way, the function of the second one obviously is to translate it into the form of the narrative itself. But the question then arises why the book was not printed in the order of that itinerary in the first place. One critic has suggested that future publishers of the novel may decide to rearrange the chapters according to this second sequence, if only to save the spines of paperbacks hard strained by the back-and-forth movements that *Rayuela* requires.[13] This proposal may seem absurd, but it raises the valid question of whether the novel would be fundamentally altered if it simply followed the non-linear sequence, a format that would make it more closely resemble those high-modernist novels whose narrative also included quotations and fragments from the most varied areas of discourse without any immediate relation to the plot. But the particular strategy of Cortázar's text consists in dissociating narrative sequence from the numerical progression of chapters and pages, and this feature distinguishes it from high-modernist experimental novels. This strategy aims not only at restricting the role of conventional printed order as a spatial icon of linear succession, but also, and perhaps more importantly, at exploring the relationship between

y el potencial del lector: Encuentro con *Rayuela* de Julio Cortázar," trans. Victor Castro, *INTI: Revista de literatura hispánica* 22–23 (1985–86): 123.

[12] These moments, which replicate to an extent the working of involuntary memory in Proust's *A la recherche du temps perdu*, are analyzed in detail by Herbert Craig in his article, "La memoria proustiana en *Rayuela* de Julio Cortázar," *Nueva revista de filología hispánica* 37 (1989): 237–45. Craig points out, however, that the past is not always recovered intact in *Rayuela*, but deformed by the experience of the present (243).

[13] Pedro Ramírez Molas, *Tiempo y narración: Enfoques de la temporalidad en Borges, Carpentier, Cortázar* (Madrid: Gredos, 1978), 127.

narrative plot and numerical sequence as opposed and yet related principles of structuring time.

One example of how *Rayuela* approaches this relationship is Chapter 55, which is omitted in the second reading itinerary and replaced instead by Chapters 129 and 133. Interestingly enough, the first part of this chapter describes a scene of reading: Traveler is in bed waiting for his wife, Talita, and reads an unnamed book to pass the time; when Talita finally returns, she tells him about the disturbing incident she has just had with Oliveira, who mistook her for Lucía and kissed her when she accompanied him to the morgue. Chapters 129 and 133, interrupted by the short Chapter 139, describe the same scene; but some of the sentences are slightly altered, and we now find out what text Traveler is reading: *La luz de la paz del mundo* (The Light of World Peace), a treatise by an Uruguayan author named Ceferino Piriz. Long passages from this text, an esoteric proposal to the United Nations on how global society and nature should be reorganized, are quoted, and accompanied by Traveler's mental comments on his reading. In and of itself, the substitution of one chapter by two somewhat different ones in the second reading itinerary foregrounds, as Barbara Hussey has suggested, the flexibility of textual composition, and the "improvisational" quality of a narrative present which exists in two versions in the same text.[14] But it is equally noteworthy that the text which is quoted in the second version is one whose very objective is to propose a system of classification for the entire known world that excludes contingency, and whose style clearly attempts to leave absolutely nothing to chance in matters of language. I will discuss the role of Ceferino Piriz and his treatise in more detail later on, but it should be mentioned here already that his proposal includes the reorganization of the nation-state into forty-five numbered "corporations," associations that group together certain kinds of conventional institutions in rather surprising ways. Whereas the double description of Traveler's reading suggests, then, that the text within which he reads is open to chance variations, the text he reads strives to exclude chance in terms of numerical as well as other systems of classification. If *Rayuela* stages the failure of

[14] Barbara L. Hussey, *"Rayuela*: Chapter 55 as Take-(away)," *International Fiction Review* 8 (1981): 56–58.

this kind of attempt at classification – Piriz' proposals are clearly absurd, and a source of constant amusement for Traveler – it is to foreground the implications of its own break with numerical progression as a way of organizing narrative visually for the reader. Since the reader cannot predict which pages and chapters will follow which others, narrative structure with beginnings and endings as well as narrative meaning is subject to the contingencies of the context that each narrative fragment happens to appear in. In this respect, *Rayuela* does take a significant step beyond its high-modernist predecessors, as the analysis of the role of various classification devices in the novel will make even clearer.

2. Lists, phonebooks, calendars

As we have seen, the shuttle movements through the text that the second itinerary of *Rayuela* imposes on the reader fulfills two functions. On one hand, it dissociates the linearity of the reading process from its representation in the sequence of printed pages. On the other hand, it breaks up the succession that is normally established by the consecutive numbering of pages and chapters; instead of a logical succession of numbers, the author offers the reader a list of numbers in the "Table of Instruction" whose structure cannot be predicted except in so far as the fifty-six chapters of the first itinerary still appear in their original sequence, although they are sometimes widely separated from each other (as, for example, in the following sequence: "24 – 134 – 25 – 141 – 60 – 26 – 109 – 27 – 28 – 130 – 151 – 152 – 143 – 100 – 76 – 101 – 144 – 92 – 103 – 108 – 64 – 155 – 123 – 145 – 122 – 112 – 154 – 85 – 150 – 95 – 146 – 29"). This apparently arbitrary listing of numbers, however, becomes the basis for a different narrative.

The "Table of Instructions" is not the only case in which a list is turned into literature in the novel: *Rayuela* abounds in enumerations and classificatory devices such as phonebooks, guest lists, schedules and calendars. During a conversation with his friend Gregorovius, for example, Oliveira accidentally discovers a list of Buenos Aires emergency pharmacies in his pocket and substitutes their addresses and phone numbers for reasoned replies to Gregorovius' accusations against him (Ch. 31). He also carries a list of classified ads for soothsayers with him (Ch. 155), and the

novel features in addition an enumeration of all the cafés he has
been to (Ch. 132), a list of Lucía's lovers (Ch. 20), Pola's PTT
calendar with the exact hours of sunrise and sunset for each day
(Ch. 101), Morelli's list of possible literary acknowledgments
(Ch. 60), a list of Burmese names that Oliveira turns into poetry
(Ch. 41), word sequences from dictionaries that he, Talita and
Traveler play games with (Chs. 40 and 41), the registry of the
mental hospital which has to be signed by the mentally handicapped in alphabetical order (Ch. 51), the designation of the
mentally handicapped not by their names, but their room
numbers (Chs. 50–56), and a conversation between Ronald and
Etienne in which each contribution is numbered, first from 1 to 7,
then in descending order down to 1 again, so that Ronald utters
all the odd- and Etienne all the even-numbered contributions
(Ch. 142).

Some, though not all, of these lists have a clear temporal or
historical dimension. The lists of Oliveira's café visits or Lucía's
lovers, for example, obviously retrace in some way the story of
their lives; but they do so by eliminating the narrative and causal
element, reducing the story to the sheer sequentiality of a
chronicle.[15] And even those lists that do not include an overtly
temporal component, such as the list of Burmese names Oliveira
finds or the dictionary words he and his friends play with, quite
clearly revolve around the problem of sequence and its relation to
meaning, since the protagonists try to turn their bare successivity
into a vehicle of aesthetic and existential significance.[16] This
becomes very clear during the conversation between Oliveira and
Gregorovius mentioned above, in which the list of emergency
pharmacies, inherently quite unrelated to their discussion about

---

[15] For a detailed discussion of the relationship between historical chronicle and
narrative, see Hayden White's essay, "The Value of Narrativity in the Representation of Reality," in *The Content of the Form: Narrative Discourse and Historical
Representation* (Baltimore: Johns Hopkins University Press, 1987), 1–25; a
different approach to this relationship is outlined in David Carr's *Time,
Narrative, and History* (Bloomington: Indiana University Press, 1986), 59–61. For
a related discussion, see also David Carr, Charles Taylor and Paul Ricoeur,
"Table ronde/Round Table: *Temps et Récit*, Volume I," *Revue de l'Université
d'Ottawa/University of Ottawa Quarterly* 55 (1985): 301–06.

[16] A detailed analysis of the elaborate language games in the novel is presented in
Luis Iñigo-Madrigal's essay, "*Rayuela*: Los juegos en el cementerio," *Lo lúdico y
lo fantástico en la obra de Cortázar,* vol. III: *Estudios particulares,* ed. Centre de
Recherches Latino-Américaines, Université de Poitiers (Madrid: Fundamentos,
1986), 275–300.

who is to blame for Lucía's disappearance, unexpectedly turns into a network of allusions to the plot of the novel:

– Y Lucía está mejor en el fondo del río que en tu cama.
– Bolívar 800. El teléfono está medio borrado. Si a los del barrio se les enferma el nene, no van a poder conseguir la terramicina.
– En el fondo del río, sí.
– Corrientes 1117 (35–1468).
– O en Lucca, o en Montevideo.
– O en Rivadavia 1301 (38–7841).
– Guardá esa lista para Pola – dijo Gregorovius, levantándose –. (31: 156)

(– And Lucía is better off at the bottom of the river than in your bed.
– 800 Bolívar. The phone number is half erased. If people in the neighborhood have a kid that gets sick they won't be able to buy terramycin.
– At the bottom of the river, yes.
– 1117 Corrientes (Tel. 35–1468).
– Or in Lucca, or in Montevideo.
– Or in 1301 Rivadavia (Tel. 38–7841).
– Keep that list for Pola – said Gregorovius, getting up –.)

Oliveira here ironically links the name of the South American liberator Bolívar with both Lucía's possible suicide and an allusion to her sick child Rocamadour; the street name "Corrientes" ("currents") turns into a metaphor for the river she may have drowned herself in, and the name of another street ("Rivadavia") into a symbol of the many random locations she might have gone to: significantly enough, the only items Lucía has left behind in her apartment are a few scribbled notes, a novel by Pérez Galdós, and a pharmacy bill, which prompts Oliveira to reflect, "Era la noche de las farmacias" (31: 156) (It was the night of pharmacies). The scene also foreshadows Oliveira's later attraction to Lucía's double in Buenos Aires, Talita, who is a pharmacist by training and takes over the management of the drug department in the mental hospital. At the same time, the telephone numbers signal the possibility of communication over long distances in ironic counterpoint to the deliberate refusal of communication in the conversation between the two men who face each other in this very scene. Finally, Gregorovius brutally returns the list to its literal meaning by associating it with Oliveira's girlfriend Pola, who suffers from breast cancer. If this scene suggests that a mere twist of coincidence can suffice to turn a list of items into a narrative of sorts, it also, and perhaps more disturbingly, signals that narrative might disintegrate into nothing more than enumeration.

The connection between alternative forms of narrative and the list as an ordering device is articulated even more directly in a chapter that deals with Morelli's reflections on his own writing practices, and his desire to create a novel that would do away entirely with the trappings of narrative logic:

Para algunos de sus lectores (y para él mismo) resultaba irrisoria la intención de escribir una especie de novela prescindiendo de las articulaciones lógicas del discurso. Se acababa por adivinar como una transacción, un procedimiento (aunque quedara en pie el absurdo de elegir una narración para fines que no parecían narrativos).*

* ¿Por qué no? La pregunta se la hacía el mismo Morelli en un papel cuadriculado en cuyo margen había una lista de legumbres, probablemente un *memento buffandi*.
(Ch. 95: 354–55)

(For some of his readers (and for himself) the intention to write a novel of sorts without the logical articulations of discourse seemed absurd. In the end, one could vaguely perceive something like a transaction, a procedure (although the absurdity of choosing narration for non-narrative ends remained).*

* Why not? Morelli himself asked that question on a piece of graph paper in whose margin there was a list of vegetables, probably a *memento buffandi*.)

Quite literally, an improvised shopping list here frames the question of why it might not be possible to write a novel without narrative; at the same time, an already purely metafictional chapter that indirectly comments on *Rayuela*'s own narrative procedures disintegrates into a series of footnotes each of which comments on the preceding one (the footnote quoted here, marked with one asterisk, refers the reader to another note, signalled by two asterisks, which in its turn ends with three asterisks that lead the reader to the next footnote, and so on – comments on the comments on the comments). This list, along with the graph paper that is usually used for mathematical equations, indicates clearly the potential as well as the danger of Morelli's reflections: a narrative structured in numerical terms would offer the possibility of doing away with the need for logical connections of the kind that shape normal discourse, but it also runs the risk of disintegrating into mere enumeration. Or into metafictional accumulation: the series of footnotes with its ever-increasing number of asterisks that makes up the bulk of the chapter functions not unlike the embedded narrations of Barth's short story "Menelaiad," which I discussed in Chapter 1, in so far as narrative progression is replaced by a potentially infinite recursion that self-consciously foregrounds problems of narrative sequence.

Jurij Lotman, in his reflection on what forces shape narrative, argues that plot depends for its existence on a plotless text of exactly the kind that Oliveira produces in his conversation with Gregorovius: a phonebook, a code of law, or any other text that classifies and organizes a certain cultural domain. Plot super-imposes itself on this order by violating its classificatory bound-aries, so that "what the plotless text establishes as an impossibility is the very thing that constitutes the content of the plot. The plot is the 'revolutionary element' in relation to the world picture."[17] This claim may be somewhat too simple in its generality, but it does capture the tension between the merely classificatory text and narrative plot that many elements of Cortázar's novel play upon. It is also this tension that shapes *Rayuela*'s experimentation with the numerical order of pages and chapters, which is precisely such a classificatory, enumerative device. Its second itinerary dissociates plot progression and narrative temporality from the numerical sequence that the format of the printed book conventionally imposes upon the novel. In so far as page and chapter numbering can be under-stood to represent a mathematical and mechanical type of tem-porality, *Rayuela*'s subversion of this order echoes the high-modernist narrative rebellion against mechanical time that I discussed in Chapter 1. But modernist novels, which frequently disrupt chronological order by flashbacks and embedded narra-tives that gradually add up to a sequence of events, do not usually extend this questioning to the numerical format of the book; *Rayuela*, by inscribing the disruption of sequence into its physical format, takes such experiments a step further to suggest that the book in its entirety is not closed in upon itself, but liable

---

[17] Jurij Lotman, *The Structure of the Artistic Text*, trans. Gail Lenhoff and Ronald Vroon (University of Michigan: Michigan Slavic Contributions, 1977), 238. Hayden White makes a similar point when he discusses the legal or pseudo-legal systems that underlie historical narrative and inform the conflicts and transgressions it describes in *The Content of the Form*, 13–14.

to be complemented by additional pieces of discourse from outside which might come to insert themselves between its chapters. While this may imply the danger of turning narrative into a mere list or accumulation of fragments, it also indicates the possibility that any fragment can become part of the narrative simply by being framed or contextualized in a certain sequence of chapters: both possibilities are indicated in the "Table of Instructions," whose central part is simply a listing of the chapter numbers in the order of the second itinerary. In a sense, *Rayuela* here plays on the relationship between storytelling and counting, terms which are etymologically related in many European languages (German *zählen* and *erzählen*, French *conter* and *raconter*) and identical in Spanish, where both are referred to by the verb *contar*.

In his structuralist theory of narrative, Roland Barthes once argued that "the mainspring of the narrative activity is to be traced to that very confusion between consecutiveness and consequence, what-comes-*after* being read in a narrative as what-is-*caused-by*. Narrative would then be a systematic application of the logical fallacy denounced by scholasticism under the formula *post hoc, ergo propter hoc.*"[18] This observation emphasizes the extent to which narrative coherence is established in the reading process as a function of the sequence of presentation: in the case of *Rayuela*, the reader will at least attempt to integrate the supplementary chapters of the second reading itinerary into the narrative in terms of their meaning. But the arbitrary numerical succession at the same time alerts the reader that connections reached in this way are not dictated by any abstract logic other than that of the reading process itself. Not even the format of the printed book, in other words, guarantees the coherence of the narrative anymore. In this respect, *Rayuela* does at least metaphorically take a step beyond those high-modernist novels which also feature accumulations of a wide variety of different voices and discourses: whereas modernist novels encourage the reader to construct these clusters as collages which do cohere in a shared narrative frame, *Rayuela*, symbolically at least, questions and explodes this frame.

---

[18] Roland Barthes, "An Introduction to the Structural Analysis of Narrative," trans. Lionel Duisit, *New Literary History* 6 (1975): 248.

3. Almanacs, treatises, encyclopedias

The implications of this procedure emerge even more clearly when one takes into consideration the role of the writers within the novel, the novelist Morelli and the essayist Ceferino Piriz, and the text's comments on their writing. As I already mentioned, Morelli, the novelist within the novel whose works and literary theories Oliveira and his friends discuss, often seems to articulate the philosophies that underlie *Rayuela* itself; the introduction of such a meta-narrative and self-referential level is common in many postmodernist novels, and lends itself to the metaleptic violations of the boundary between embedded and frame text that I discussed in Chapter 1. But here again, *Rayuela* at first sight seems to deploy a potentially postmodernist device in rather modernist ways: Morelli's actual works are neither described in very concrete detail nor quoted at any length, so that no metaleptic collision between them and the actual text of *Rayuela* is allowed to occur; neither does Morelli ever enter into direct confrontation with the narrator of *Rayuela*.[19] As a consequence, the reader gets to know Morelli's theories much better than his novels. In one discussion, Oliveira's friend Etienne observes that Morelli detests the linearity of the conventional narrative text:

Por ejemplo, le revienta la novela rollo chino. El libro que se lee del principio al final como un niño bueno. Ya te habrás fijado que cada vez le preocupa menos la ligazón de las partes, aquello de que una palabra trae la otra . . . Cuando leo a Morelli tengo la impresión de que busca una interacción menos mecánica, menos causal de los elementos que maneja; se siente que lo ya escrito condiciona apenas lo que está escribiendo, sobre todo que el viejo, después de centenares de páginas, ya ni se acuerda de mucho de lo que ha hecho.   (Ch. 99: 364)[20]

(For example, he can't stand the Chinese-scroll novel. The book that one reads from beginning to end like a good child. You've probably noticed already that he gets less and less worried about joining the parts together, that concern of one word's leading to another . . . When I read Morelli I have the impression he's looking for a less mechanical, less causal interaction of the elements he works with; one feels that what has

---

[19] In this respect, *Rayuela* is much more similar to a modernist metanarrative text such as Huxley's *Point Counter Point* than to most postmodernist metafiction.
[20] The elision marks form part of the original text.

already been written hardly conditions what he is writing, especially since the old man, after hundreds of pages, doesn't even remember much of what he's done.)

Morelli's composition process, according to this observation, relies on a temporality without memory which suspends causation in favor of a "less mechanical . . . interaction." But this does not mean that Morelli simply advocates the loosening or randomization of story order. In his writing, he shows a curious mixture of pedantic, even obsessive concern with ordering on one hand, and carelessness about whether this order is ultimately sustained, on the other. The former surfaces in "su lado Bouvard et Pécuchet, su lado compilador de almanaque literario (en algún momento llama 'Almanaque' a la suma de su obra)" (Ch. 66: 303) (his Bouvard and Pécuchet side, his side as compiler of a literary almanac [at some point he calls his entire work an "Almanac"]).[21] This aspiration, obviously incompatible with tolerance for any kind of disruption or alteration of order, emerges when Etienne and Oliveira visit him at the hospital. He entrusts them with some of his most recent writings and the key to his apartment so that they can incorporate these writings into his work and send them to the publisher. Oliveira warns him that their interference might result in a complete confusion of the text; but Morelli replies:

No, es menos difícil de lo que parece. Las carpetas los ayudarán, hay un sistema de colores, de números y de letras. Se comprende en seguida. Por ejemplo, este cuadernillo va a la carpeta azul . . . Número 52: no hay más que ponerlo en su lugar, entre el 51 y el 53. Numeración arábiga, la cosa más fácil del mundo.   (Ch. 154: 461)

(No, it's less difficult than it seems. The folders will help you, there's a system of colors, numbers and letters. You'll understand it at once. For example, this notebook goes in the blue folder . . . Number 52: all there is to it is putting it in its place, between 51 and 53. Arabic numerals, the easiest thing in the world.)

The elaborate filing system with folders classified by "colors, numbers and letters" does not bespeak a writer careless of order, but on the contrary an unusual degree of pedantry. Morelli's

---

[21] On the basis of this remark, Anthony Percival calls the expendable chapters "a potential avant-garde almanac" ("Reader and *Rayuela*," *Revista canadiense de estudios hispánicos* 6 [1982]: 248).

casual observation that Arabic numerals are "the easiest things in the world" when it comes to keeping track of sequence ironically points to the structure of *Rayuela* itself, in which these very numbers give no clue whatever as to the order of the items they designate. Cortázar's novel, then, functions like a work of Morelli's after a mix-up or break-down of the filing system. Oliveira fears he may create precisely such a mix-up, and mentions that he and Etienne have already debated for hours whether a complication in Morelli's first volume could have arisen due to a printing error; but Morelli counters his concern with the surprisingly insouciant remark, "Ninguna importancia . . . Mi libro se puede leer como a uno le dé la gana. . . . Y en el peor de los casos, si se equivocan, a lo mejor queda perfecto" (Ch. 154: 461) (No matter . . . You can read my book any way you want to. . . . And in the worst case, if you do make a mistake, it might just turn out perfect).

Morelli's conviction that an accidental filing error might give his work its perfect shape raises the question of why, in this case, he bothers with an elaborate ordering system in the first place. But the answer lies in the question itself: Morelli relies on the power of contingency, not total randomness, and contingency can only become operative if there is an order or expectation it can break with. Without the filing system, there could be no filing error, and therefore no way of creating the dialectic of order and contingency his writing relies on. For the novel *Rayuela*, this principle implies that the text should indeed never be printed according to the second reading itinerary, as Ramírez Molas suggests, since the point is precisely its deviation from the numerical order (*contar* understood as counting) that usually structures the printed text; neither is the first, linear reading itinerary a trap for the incompetent readers the narrator occasionally derides,[22] since it exemplifies the kind of narrative succession (*contar* understood as storytelling) the second itinerary defines itself against.

Morelli's idiosyncratic approach to narrative order and its relation to the novel in which he appears takes on added significance when we take into account the writer who functions as a double or complementary figure for him in the Buenos Aires

---

[22] See Percival, "Reader and *Rayuela*," 243–44.

section, where Morelli himself is hardly mentioned at all:[23] the Uruguayan Ceferino Piriz, author of *La luz de la paz del mundo*. This treatise articulates in great detail a hallucinatory vision of a totalizing world order in which all national and international affairs and institutions are completely reclassified and reorganized in terms of such categories as the color spectrum and the signs of the zodiac. Traveler, Talita and Oliveira, who read *La luz de la paz del mundo* with exhilaration, admiration and profound bewilderment, discuss it as intensely as the Serpent Club debated Morelli's work in Paris; but in contrast to Morelli's novels, Piriz' text is quoted at length. For example, he divides the history of civilization into three periods, the first from the "immemorial past" to 1940, the second from 1940 to 1953, and the third from 1953 to 2000. Humankind is divided into six races, white, yellow, brown, black, red and "pampa," each of which constitutes one chamber in the Society of Nations, a kind of world administration. And the ideal country, according to Piriz, is organized into forty-five National Corporations, among which figure such abstruse organizations as the "CORPORACION NACIONAL DE LOS DETECTIVES CIENTIFICOS EN LO ANDANTE Y SUS CASAS DE CIENCIAS" (National Corporation of Scientific Detectives-Errant and their Houses of Science), which includes detectives, investigation police, explorers and travelers (Ch. 133: 424), the "CORPORACION NACIONAL DE LOS BEATOS GUARDADORES DE COLECCIONES Y SUS CASAS DE COLECCION" (National Corporation of Blessed Guardians of Collections and their Houses of Collection), which brings together deposits, warehouses, archives, museums, cemeteries, jails, asylums, homes for the blind, and all their employees (Ch. 133: 425), and the "CORPORACION NACIONAL DE AGENTES COMISIONADOS EN ESPECIES COLORADAS DEL AMARILLO Y CASAS DE LABOR ACTIVA PRO ESPECIES COLORADAS DEL AMARILLO: . . . animales de pelaje amarillo, vegetales de flor amarilla, y minerales de aspecto amarillo" (National Corporation of Agents Commissioned for Species Colored in Yellow and Houses of Active Labor for the Benefit of Species Colored in Yellow: . . . animals

---

[23] The doubling of the major characters in the novel is analyzed in detail by Ana María Barrenechea in "Los dobles en el proceso de escritura de *Rayuela*," 812–27, and by E. D. Carter Jr. in "La sombra del perseguidor," 67–99. Neither Barrenechea nor Carter, however, mention the parallel between Morelli and Piriz.

with yellow fur, plants with yellow flowers, and minerals with a
yellow look), with analogous corporations for all other colors
(Ch. 133: 426). "¡Purista, racista Ceferino Piriz! ¡Un cosmos de
colores puros, mondrianesco a reventar!" Traveler reflects when
he peruses this catalogue of corporations (Purist, racist Ceferino
Piriz! A cosmos of pure colors, Mondrianesque beyond endur-
ance!) (Ch. 133: 427). But there is a point to this apparent
madness. Through the rigorous application of arbitrary classification criteria (such as "collection" to group together museums and
jails), Piriz creates, as Traveler recognizes, nothing less than a
new and different universe, more fantastic than anything fictional
literature could produce. It is a vision inspired by an unyielding
obsession for completeness and rigorous symmetry, in which no
detail is left to chance. This obsession is reflected even in Piriz'
style, which spells out all the categorizations and subcategoriz-
ations of this alternative universe by means of symmetrical
sentence structures and repetitions of identical phrases, resorting
to "etc." or "idem" only in extreme cases. Piriz argues, for
example, that according to the order he proposes,

si un herrero italiano gana lo mismo dicho, entre $8,00 y $10,00 por
jornada, entonces un herrero español también ha de ganar entre $8,00 y
$10,00 por jornada; más: si un herrero español gana entre $8,00 y $10,00
por jornada, entonces un herrero ruso también ha de ganar entre $8,00 y
$10,00 por jornada; más, si un herrero ruso gana entre $8,00 y $10,00 por
jornada, entonces un herrero norteamericano también ha de ganar entre
$8,00 y $10,00 por jornada; etc.   (Ch. 133: 422)

(if an Italian blacksmith earns the aforementioned [amount], between 8
pesos and 10 pesos a day, then a Spanish blacksmith must also earn
between 8 pesos and 10 pesos a day; plus: if a Spanish blacksmith earns
between 8 pesos and 10 pesos a day, then a Russian blacksmith must
also earn between 8 pesos and 10 pesos a day; plus, if a Russian
blacksmith earns between 8 pesos and 10 pesos a day, then an
American blacksmith must also earn between 8 pesos and 10 pesos a
day; etc.)

This type of discourse creates a background against which the
slightest logical or stylistic variations, such as the final "etc.,"
stand out as unusual and deviant, "[c]uriosas infracciones a la
simetría, al rigor implacable de la enumeración consecutiva y
ordenada, que quizá traducían una inquietud, la sospecha de que
el orden clásico era como siempre un sacrificio de la verdad a la

belleza" (Ch. 129: 416), as Traveler reflects (curious infractions of symmetry, of the implacable rigor of consecutive and orderly enumeration, which betrayed perhaps an uneasiness, the suspicion that classical order was, as always, a sacrifice of truth to beauty). In Piriz' writing, such transgressions of the enumerative order are, at least in Traveler's view, only tolerated with considerable reluctance on the part of the writer, as exceptional favors to the reader that violate the totalizing scheme by means of which Piriz attempts to organize the world. As Traveler observes, "se podía saltar la enumeración, *pero no era lo mismo* . . . ; no era en absoluto lo mismo, porque el pensamiento de Ceferino era cristalográfico, cuajaba con todas las aristas y los puntos de intersección, regido por la simetría y el *horror vacui*" (Ch. 129: 415; original emphasis) (one could skip the enumeration, *but it wasn't the same* . . . it was not the same at all, because Ceferino's thought was crystallographic, it covered all the edges and points of intersection, ruled by symmetry and *horror vacui*).

Both Morelli and Piriz, then, show an unusual concern with sequential ordering and enumeration in their writing, but whereas Morelli gives chance ample space to alter any order that he might have created, Piriz strenuously seeks to exclude anything merely contingent. Contingency therefore functions as an essential creative force in Morelli, but remains an accidental destructive factor in Piriz. Or does it? In the introduction to the edition Traveler reads, Piriz announces that the reader will in fact never see the entire text composed with such minute attention to completeness: ". . . yo en este anuncio me limito solamente a enviar algunos extractos de cuya obra" (Ch. 129: 413) (I limit myself in this notice to convey only some extracts from the aforementioned work). The reason, he explains, is that the treatise has been submitted for an international competition, and that the journal in which it will appear does not allow him to publish it in its complete form elsewhere. Due to this restriction, Traveler never gets to read the entire text of *La luz de la paz del mundo*, and readers of the novel *Rayuela* in their turn see only fragments of what Traveler reads. In addition, as I mentioned earlier, the chapter which contains Traveler's reading of Piriz appears in the novel twice in slightly different versions. Through this double editing in the printed transmission of the text, Piriz' exhaustive classification of the world comes to the reader of *Rayuela* in twice-abbreviated shape, a partial, fragmented version whose very form is an ironic comment on the aspirations of the original work. But for the reader, this incomplete version is all there is of Piriz' writing within the framework of the novel. Morelli's work is subject to an even more radical editing: the readers of *Rayuela* see and hear annotations, theoretical reflections and interpretive discussions of a work which they never actually get to read even in excerpt. Therefore, although Morelli and Piriz appear to be diametrically opposed to each other on the surface – Morelli invites contingency whereas Piriz attempts to exclude it as much as possible from his text – their works turn out to share a crucial feature: both are designed in terms of an ideal numerical order that is scrambled and mutilated in its transmission through print.

This divergence between the order imposed by numbers and a text that emerges out of its violation is obviously also at stake in *Rayuela*'s second reading itinerary with its scrambled chapter sequence. As I already indicated, this scrambling might at first sight seem to articulate a critique of rational, mechanical progression that the literary text is defined against, an interpretation that could be supported by Oliveira's frequent and explicit attacks on rationality.[24] But whereas such a reading would align *Rayuela* with many high-modernist novels whose narrative organization is designed to express a similar critique, it does not really explain Cortázar's novel satisfactorily. In the case of Morelli and Piriz, the numerical order is designed by the writers themselves, whereas the creative disruption occurs precisely during the mechanical reproduction and distribution of the texts: filing and printing errors alter Morelli's novels, and the totalitarian aspirations of Piriz' treatise are subverted by the intricacies of copyright law. As they are by his readers: if Traveler, Talita and Oliveira feel a certain awe vis-à-vis Piriz' imaginative power, they also and primarily get many a good laugh out of the bizarre universe he creates. The writer, then, turns out to have no ultimate control over how the text is altered in its reproduction, dissemination and reception. This includes the temporal order of the text, which in both Morelli and Piriz strives toward the

---

[24] A detailed and critical analysis of Oliveira's attitude toward rationality and irrationality is presented in Rodger Cunningham's "Falling into Heaven: Pre-Adamism and Paradox in *Rayuela*," *INTI: Revista de literatura hispánica* 34–35 (1991–92): 93–106.

regularity of numerical sequence only to be radically distorted in its transmission to the reader.

The fate of the texts that are written and read within *Rayuela* lends a curious ambiguity to the "Table of Instructions" at the beginning of the book. It is obviously meant to control the deviations from the normal sequence that might occur in the reading even as the texts within the text demonstrate that such control is both impossible and unnecessary. Here again, *Rayuela* proves to be historically hybrid in its methods and intentions: whereas the metafictional writings within the novel clearly stage the loss of mechanical ordering devices and the important role of pure chance in the process of reception, the "Table of Instructions" acknowledges the possibility of such contingency for *Rayuela* only to try to recuperate it immediately afterwards by means of the chapter list that defines the second itinerary. In an uncertain transition from the openness of modernist narrative to the aleatoriness of the postmodern, *Rayuela* uses numerical order to exclude chance, and chance to subvert numerical order.

4. Endgames

This interplay between numerical order and chance is also reflected in the novel's title game, *Rayuela* or Hopscotch. The game is based on a symbolic drawing of the universe that appeared on the cover of *Rayuela*'s first edition: a square at the bottom called "Earth" and a half-circle at the top named "Heaven," linked by a series of squares with ascending numbers from 1 to 9. At first sight this appears like a perfectly closed spatial figuration of the cosmos, predicating a unidirectional and teleological movement from one end of the diagram to the other which might variously be understood to refer to progress through life toward fulfillment, the transition from earthly labor to heavenly reward, from mortality to eternity, or, less metaphysically, from life to death. The pebble pushed along by the player's foot would correspondingly signify the constantly shifting moment of the present during this linear and closure-oriented spatio-temporal trajectory. But the way in which the game is played subverts this linearity: once the players have reached Heaven, they must turn back and return to Earth by the same procedure, hopping on one leg and pushing the pebble along without touching any of the chalk-traced lines. And neither does the game end here: if the player has succeeded in avoiding contact with the chalk lines and in keeping the pebble in the right squares, the journey starts over again toward Heaven, this time starting from square 2, in the next cycle from square 3, and so forth. Once an entire round has been completed without error, additional complications can be introduced: hopping on the other foot, backwards, skipping a square, or other variations. As a consequence, the game has no fixed endpoint and no clearly defined objective: it is potentially infinite.[25] As Enrique Giordano has argued, this infinitude becomes particularly clear in a scene in which several of the mentally disabled play the game:

El 8 jugaba casi toda la tarde a la rayuela, era imbatible, el 4 y la 19 hubieran querido arrebatarle el Cielo pero era inútil, el pie del 8 era un arma de precisión, un tiro por cuadro, el tejo se situaba siempre en la posición más favorable, era extraordinario. . . . En su cama, cediendo a los efectos de un centímetro cúbico de hipnosal, el 8 se estaría durmiendo como las cigüeñas, parado mentalmente en una sola pierna, impulsando el tejo con golpes secos e infalibles, a la conquista de un cielo que parecía desencantarlo apenas ganado.   (Ch. 54: 258)

(Number 8 played hopscotch all afternoon, he was unbeatable, Number 4 and Number 19 would have liked to take Heaven away from him, but it was useless, Number 8's foot was a precision tool, one throw per square, the stone always ended up in the most favorable position, it was extraordinary. . . . In his bed, under the influence of a cubic centimeter of sedative, Number 8 would probably fall asleep like the storks, mentally standing on one leg, moving his stone with brisk, unerring strokes towards the conquest of a heaven that seemed to disappoint him as soon as he had reached it.)

Heaven, which looks at first like the objective and endpoint of the game, here turns out to be just a renewed point of departure, and the game develops as a series of self-reversing and repetitive journeys,[26] aptly symbolized by the player's "name," Number 8, which is itself a figure of infinity. The narrative development of the actual game, then, has a defined beginning but only an aleatory ending, and the time between the two is structured by

[25] This description of the game follows the one given by Enrique Giordano, "Algunas aproximaciones a *'Rayuela'*, de Julio Cortázar, a través de la dinámica del juego," *Homenaje a Julio Cortázar: Variaciones interpretativas en torno a su obra,* ed. Helmy F. Giacoman (Long Island City: L.A. Publishing, 1972), 97–98.
[26] Ibid., 99.

reversions, repetitions and contingencies. Hopscotch is therefore built on the dualism between the closed, unidirectional temporal structure suggested by its spatial configuration, and the reversible time that emerges through the way in which it is played.[27] Clearly, this game functions as a central metaphor for the novel itself and its suspension between two different types of temporality, although, as I will argue below, *Rayuela's* first itinerary does not have as unambiguous an endpoint as the hopscotch diagram. The analogy resides not only in the way certain sequences of numbers (of squares, pages or chapters) succeed or fail to give rise to a certain temporal order, however; strikingly, in the scene quoted, the players themselves are numbers, since this is the way the hospital's inmates are habitually designated by the staff. They seem as much to form part of the hopscotch, of its numerical structure, as they are subjects who act upon it, and cannot seem ever to separate from it, at least in Oliveira's fantasy of Number 8 continuing the game even in his sleep. This integration of the players into the game also assumes crucial importance in the novel's two different endings.

The first, linear itinerary leads the reader to an ending that is quite literally suspended as Oliveira leans out of the window contemplating suicide, but nevertheless bears all the formal marks of closure:

Era así, la armonía duraba increíblemente, no había palabras para contestar a la bondad de esos dos ahí abajo, mirándolo y hablándole desde la rayuela, porque Talita estaba parada sin darse cuenta en la casilla tres, y Traveler tenía un pie metido en la seis, de manera que lo único que él podía hacer era mover un poco la mano derecha en un saludo tímido y quedarse mirando a la Maga, a Manú, diciéndose que al fin y al cabo algún encuentro había, aunque no pudiera durar más que ese instante terriblemente dulce en el que lo mejor sin lugar a dudas hubiera sido inclinarse apenas hacia afuera y dejarse ir, paf se acabó.

(Ch. 56: 284–85)

(That's how it was, the harmony lasted incredibly long, there were no words to answer the goodness of those two down there, looking at him and talking to him from the hopscotch, because Talita stood in square

---

[27] Zunilda Gertel calls it a "juego infinito en la finitud espacial del texto" (infinite game in the spatial finiteness of the text) in *"Rayuela,* la figura y su lectura," *Hispanic Review* 56 (1988): 303; see also Alberto Sacido Romero, "El espacio, esqueleto representacional en la crisis lúdica de la *Rayuela," INTI: Revista de literatura hispánica* 32–33 (1990): 86.

three without realizing it, and Traveler had one foot in the six, so that the only thing that he could do was to move his right hand a bit in a timid salute and keep looking at la Maga, at Manú, telling himself that finally there was some meeting after all, even though it might not last longer than that terribly sweet moment in which the best thing unquestionably would have been to lean a little farther out and let himself go, bang, over.)

"Armonía," "encuentro," "al fin y al cabo," "paf se acabó": in its vocabulary the passage marks closure rhetorically just as the coincidence of all major figures and the novel's central symbol does structurally. The last words, "paf se acabó," echo almost literally a scene from the very first chapter, in which Lucía and Oliveira throw away a broken old umbrella: "Terminado. Se acabó" (Ch. 1: 12) (Finished. Over), and the phrase "no había palabras" (there were no words) can be understood to refer not only to the narrated scene, but also to the end of narration. At the same time, however, these indicators point to a potential rather than an effective moment of closure: whether Oliveira does indeed bring about the "bang" of the end by committing suicide remains open.[28] Just as Talita and Traveler, in this final panorama, seem to become part of the hopscotch diagram by occupying squares 3 and 6, the novel foregrounds how much its own temporality resembles that of the game: whereas it emphasizes closure in its rhetoric, it denies it in its plot, just as the hopscotch game subverts its closed spatial structure by its open temporality.

The second itinerary goes beyond this modernist open end in a series of chapters which project possible alternative endings: Oliveira throws himself out the window and dies; he might also throw himself out the window and continue to live; in another reading of the end, Oliveira turns mad and becomes one of the inmates of the asylum; in yet another, he returns home to Gekrepten and is taken care of by his friends.[29] The novel

---

[28] Cortázar himself indicated in an interview that he did not think Oliveira committed suicide, and, curiously enough, expressed pity for the readers who drew this conclusion, at the same time that he confirmed the openness of the ending (Evelyn Picón Garfield, *Julio Cortázar* [New York: Ungar, 1975], 106; see also Simpkins, "'The Infinite Game,'" 75, n. 5).

[29] Boldy, *The Novels*, 89; Cynthia Stone, "El lector implícito de *Rayuela* y los blancos de la narración," *Los ochenta mundos de Cortázar: Ensayos*, ed. Fernando Burgos (Madrid: EDI-6, 1987), 180.

recounts this last scenario in at least seven different versions: two episodes in which Gekrepten takes care of him, one in which Talita gives him cold compresses, one in which Traveler administers a tranquilizing shot, and one in which Ferraguto, the director of the asylum, dismisses him from his job (Chs. 135 and 72, 63, 88, 77). But the most important final chapters are the two which refer to each other at the very end in a movement which seems to invite an infinite number of rereadings: 131 and 58. In Chapter 131, Oliveira is in bed and talks to his friend Traveler, with whom he playfully considers the possibility of entering the "corporación nacional de los monjes de la oración del santiguamiento" (national corporation of monks of the prayer of the sign of the cross) (Ch. 131: 419), one of Ceferino Piriz' projected institutions. When Traveler mentions Piriz' mysteriously tautological "lugares de paraje" (sites of places), Oliveira adds "como desde lejos" (as if from far away) that he himself is now in one of them, and that it is "un lugar de paraje clavado" (a nailed-up site of a place) (Ch. 131: 419) – no doubt an allusion to a coffin. Almost at the same time, he remembers that Piriz is Uruguayan, a fact that can only be significant to him in so far as Lucía was also from Uruguay: the representative of the most rigorous order imaginable and the figure persistently associated with chaos turn out to proceed from the same place of origin. The scene ends with a literal quote from Piriz: as Doctor Ovejero comes in to look after his patient, Oliveira utters the phrase, "Monjes que han de combatir siempre todo mal espiritual" (Ch. 131: 419) (monks who must always combat all spiritual evil), a quotation from Piriz' text. To Ovejero, who is unacquainted with Piriz, this sentence must seem purely random, and he visibly takes it as a symptom of Oliveira's disturbed state of mind. The reader, aware of the jokes that preceded Ovejero's arrival, is more likely to take it as a sign of Oliveira's recovery. But the references to Piriz in this chapter stand for more than comic relief. They signal a peculiar kind of closure in so far as they project the integration of Oliveira and Traveler into Piriz' totally categorized and numbered universe: narrative temporality ends by merging with the numerical series, since the protagonists become members of National Corporation no. 32. If the boundary between madness and sanity is in question in this chapter, it is not so much because the reader has any reason to believe Oliveira is not his usual self, but because both he and Traveler begin to resemble the numbered asylum inmates that seem to form part of the hopscotch universe as much as they are its players: the two protagonists of the novel, too, at least imaginatively merge into a universe they had only toyed with before, and this universe has as rigid a numerical structure as the hopscotch diagram.

In the complementary closing chapter, 58, Oliveira is apparently at home with Gekrepten, Talita, Traveler and Doctor Ovejero, who look after him and offer varied and contradictory advice about how to get well. But halfway through the scene, the other characters begin to refer to Oliveira in the third rather than the second person, as if he had fallen asleep. Oliveira continues, however, to contribute to the conversation, as do a number of other characters whose presence seems somewhat incongruous in this context: Remorino, the asylum attendant, Director Ferraguto, his wife Cuca, and even the inmate who helped Oliveira build his "defense system," Number 18. Gradually the reader realizes that almost everything that is said in this scene is a more or less literal repetition of sentences that were already uttered in earlier episodes, so that it becomes increasingly doubtful where and when this scene takes place, who is present, and how much of it "actually" occurs and how much of it is Oliveira's memory, hallucination or dream. This is even true of the very last words, "Muera el perro" (Death to the dog), which Number 18 pronounces. They ring ominous in this chapter because Oliveira had on several occasions described his existential project as becoming "a dog among humans" (especially in Chapter 125). But Number 18 is only repeating a phrase which the inmates had been reiterating since the day Ferraguto took the clinic over, without any of the staff ever being able to find out what, if anything, it referred to. Again, it remains unclear whether the sentence has any present significance, or merely echoes the past. Ana María Barrenechea aptly observes that "[e]n una especie de torre de Babel, el cap. 58, [*sic*] mezcla los dos espacios – la casa y el manicomio – y los dos tiempos – las cinco y las ocho de la mañana – en conversaciones alternadas de Horacio con Gekrepten, o de Horacio con todo el grupo de personajes del manicomio (y aun dentro de éste en dos situaciones distintas, la de atender a Horacio enfermo o la de echarlo junto con sus amigos)" (in a sort of Tower of Babel, Chapter 58 mingles two spaces – home and the asylum – and two moments in time – five o'clock and eight o'clock in the morning – in alternating conversations of Horacio with Gekrepten or Horacio with the entire group of characters from the asylum [and even, in the latter, in two distinct situations, Horacio taken care of in his sickness or fired together with his friends]).[30] This chapter, in other words, collapses a succession of different episodes into a temporal amalgam from which the reader can no longer infer any consistent narrative development: the various episodes that are alluded to not only merge different times and spaces but in fact offer alternative scenarios of Oliveira's departure from the asylum. In addition, the relation of this scene with the one in Chapter 131 remains open: since Dr. Ovejero is present and looking after Oliveira in both, one might again surmise that they are alternative renderings of what is essentially the same scene.

Clearly, the juxtaposition of these two final chapters as well as the internal structure of Chapter 58 differ fundamentally from the ambiguous ending of the first itinerary. If the possibility of Oliveira's suicide made the first ending an essentially modernist and open one, the ending of the second reading itinerary takes a step beyond mere openness by breaking up into the alternative temporal universes that characterize postmodernist narrative. This break-up is a step not only beyond the first itinerary but also beyond the typical structure of the second one: as I pointed out earlier, the second reading route does *not* usually include any material that contradicts or subverts the first narrative. The two readings are generally complementary rather than alternative. This, however, is not true of the various endings of the second book, which take up the narrative possibilities implied in the open ending of the first itinerary and convert them, if only briefly, into precisely the kind of alternative plot lines that are imagined in Borges' "Jardín de senderos que se bifurcan" and realized in a great number of postmodernist texts. Only in the end, then, does Cortázar effectively deploy the alternative temporalities that were possible in the structure of *Rayuela* all along.

It is probably unnecessary to stress that the analysis I have proposed here in no way implies that *Rayuela* is somehow a less

[30] Ana María Barrenechea, "La estructura de *Rayuela* de Julio Cortázar," *Nueva novela latinoamericana*, vol. II: *La narrativa argentina actual*, ed. Jorge Lafforgue (Buenos Aires: Paidós, n.d.), 246.

successful or aesthetically inferior novel when compared to other texts that are articulated in a more fully postmodernist mode. On the contrary, the particular interest of this novel lies in the way in which it negotiates a narrative idiom in between modernist and postmodernist strategies and goals. If its collage of different types of discourse, the juxtaposition of two readings that complement rather than contradict each other, the embedding of writers and writings into the text that remain distinguishable from the novel itself, and the open ending of the first itinerary obey a largely modernist aesthetic of narrative, *Rayuela*'s play with the order of chapters, its persistent reflection on various alphabetical or purely numerical ordering devices as ways of organizing and indeed creating narrative universes, its foregrounding of the contingency of the text and the alternative endings of the second itinerary stem from a postmodernist inspiration. If one were to strike a balance, *Rayuela*'s modernist elements would no doubt outweigh the postmodernist ones in importance. But the principal task of this analysis has not been to come to any unequivocal categorizations that are, at any rate, likely to simplify the complexity of Cortázar's text, but to show in what ways this novel works at the borders and in the interstices of modernist and postmodernist narrative modes. It is its peculiar combination of both modes that makes for *Rayuela*'s intricacy, and that maps some of the literary historical path to the more unambiguously postmodernist novels that will form the object of the following chapters.

3

"Repetitions, contradictions and omissions": Robbe-Grillet's *Topologie d'une cité fantôme*

A theorist as well as a practitioner of experimental fiction, Alain Robbe-Grillet has commented on his own works on numerous occasions. In these theoretical reflections, the redefinition of the relationship between narrative sequence and consequence emerges as one of the fundamental concerns of the *nouveau roman*:

Causality and chronology are really the same thing in a traditional narrative. The succession of facts . . . is based entirely on a system of causalities: what follows phenomenon A is a phenomenon B, the consequence of the first; thus, the chain of events in the novel. The very order of traditional narration will be causality and temporality as causality. Now if one takes a Nouveau Roman . . . what happens is entirely different. Instead of having to deal with a series of scenes which are connected by causal links, one has the impression that the same scene is constantly repeating itself, but with variations; that is, scene A is not followed by scene B but scene A', a possible variation of scene A. Nevertheless, these scenes follow each other in an order which should be that of temporality and causality.[1]

This observation is obviously based on Roland Barthes' earlier claim, already alluded to in the previous chapter, that

the mainspring of the narrative activity is to be traced to that very confusion between consecutiveness and consequence, what-comes-*after* being read in a narrative as what-is-*caused-by*. Narrative would then be a systematic application of the logical fallacy denounced by scholasticism under the formula *post hoc, ergo propter hoc* . . .[2]

[1] "Order and Disorder in Film and Fiction," trans. Bruce Morrissette, *Critical Inquiry* 4 (Autumn, 1977): 5.
[2] "An Introduction to the Structural Analysis of Narrative," trans. Lionel Duisit, *New Literary History* 6 (1975): 248. On the connection of narrative time and

The New Novel, according to Robbe-Grillet, aims at breaking up this conjunction, in a process that, as we shall see, does not so much abolish narrative temporality as redefine it. In his early novels, Robbe-Grillet dissociated time and causation by leaving crucial gaps in the narrative chronology (*Le voyeur*), by ending a story with the event that supposedly triggered it in the first place (the murder in *Les gommes*) or by repeating almost identical scenes over and over again (*La jalousie*). Enigmatic and alienating though these novels appeared at the time of their publication, they proved less resistant to conventional interpretive recuperation than Robbe-Grillet's theoretical reflections lead one to believe. Most prominently, American critic Bruce Morrissette's ground-breaking study *Les romans de Robbe-Grillet* proposed quite traditional hermeneutic and humanistic readings of the early novels, which nevertheless led to stunningly convincing results even in the novelist's own eyes. Morrissette's reading of *Les gommes* as a postmodern version of the Oedipus myth, for example, allows one to naturalize and connect even the apparently most disparate elements of the novel.[3]

But such readings have become increasingly difficult with Robbe-Grillet's later works, the so-called *nouveaux nouveaux romans*, which abandon even those elements that ensured a certain continuity in the earlier novels: consistency of narrative voice, recognizable characters, networks of motifs and allusions, and a plot structure which, although deformed, nevertheless left the reader in no doubt as to how it differed from more conventional fiction.[4] Novels such as *La maison de rendez-vous, Projet pour*

causation, see also Tzvetan Todorov, *Introduction to Poetics*, trans. Richard Howard (Minneapolis: University of Minnesota Press, 1981), 41–45; Seymour Chatman, *Story and Discourse: Narrative Structure in Fiction and Film* (Ithaca: Cornell University Press, 1978), 45–48; and Jonathan Culler's essay, "Story and Discourse in the Analysis of Narrative," *The Pursuit of Signs: Semiotics, Literature, Deconstruction* (Ithaca: Cornell University Press, 1981), 169–87.

[3] The humanistic tendency of Anglo-Saxon interpretations of Robbe-Grillet has, however, been consistently rejected by his French critics, who generally prefer to see his novels as the meaning-resistant expression of pure *chosisme*: see Barthes' preface to Bruce Morrissette's *Les romans de Robbe-Grillet* (Paris: Minuit, 1963), 8–16; Thomas O'Donnell, "Robbe-Grillet's Ghost Town," *Yale French Studies* 57 (1979): 195–96; David R. Ellison, "Reappearing Man in Robbe-Grillet's *Topologie d'une cité fantôme*," *Stanford French Review* 3 (1979): 97–98.

[4] Ellison, "Reappearing Man," 98; see also Ronald L. Bogue, "Meaning and Ideology in Robbe-Grillet's *Topologie d'une cité fantôme*," *Modern Language Studies* 14 (1984): 36. For Robbe-Grillet's own assessment of the differences between his earlier and later works and generally, between the *nouveau roman*

une révolution à New York or *Souvenirs du triangle d'or* cannot be understood in terms of the kind of symbolic or psychological reading that was proposed for the earlier works. Much more radical experiments with repetition and recursion than Robbe-Grillet's work from the 1950s, they redefine time as a realm of simultaneity in which past and future are indistinguishable, and in which the present manifests itself only as the difference between two versions of the (almost) same.[5] These rather striking differences between Robbe-Grillet's *nouveaux romans* from the 1950s and his *nouveaux nouveaux romans* roughly from the mid-60s onward can, in keeping with the criteria I outlined in Chapter 1, be understood to mark the transition from a mostly late-modernist to a clearly postmodernist mode of narration.[6]

Topologie d'une cité fantôme from 1976 belongs to the later series of novels. Even its process of composition eludes any sense of temporal or intentional coherence, since it originated as a collage or "intertextual assemblage," as Morrissette calls it, from collaborative efforts Robbe-Grillet had previously undertaken with painters and photographers such as Robert Rauschenberg, Paul Delvaux, David Hamilton, and from a project based on the works of Surrealist painter René Magritte, *La belle captive*. Only a very small part of the text was originally written for the novel,[7] which is, moreover, studded with references to Robbe-Grillet's own earlier works. And finally, in a curious inversion of the creative and critical process that Françoise Meltzer refers to as "back-formation," Robbe-Grillet derives some of novel's most important structural principles from the theories of his own critic, Bruce Morrissette.[8] Morrissette had already proposed in 1972 that the mathematical notion of topology, the study of geometric forms as

and the *nouveau nouveau roman,* see his interview with Katherine K. Passias, "New Novel, New New Novel," *SubStance* 13 (1976): 131–32.

[5] See Roland Barthes, "Littérature objective," *Essais critiques* (Paris: Seuil, 1964), 36.

[6] In associating Robbe-Grillet's *nouveaux romans* with late modernism and his *nouveaux nouveaux romans* with postmodernism, I am following Brian McHale's analysis (*Postmodernist Fiction* [New York: Methuen, 1987], 13–15).

[7] Bruce Morrissette, *Intertextual Assemblage in Robbe-Grillet from Topology to the Golden Triangle* (Fredericton: York, 1979), 79–80. For a detailed exploration of Robbe-Grillet's use of material from the visual arts in the novel, see Lillian Dunmars Roland, *Women in Robbe-Grillet: A Study in Thematics and Diegetics* (New York: Peter Lang, 1993), 137–69.

[8] Françoise Meltzer, "Preliminary Excavations of Robbe-Grillet's Phantom City," *Chicago Review* 28 (1976): 41; Ellison, "Reappearing Man," 99.

they undergo shifts, distortions and inversions, might serve as an explanatory metaphor for the structures underlying New Novels; the title of *Topologie* as well as many of its structural features arise out of the systematic exploration of this concept.[9] Furthermore, Morrissette published a seminal analysis of the principle of self-generation in postmodern fiction, focusing on the processes by which contemporary narrative texts develop out of a limited inventory of phonetic, lexical, semantic or situational "generators."[10] Robbe-Grillet, who has frequently collaborated with Morrissette, foregrounds the application of this principle quite ostentatiously in the text of the novel. *Topologie*, then, is "a meeting place for extratextual and intertextual discourses," a complex web of responses to and repetitions of earlier works, both visual and textual, creative and critical.[11]

1. The Gradiva matrix

Many of these earlier works and artists are either mentioned explicitly in the novel or represented by some of their most characteristic and easily recognizable features: the photos of David Hamilton, some paintings of René Magritte, and Robbe-Grillet's own earlier novel *Les gommes*, to name only a few, are repeatedly referred to in detailed descriptions and linguistic puns. But *Topologie*'s most important thematic and linguistic matrix is only alluded to much more indirectly: Wilhelm Jensen's German novel *Gradiva* from 1903, subtitled *Ein pompejanisches Phantasiestück* (A Pompeiian Fantasy), which achieved notoriety through a psychoanalytic study by Freud, "Der Wahn und die

---

[9] "Topology and the French *Nouveau Roman*," *Boundary* 2 1 (1972): 46–52. See Daniel P. Deneau, "Another View of the *Topologie d'une cité fantôme*," *Australian Journal of French Studies* 17 (1980): 195; Ben Stoltzfus, "A Dialectical Topology," *Alain Robbe-Grillet: The Body of the Text* (Cranbury: Associated University Presses, 1985), 102–03, 112–16. Stoltzfus also explores the application of topological operations to other novels and films by Robbe-Grillet (*ibid.*, 103–12).

[10] "Post-Modern Generative Fiction: Novel and Film," *Critical Inquiry* 2 (1975): 253–62.

[11] Ilona Leki, *Alain Robbe-Grillet* (Boston: Twayne, 1983), 119. Several critics have suggested that the word "cité" in the French title might in fact be a pun on its two meanings as the word for "city" and the past participle of "citer" ("to quote") (Thomas O'Donnell, "Robbe-Grillet's *Métaphoricité Fantôme*," *Studies in Twentieth-Century Literature* 2 [1977]: 59; Françoise Dupuy-Sullivan, "Jeu et enjeu du texte dans *Topologie d'une cité fantôme* d'Alain Robbe-Grillet," *Les lettres romanes* 44 [1990]: 211).

Träume in W. Jensens *Gradiva*" (Illusion and Dreams in W. Jensen's *Gradiva*).[12] The protagonist of this novel, the German archaeologist Norbert Hanold, becomes obsessed with the figure of a woman he first sees represented in an ancient relief; he names her "Gradiva," after an epithet of the God Mars, *Gradivus*, that signifies "the marcher," for reasons that I will explain shortly. During a visit to the ruins of Pompeii he imagines he actually sees Gradiva alive, walking among the dilapidated buildings. When he finally confronts this enigmatic figure, she turns out to be a friend of his youth, Zoe, to whom he was once affectionately attached and who now, in an erotic renewal of their childhood bond, becomes his fiancée. The name "Gradiva" is a transparent anagram of the Latin "gravida" ("pregnant"), and hence a particularly apt matrix for a "generative" novel. This name itself is deliberately elided from the text of *Topologie*, but it surfaces in multiple variations and anagrammatic rearrangements that shape the novel's narrative materials.[13]

Most importantly, "Gradiva" anagrammatically generates the name of the perhaps antique phantom city Vanadium and its goddess Vanadé (Vanadis), both of which are in the novel often represented simply by the letter V. In a passage that has attracted much critical attention, the novel turns the letters of Gradiva, Vanadium and Vanadis into a phonological matrix from which "the central theme of *Topologie*" emerges – the story of the raped virgin:[14]

Tout en haut du mât, l'oriflamme, vue de plus près, apparaît comme une longue banderole effilée, terminée par une extrémité bifide et portant, brodée en son centre, une lettre G de couleur rouge vif. Cette lettre donne la série suivante, à laquelle d'ailleurs on devait s'attendre:

---

[12] O'Donnell, "Robbe-Grillet's Ghost Town," 199–200. For the essay and the text of Jensen's short novel, see Sigmund Freud, *Der Wahn und die Träume in W. Jensens "Gradiva" mit dem Text der Erzählung von Wilhelm Jensen*, ed. Bernd Urban and Johannes Cremerius (Frankfurt: Fischer, 1973).

[13] O'Donnell, "Robbe-Grillet's Ghost Town," 200–01. Robbe-Grillet himself insists on the importance of Gradiva as what he calls *Topologie*'s "missing character" ("Interview," with Vicki Mistacco, *Diacritics* 6.4 [1976]: 39), with an obvious pun on the double meaning of "character" as "figure" and "letter" (*ibid.*, 39–40).

[14] Robbe-Grillet, Interview with Vicki Mistacco, 40. For comments on the passage, see Morrissette, "Intertextual Assemblage as Fictional Generator: *Topologie d'une cité fantôme*," *International Fiction Review* 5 (1978): 9; Bogue, "Meaning and Ideology," 36; Dupuy-Sullivan, "Jeu et enjeu," 212; Ellison, "Reappearing Man," 104.

vanadé – vigie – navire
danger – rivage – devin
nager – en vain – carnage
divan – vierge – vagin
gravide – engendra – david

et il est aisé de voir, d'après la disposition des consonnes, que le nom complet de cet enfant serait en fait David G. Voici l'histoire: . . .[15]

(Seen from closer up, the streamer at the very top of the mast appears as a long, tapering banderole that splits into two ends and displays in its center an embroidered letter G in a bright red color. This letter yields the following sequence, which at any rate was to be expected:

vanadis – vigil – vessel
danger – shore – diviner
dive – in vain – carnage
divan – virgin – vagina
gravid – engendered – david

and it is easy to see from the arrangement of the consonants that the full name of this child would in fact be David G. Here is the story: . . .)[16]

In a movement that is typical of *Topologie*'s narrative procedures, the passage begins with a concrete visual description of the letter, but leaves open in what sense this letter "yields" or "gives rise to" the series of words that follows. The story that emerges from the phonological play on /v/, /g/, /n/, /d/, /a/ and /i/ revolves around the attack of a ship of soldiers on the ancient city of Amazons, Vanadium. According to this story, all of the women except the one who is on guard are killed; the survivor is gang-raped by the soldiers and then escapes by throwing herself into the ocean. The water, mixed with her dead companions' blood, impregnates her, and she gives birth to a hermaphrodite, David. This "David G." reappears in various versions throughout the novel: in other parts of the text, he becomes David H. by alphabetical shift and then returns as D. H., David Hamilton, Mrs. Hamilton's son, or as Gustave Hamilton. The quoted

[15] *Topologie d'une cité fantôme* (Paris: Minuit, 1976), 49–50. All future page references to the novel will be given parenthetically and refer to this edition. Translations are mine, but I would like to acknowledge my indebtedness to the model of J. A. Underwood's translation of the novel: *Topology of a Phantom City* (New York: Grove, 1977).

[16] In my translation of this phonological poem, following Underwood's example, I have attempted to render the sound pattern as well as the content and have therefore not always chosen the word that would most precisely translate the French original.

passage emphasizes the role of the phonological matrix as the origin of this plot by insisting that the letter G generates all the other words, and that the name "David G." arises logically out of this pattern. Clearly, this causality is largely arbitrary, since a single letter can give rise to any number of words, and the matrix could easily have led to a different proper name. In keeping with the overall plot structure of *Topologie*, the text converts a pattern of repetition into a pseudo-causal chain that emphasizes that the words do not so much refer to extratextual referents as they are generated by intratextual principles and rules of derivation.

However absurd this process of "derivation" may appear, it fulfills an important function for the novel. In this passage, the text pretends that it does not really originate with an author, but that it emerges instead with inescapable logic out of a linguistic schema, an arrangement of signifiers. We will see the same pattern repeated later in the novel when a criminal investigation of a series of murders leads the police not to the killer, but to the discovery of a geometrical schema that supposedly underlies the choice of the sites where the crimes were committed. In both cases, human agency and intention are replaced by an abstract conceptual pattern whose own origin and meaning can apparently not be traced: nobody asks the question *why* the murderer chooses to kill his victims according to this particular schema, or whether he is indeed conscious of it at all; and the police do not seem any closer to finding out his identity after they have recognized the pattern. In the case of the phonological matrix that *Topologie* is based on, or at least claims it is based on, the question of origins is somewhat more complex since this matrix does in fact have a prior history that the novel calls upon: Wilhelm Jensen's novel and Freud's interpretation. In Freud's reading of *Gradiva*, Norbert Hanold's obsession with an ancient artwork, his journey to Pompeii, and many of his thoughts and perceptions during this trip and his strolls through the ruined city can be traced back to his unconscious desire for Zoe, his childhood friend. The most striking evidence of this connection is the peculiar posture of the female figure in the ancient relief, who is shown walking with her foot held in an almost vertical position; this idiosyncrasy prompts Hanold to call her Gradiva, "the marcher." Zoe, it turns out, walks exactly in this unusual manner, which is what gives Hanold the illusion that he sees Gradiva herself wandering around Pompeii, and ultimately what caused him to become so attached to the relief in the first place. His desire is so thoroughly repressed, however, that Zoe has to remind him explicitly of the time they spent together when they were younger, and the affection they had for each other, before their new relationship can take its course. In Freud's reading, the archaeological motif that dominates Jensen's novel is therefore a complex metaphor for the operation of the unconscious as the buried and invisible layer of the mind. By breaking down the title of a novel that is most famous for its psychoanalytical interpretation into a matrix for random linguistic permutations that stubbornly resist the search for any deeper meaning, Robbe-Grillet implicitly rejects this psychoanalytical model of reading and writing. His text does not conceal any hidden depths of mind or time, and its multiple returns to the past do not lead to any primal scene that would provide the key for interpretation. Its emphasis on "self-generation" is therefore a device that is designed to block certain modernist types of interpretation – among others, the psychological or specifically psychoanalytical understanding of temporality. It goes without saying that the text's claims about itself (as well as the author's assertions about it) need not prevent one from undertaking an analysis that would invalidate these claims, a point that I will return to in the conclusion to this chapter. But for the moment, I would like to emphasize the implications of the process of textual self-generation that *Topologie* enacts with the Gradiva matrix for the understanding of its temporal organization: by subjecting this name to continuous fragmentations and recombinations, the novel emphasizes that there is no continuous temporality, and in particular no past that could be called upon to elucidate the present. The past co-exists with the present, and both temporal dimensions connect and collide ceaselessly throughout the novel, without either of them assuming causal priority over the other.[17]

Given the novel's emphasis on self-generative procedures, it is no accident that its first chapter begins with a scene in a prison

---

[17] *Topologie d'une cité fantôme* thereby illustrates rather strikingly what Fredric Jameson calls the "new depthlessness" of postmodernist art; among the depth models rejected by this type of art, he specifically includes "the Freudian model of latent and manifest, or of repression" (*Postmodernism, or, The Cultural Logic of Late Capitalism* [Durham, NC: Duke University Press, 1991], 6 and 12).

cell that is referred to as a "cellule génératrice" or "generative cell,"[18] and the theme of the raped or murdered virgin from the phonological matrix recurs obsessively throughout the text. But the "pregnant" name Gradiva not only produces the novel's diegetic nucleus, it also functions as a numerical and geometric generator. As Françoise Meltzer has pointed out, the symbol V is not only short for Vanadis and Vanadium, but also represents the number five in Latin and geometrically forms a triangle. Patterns of fives run through the entire text: its five chapters or "spaces," five possible murder locations, temples supported by five columns, prison windows blocked by five bars, game scores kept in groups of five pencil strokes, and so forth.[19] Similarly, V-shaped inscriptions and objects appear again and again: women's genitals, temples with triangular pediments, V-shaped slices of watermelon, rocks engraved with V-shaped strokes; turned sideways, the V becomes a Greek Delta, and Ds equally abound in the text.[20] The triangular shape of the V also gives rise to multiple series of threes: for example, groups of three women, the 333 steps of a staircase, or three groups of actresses playing in a theater with three thousand seats.[21] These numerical matrices are accompanied by omnipresent geometrical figures like the triangle, the rectangle and the oval, each of which dominates certain sections of the text. The "generative" prison cell of the first chapter, for example, is described in terms of rectangles and fives, but when the scene is subsequently transposed on stage, the text suddenly renders it in threes, circles and ovals – apparently because the narrator has suddenly realized that what he had remembered as wooden prison chairs were in fact iron garden chairs with curved shapes.[22] The V of Gradiva's elided name thus becomes a structural hinge on which the overall structure of the novel as well as much of the detail of individual scenes depends.[23]

[18] See Dupuy-Sullivan, "Jeu et enjeu," 212.
[19] Meltzer, "Preliminary Excavations," 44; Leki, *Robbe-Grillet*, 119–20.
[20] Meltzer, "Preliminary Excavations," 45; Leki, *Robbe-Grillet*, 125.
[21] Vicki Mistacco, "The Theory and Practice of Reading Nouveaux Romans: Robbe-Grillet's *Topologie d'une cité fantôme*," *The Reader in the Text: Essays on Audience and Interpretation*, ed. Susan R. Suleiman and Inge Crosman (Princeton: Princeton University Press, 1980), 377.
[22] Mistacco, "Theory and Practice," 376; Stoltzfus, "Dialectical Topology," 112.
[23] Other insistently recurring motifs, such as windows and doors, mark points of entry and exit in the topologically constructed world of the phantom city, just

The temporal and causal consequences of this procedure emerge in a scene from *Topologie*'s first chapter which obliquely comments on the paradoxes of the novel's self-generation. In this scene, a nurse reads a story from a tourist guidebook to Vanadis, a girl recovering from an illness. The story describes the destruction of the city of Vanadium by a volcanic eruption in 39 B.C. The disaster appears to be recorded, although in a somewhat enigmatic fashion, in the inscription on a temple. But according to the guidebook, the type of writing used in this inscription had already become obsolete three hundred years prior to the moment it describes:

Le dessin particulier des lettres a révélé aux historiens qu'il devait s'agir là de l'une des dernières apparitions de cette écriture dans la région côtière, où l'on avait d'ailleurs cessé de l'employer sur les monuments publics depuis près de trois siècles. Pourtant, le texte paraît faire allusion au désastre lui-même qui anéantit la cité, et serait donc postérieur à celui-ci. La contradiction chronologique qui existe ainsi entre les caractères et ce qu'ils racontent posent [*sic*] une énigme que personne n'a encore résolue. (41–42)

(The peculiar shape of the letters revealed to the historians that this had to be one of the last manifestations of this type of writing in the coastal area, where it had anyway ceased to be used on public monuments almost three centuries before. However, the text seems to allude to the very disaster that annihilated the city, and would therefore postdate it. The chronological contradiction which thus exists between the letters and what they tell poses an enigma that nobody has yet solved.)

This temporal problem is accompanied by a causal one. The text in the guidebook shows a picture of the temple in question with the caption, "L'inscription destructrice de Vanadium" (42), which could translate as either "the inscription of the destruction of Vanadium" or as "the inscription that destroyed Vanadium." If the mere existence of the inscription implies a chronological reversal, this inscription about the inscription effects an additional causal inversion, in which the telling of the disaster story would not only precede the disaster, but in fact bring it forth. In other words, narrative, which purports to render an event that occurred prior to it, in fact turns out to generate this event at the

---

as an abundance of mirrors signals the recurrent inversion and confusion of inside and outside spaces (Deneau, "Another View," *passim*; Stoltzfus, "Dialectical Topology," 91–92).

same time that it makes its occurrence logically and temporally paradoxical. The paradox arises from the temporality that inheres in the writing itself, regardless of its referent; as it generates narrated time, the act of writing cannot erase its own temporality and is therefore inevitably included in the chronology which is its signified. Through this temporal loop, narration is presented as necessarily self-reflexive since it is situated in time by the text it generates; analogous logical loops structure the novel's self-generation out of its own phonological components.

The guidebook scene, then, foregrounds the problem of the temporal and causal relationship between the narrated moment and the moment of narration; through the temporal and causal loops which lead from one moment to the other and back, beginnings and origins are lost, since every attempt to go back in time only succeeds in regenerating the present moment without illuminating it. As in the allusions to psychoanalytical interpretation, the recuperation of the past gives rise to paradoxes, not to causal linkages. These paradoxes are developed further through the "archaeological" structure of the novel.

2. Archaeology of a postmodern ghost town

Bruce Morrissette has noted that although Robbe-Grillet's novels gradually abandon chronological order in the stories they tell, they nevertheless preserve a stable "textual chronology" since Robbe-Grillet has not, like other postmodern authors, experimented with loose-leaf texts or variable reading orders.[24] But through the narrative strategies he deploys, Robbe-Grillet succeeds in creating a temporal structure that traces alternative itineraries much more effectively than that of, for example, Cortázar's *Rayuela*. In *Topologie d'une cité fantôme*, the most diverse historical epochs are made to co-exist simultaneously through the central motif of the archaeologically layered phantom city and its array of "[t]héâtres, prisons, harems, temples et lupanars" (theaters, prisons, harems, temples and brothels).[25] Through its explorations of the history and spatial configuration of this city, the novel defines a space from which all

[24] "Intertextual Assemblage as Fictional Generator," 7–8.
[25] I take this phrase from Robbe-Grillet's own summary-description of the novel on the back of the Minuit edition.

moments in time seem to be equally accessible, and whose own present or placement in history becomes increasingly elusive as it appears in more and more varied historical contexts. A textual site generated by what Jameson, as we already saw, calls post-modernism's "omnipresent and indiscriminate appetite for dead styles and fashions,"[26] Robbe-Grillet's phantom city becomes the scenario of serial murders which also call up diverse historical settings. From the vestal virgins of Antiquity to the disarticulated mannequins left behind by postmodern consumer culture, the narrator, perhaps a detective, perhaps a spectator and perhaps a murderer, conjures up wildly incompatible historical frameworks in a narrative which has abandoned any sense of progress and explores the past as a set of variations on a split and dispersed present.

Not only is the urban space of *Topologie* the background for scenes of violence usually directed against women, it also bears the marks of catastrophe itself.[27] Typically, it is described as partially or entirely destroyed by a past disaster of historical dimensions. The chronologically earliest stratum seems to be the antique city of Vanadium, annihilated by a volcanic eruption in 39 B.C. according to the embedded story I discussed earlier; quite obviously, this is *Topologie*'s version of Wilhelm Jensen's Pompeii (First Space, Section IV: "L'inscription" [The Inscription]). But in the account generated by the phonological matrix, Vanadium is a city of Amazons attacked by soldiers who slaughter all its inhabitants (First Space, Section V: "Le navire à sacrifices" [The Ship of Sacrifice]). In a third version, Vanadium appears to be merely the setting of a play performed in the municipal theater of a contemporary city that the narrator attends, apparently more than once. In some sections of the novel, this modern city is said to have a "historical center" which has recently been in part destroyed or damaged by an explosion; the shored-up ruins are to be converted into an amusement park (Third Space, Section I: "Mise au point" [Rectification]). Later in the same chapter, however, the narrator also mentions archaeological excavations

---

[26] *Postmodernism*, 286.

[27] Several critics have pointed out that the novel encourages the metaphoric superimposition of the city and the virgin through the confusion of "ville" and "fille," words which the text on at least one occasion substitutes for each other (Bogue, "Meaning and Ideology," 39; O'Donnell, "Métaphoricité," 60–61).

that are taking place somewhere in the city. It remains unclear whether the historical center and the archaeological project designate the same area, or whether they are in fact distinct or not even located in the same city. Additionally, the "Incipit" section, which precedes the first "space," describes a city devastated by fire, a detail that does not match any of the other versions. The novel's setting, then, switches uneasily back and forth between an antique and a contemporary space which sometimes exclude and sometimes frame each other, since Vanadium is at times the plot's "real" background and at others just a fictional space in the modern city (the theater) or a vestige of its past (the historical center and the excavations). The difference between these variants is persistently foregrounded and yet does not seem to matter much for the plot: more than any however defined historical reality, the "city" in *Topologie* simply designates a moment in time at which all other moments of the past and present have become equally available.

As a consequence, none of the details which define it can be held on to throughout the text – except one: in practically all versions, the urban landscape of the novel is in ruins. The disaster that destroyed it is often described in uncertain or contradictory terms, but the post-apocalyptic tone persists regardless of the historical context. For instance, in the first chapter, the narrator's visual focus moves from the inside of the "generative" prison cell through a barred window out into an antique landscape with a temple:

Au-delà de cette grille, ce que l'on voit par l'ouverture béante qui laisse entrer à flots l'air brûlant du dehors, ou plutôt ce que l'on verrait si cette ouverture n'était placée si haut, ce devrait être, normalement, un paysage de la Grèce antique, ou de Sicile, ou bien d'Anatolie, une route de pierraille qui monte . . . vers le petit temple d'allure massive situé au sommet d'une colline: un fronton triangulaire soutenu par cinq colonnes épaisses . . . le second fût à partir de la gauche se trouvant mutilé de telle façon que seuls demeurent en place sa base cubique et son chapiteau curieusement resté suspendu en l'air. (27–28)

(On the other side of this grating, what one sees through the gaping aperture that lets in waves of burning hot air from outside, or rather, what one would see if this opening weren't placed so high up, should normally be a landscape of ancient Greece, or of Sicily, or of Anatolia, a gravel road that climbs . . . toward the small, massive temple at the

summit of a hill: a triangular pediment supported by five thick columns
. . . the second pillar from the left being so mutilated that the only parts
remaining are its square base and its capital, strangely suspended in the
air.)

But only half a page later, the narrator revises this description
and replaces the antique landscape with a contemporary scene:

Non, ce modèle d'architecture est vraiment par trop improbable, et trop
improbable aussi cette colonne ruinée dont les restes défieraient ainsi les
lois élémentaires de la pesanteur. Ce qu'il y a, dehors, ce sont seulement
des rues, les rues d'une ville aux trois quarts détruite, mais d'une ville
moderne, ou du moins dont les constructions n'étaient vieilles que d'un
siècle au plus. Sous l'effet de quelque cataclysme – incendie géant, peut-
être, ou bombardement aérien – toutes les maisons . . . se sont partielle-
ment effondrées, et aucun îlot habitable ne semble être resté debout.   (28)

(No, this architectural model is really too improbable, and too improbable also this ruined column whose remains would challenge the
elementary laws of gravity in this way. What there is, outside, is only
streets, the streets of a city that is three quarters destroyed, but of a
modern city, or at least one whose buildings were not more than at most
a century old. Under the impact of some cataclysm – a gigantic fire,
perhaps, or aerial bombardment – all the buildings . . . have partially
collapsed, and no inhabitable block seems to be left standing.)

The fictionality of both scenarios is emphasized not only by the
narrator's correction of details that might appear implausible, but
also by the fact that he could not have seen the antique landscape
even if it existed because the window is placed too high up for
him. Clearly, whether the outside consists of a temple with a
ruined pillar or a cityscape reduced to rubble by an air-raid does
not matter so much as the sense of a space that reaches back in
time through the marks of its own destruction. Never do we
encounter a space that is fully present unto itself and displayed
intact at the moment of (perhaps imagined) observation. All the
cities of *Topologie* – if indeed there is more than one – are
dispersed in a history which it seems impossible to envision
except as cataclysm.

The shift from one moment in time to another is often accomplished by means of a relatively minor spatial displacement. In
the scene just quoted, the transfer of the narrator's gaze from the
inside to the outside of the prison cell propels the reader from one
historical era to another: as long as the female prisoners in the cell

are described, the time must be one in which the building serves a well-defined function, whether it be that of prison, harem or house of prostitution. As the focus moves to the ruined but carefully cleaned-up streets outside, however, the building suddenly turns into one old monument among others, part of what is now a strolling ground for a group of nineteenth-century bourgeoises with the "sourire absent, vaguement ennuyé, des visiteuses de musées" (the absent-minded, vaguely bored smile of visitors in a museum) (30). But if the story seems to have shifted simply from one time frame to another, the next scene brutally confronts the two moments with each other. After an initial moment of motionlessness ("A l'intérieur, cependant, personne ne bouge" {Inside, however, no one moves] [33]), it describes the sudden gesture of one of the prisoners inside, who picks up a pebble and throws it out the window, eliciting a cry of pain from one of the visitors, which is answered by a similar cry from one of the inmates attacked by another with a carving knife. The scene ends in a paragraph which cuts back and forth between inside and outside, foregrounding not only the visual parallels between the two spaces but their causal connectedness: a stone thrown from inside injures a person outside, and a cry in the prison causes the women outside to assemble beneath the window, looking up in amazement. Tearing the two incompatible historical moments from their contexts, the novel juxtaposes them in a paradoxical simultaneity.

This simultaneity also defines the moment of the narration in relation to what is narrated in *Topologie*. "C'est le matin, c'est le soir" (It is morning, it is evening), the narrator declares in one breath in the "Incipit" section (10). "Je suis là. J'étais là. Je me souviens" (I am there. I was there. I remember) (11), and he then proceeds to describe, through a series of negations, a ruined cityscape from which all the elements which define it in subsequent chapters are absent:[28]

Mais il n'y a plus rien, ni cri, ni roulement, ni rumeur lointaine; ni le moindre contour discernable accusant quelques différences, quelque relief, entre les plans successifs de ce qui formait ici des maisons, des palais, des avenues. La brume qui progresse, plus dense d'heure en

---

[28] Ellison, "Reappearing Man," 103; Morrissette, "Intertextual Assemblage as Fictional Generator," 8.

heure, a déjà tout noyé dans sa masse vitreuse, tout immobilisé, tout éteint.

. . .

Voici. Je suis seul. Il est tard. Je veille. Dernière sentinelle après la pluie, après le feu, après la guerre, j'écoute encore . . .

Mais il n'y a plus rien, ni choc, ni craquement, ni rumeur lointaine, ni le moindre contour encore discernable, avant de m'endormir.   (9–10)

(But there is nothing anymore, neither scream, nor roar, nor distant rumbling; not the slightest outline visible indicating any differences, any depth in the successive surfaces that formed houses, palaces, avenues here. The spreading fog, thicker by the hour, has already drowned everything in its glassy mass, paralyzed everything, extinguished everything.

. . .

Here. I am alone. It is late. I stay awake. The last guard after the rain, after the fire, after the war, I still listen . . .

But there is nothing anymore, neither crash, nor cracking, nor distant rumbling, not the slightest outline visible, before I fall asleep.)

This "Incipit," rather than situating the narrator in time, makes time itself radically ambiguous by placing the moment of narration simultaneously at the beginning and after the end of the story:[29] the scene apparently initiates the plot, but the guard who seems to be at the same time awake and about to fall asleep describes himself as the last human being left in a landscape that has already gone through a disaster whose nature remains uncertain. His sketch of the foggy shapes around him outlines in reality a moment of the "no longer" in which all the distinctions which allowed the story to come into being have already been erased. Nevertheless, the story follows, a "Construction of a Temple in Ruins," as the first space is titled, in another phrase which collapses the moments before the beginning and after the end.[30]

3. Mythical births and serial killings

This procedure of juxtaposing the moment before and the

[29] "Robbe-Grillet's annihilation of time . . . shifts the narrative into a mythical present," Stoltzfus observes regarding this passage ("Dialectical Topology," 113).

[30] See Ellison, "Reappearing Man," 103.

moment after a crucial event shapes the plot of *Topologie* throughout, and leads to the elision of precisely those causal links that would have established a connection between successive points in time. It also entails shifts and slides of temporal and narrative logic which would not occur if what seem to be the obvious causal nexi were spelled out.[31] We already saw one example of this strategy in the disasters which befall the phantom city of *Topologie*; since it is never very clear just why the city came to be as ruined as it is at any given moment, the text simply slides from one historical period to the other, never actually specifying or describing any of the catastrophes. Observing large amounts of debris at one of the mysterious sites he inspects, for example, the narrator comments: "Il doit s'agir, non de destructions liées aux récents événements (dont le souvenir exact m'échappe, à l'instant: bombardement, mise à sac, ou séisme?), mais de travaux archéologiques beaucoup plus anciens" (It must come not from destructions related to the recent events [whose exact nature slips my mind at the moment: bombardment, conquest, or earthquake?], but from much older archaeological work) (177). In the one case where there does seem to exist an inscription which records the disaster, this writing is itself riddled with logical paradox, as we already saw. Nevertheless, precisely through these moments of elided destruction, the city layers itself through the ages from Antiquity to the narrator's contemporary environment.

A similar causal shift occurs in the story of the sack of Vanadium, the ancient Amazon city. The phonological matrix of this narrative, which I quoted earlier, gives the reader the impression, with the lines "divan – vierge – vagin/gravide – engendra – david" (49), that the demigod David is conceived during the rape of the surviving Amazon by the invading soldiers. But the story that immediately follows the phonological poem gives a different genealogy by suggesting that it was not the gang-rape that impregnated the Amazon, but the ocean water mixed with the blood of her murdered companions: "De cette étrange union naquit le demi-dieu David. La suite de l'histoire a déjà été rapportée" (Out of this strange union the demigod David

---

[31] See Roy Jay Nelson, *Causality and Narrative in French Fiction from Zola to Robbe-Grillet* (Columbus: Ohio State University Press, 1990), 201–02.

was born. The rest of the story has already been told) (52). In fact, however, the story of David as it was told before contradicts both of these versions:

Ce David, on le sait, était le double masculin de Vanadé, divinité hermaphrodite du plaisir. Il régnait en maître sur ce peuple de filles, ayant lui-même un corps de femme mais pourvu par surcroît d'un sexe mâle, bien visible sur les images où le dieu-déesse figure dans le ciel, volant vers ses innombrables épouses ... Cette fécondation à demi homosexuelle assurait – selon la légende – la reproduction de l'espèce, mais ne créait encore que des femelles, dont la lignée parthénogénétique se poursuivait ainsi de générations en générations, jusqu'à l'irruption périodique des soldats ennemis dans la cité vaincue.   (44–45)

(This David, as is well known, was the masculine double of Vanadé, the hermaphrodite divinity of pleasure. He ruled as lord over this people of girls, having himself the body of a woman, but being endowed in addition with male genitals that are clearly visible in pictures where the god-goddess appears in the sky, flying toward his innumerable spouses ... This half homosexual fertilization ensured according – to the legend – the reproduction of the species, but produced again nothing but females, whose parthenogenetic procreation thereby continued from generation to generation, until the periodic irruption of enemy soldiers into the defeated city.)

According to this account, David not only existed long before the invasion of Vanadium, but is in fact parent to all the Amazons that are killed in the battle, whereas the story of the invasion itself suggests that he is an offspring conceived during this battle. Without David, there could be no Amazons; but without the Amazons, David could not have been born: the two versions, reproduction through self-generation and reproduction through violence, entangle the narration in an irresolvable logical and temporal circle.

The plot of *Topologie* is structured as a series of such temporal gaps and causal contradictions, many of which revolve around the novel's central topic, the rape or murder of a virgin. The crime itself is never described directly, and the text focuses instead on scenes before or after, sometimes even conflating the two. This procedure builds in principle on the hermeneutic time structure of the classical mystery novel, in which the detective enters the scene *after* the crime has been committed, and has to read clues and traces so as to reconstruct what happened *before*.

But whereas conventional mysteries leave the reader in no doubt
that the crime has in fact occurred and usually end with a precise
account of how and why it happened, *Topologie* distorts time in
such a way that the reader cannot be certain whether the crime
has already been committed or lies still in the future.[32] The
abundance of clues and connections between the various murder
cases that the narrator uncovers never leads to the conviction of
the murderer, but seems on the contrary designed to provide the
material for yet another serial killing – possibly committed by the
narrator himself.

Time shifts and logical contradictions characterize, for
example, the events of the novel's third chapter, which begins,
ironically, with the narrator's reassurance that he will now clarify
what has remained obscure in his account so far:

Ah! ah! je vois que les choses se compliquent. Si l'on ne veut pas s'y
laisser prendre, il serait temps sans doute, à présent, de tirer au clair un
certain nombre de détails restés indécis ou contradictoires, et cela sans
préjuger de leur importance finale pour l'ensemble du texte.   (93)

(Aha! I see that things are getting complicated. To avoid getting trapped,
it would undoubtedly now be time to clarify a certain number of details
that have remained imprecise or contradictory, without prejudging their
final importance for the text as a whole.)

The details are indeed far from clear, but if the narrator promises
to explain the plot, the ensuing chapter falls far short of fulfilling
this promise. At the beginning, the city's historical part has been
severely damaged by an explosion of unexplained origin; a
young prostitute has been murdered, and the police have not
been able to trace the murderer. Rumors are spreading that a
secret society has been discovered which meets on prearranged
dates to perform mysterious and barbaric rites. But instead of
pursuing possible solutions to these enigmas, the narrator proceeds to tell us about the dress rehearsal of a play named *David* at
the Grand Theater. Initially he claims that he only stayed for the
first scene, in which groups of girls were walking among ruined
buildings, a scenario similar to the one which started out the

---

[32] For a brief discussion of the gaps in the mystery structure of several Robbe-
Grillet novels, see Alain-Michel Boyer, "Le récit lacunaire," *Textes et langages
XII: Normes et transgressions en langue et en littérature* (n.p.: Université de Nantes,
1986), 115–23.

novel. After this, the narrator says, he left the theater; only on the following day did he hear the news that at the moment one of the courtesans was to be sacrificed on stage, a young woman was stabbed to death in the audience. But through a sudden textual shift, we find the narrator back in the theater audience on the night of the première, as he now calls it, and he describes how he made his way through the crowd to the place where the victim lay, and where photos and measurements were taken by a detective. After this, he says, he left. The two versions of this event exemplify the temporal shifts and gaps typical of *Topologie*: according to the narrator's first account, he left *before* the murder happened, and only hears about it *afterwards* on the radio; according to the second version, he was present in the theater immediately *after* the murder, but if this seems to imply that he must have been an eye-witness to the deed, he nonetheless never confirms that this is so. Moreover, the first version claims that the crime occurred on the night of the dress rehearsal, whereas the second one shifts the event without any explanation to the night of the première. The two versions, in other words, are built around a gap and shift which let the killer escape by suspending the murder in a temporal void. Not impossibly, this killer could be the narrator himself, and the self-contradictions of his testimony might be motivated by his desire to hide his presence in the theater at the time of the murder. But self-protection does not explain the confusion concerning the day on which the crime occurred, or the strange simultaneity between the feigned murder on stage and the "real" one in the audience; both details make one wonder whether indeed the lurid killing took place at all.

Later the same week, a third woman is found murdered in the city; she is discovered underground, stabbed to death in the crypt of a ruined temple unearthed by archaeological excavations. The victim was slashed five times in the thighs and belly, and the narrator seems to imply that the same wounds were also found on the previous victims. According to his own version, however, the woman killed at the theater was only stabbed once in the breast. But with this additional murder, the police succeed in identifying a geographical plan behind the murders that I already mentioned earlier:

A partir des données topographiques fournies par les trois points où se sont produits les trois sacrifices successifs, l'équipe des métreurs professionnels de la police judiciaire détermine sans mal sur la carte l'existence d'un quatrième emplacement, qui est le quatrième sommet d'un carré parfait. Ils constatent en outre que le centre de ce carré est occupé de façon rigoureuse par l'ancienne tour de guet ... dont il a déjà été question dans le texte à plusieurs reprises. Les enquêteurs ont reconnu là, aussitôt, le schéma générateur initial. Ils se précipitent donc au point manquant qu'ils viennent ainsi de calculer, et ne sont guère surpris d'y découvrir une vaste bâtisse de trois étages, à demi en ruine, qui ne peut être évidemment que la maison si longtemps recherchée par les inspecteurs, celle dont les photographies figurent sur le rouleau de pellicule abandonné, non développé, au fond d'un pot à eau vide en porcelaine blanche, dans la chambre du premier meurtre. (113)

(On the basis of the topographical data provided by the three places where the three successive sacrifices occurred, the team of professional surveyors from the police effortlessly locates a fourth site on the map that is the fourth corner of a perfect square. They realize in addition that the center of this square is taken up precisely by the old watchtower . . . that has already been mentioned in the text on several occasions. The investigators here immediately recognize the initial generative pattern. So they rush to the missing site that they have calculated in this way, and are hardly surprised to find there a large building with three floors, half ruined, which can only be the building the inspectors searched for so long, the one that was photographed on the abandoned, undeveloped roll of film in an empty water pot made of white porcelain, in the room of the first murder.)

The police investigation leads to the discovery not of the killer, but of an abstract geometric pattern as the origin of the homicides, which are already referred to as "sacrifices" rather than as "murders" in this passage. The clues found at the different points of this spatial design refer to each other in a network that cannot be accidental, but they do not reveal the killer's identity: this is the logical dead end of Robbe-Grillet's mystery story. Yet the chapter does not end here. In the following scene, it is not the police but the narrator himself who inspects the abandoned and badly damaged house pinpointed by the schema. The reader at this point expects him to discover a fourth body, but instead the narrator simply notes that some preservation work has been done on the building and then comes to the surprising conclusion:

Mais le plus périlleux sera, sans aucun doute, la construction du Saint des Saints (dans la partie souterraine) qui doit comporter un bûcher pour les holocaustes. De toute manière, il n'est plus question de remettre en cause, maintenant, le choix de cette construction en ruine pour l'établisse-ment du sanctuaire. (119–20)

(But the most dangerous [operation] will undoubtedly be the construc-tion of the Holy of Holies (in the basement), which has to include a stake for the holocausts. At any rate, it is out of the question now to reconsider the choice of this construction in ruins for the establishment of the sanctuary.)

These ominous words, which harken back to the human "sacri-fices" that were mentioned before, seem to indicate that there is indeed a criminal secret society which performs pseudo-religious murders, as had been rumored at the beginning of the chapter, and that the narrator forms part of it. But again, the details of the scene do not fit in smoothly with the chronology of events as it has been laid out in the rest of the chapter. If indeed the narrator knew the spatial pattern underlying the murders all along, there was no reason for him to wait with the inspection of the building until after the police had discovered it; neither would such an inspection make much sense at that point, since it would pre-sumably be under police surveillance. His visit, therefore, must precede the intervention of the police. The construction of a "Holy of Holies" underground suggests that the narrator is in fact mentally preparing the third murder, which took place in just such a location. In other words, just when the investigation following the third murder had led the reader to expect the discovery of a fourth body, the text shifts back to a moment which could only have occurred before the third crime. Intrigu-ingly enough, this episode occupies a section of the novel that is entitled "Maquette provisoire du projet" (Provisional Model of the Project), a phrase which might refer either to the schema that the police discover or to the secret project the narrator considers at the end. By unfolding this ambiguity in narrative, the chapter moves from a moment *after* a murder, when the body has already been discovered, to a moment *before* what appears to be a human sacrifice; whether the victim is the same in both cases, or whether the third murder has already generated plans for the fourth one, remains undecidable and opens the text up for further repeti-tions.

Similar time shifts occur again and again in the complicated plot of *Topologie*. In the second chapter, for example, David H. walks slowly up and down the floors of an immense old building. He arrives at a room where an adolescent girl is looking at herself in a mirror; but when she turns around, presumably to meet David H.'s gaze, the latter is already climbing the stairs to the attic. Did she just miss him by seconds, or is there a longer time span and perhaps an unspecified event elided between her turning around and David climbing the stairs? Again, in the last room he enters, David H. takes a picture of a group of women. In the following chapter, a roll of film is found in association with the first murder, but it shows no figures at all – only empty rooms in a dilapidated building very much like the one where David H. took his picture, and on the basis of which the police later identify the building that completes the geometric pattern of murder sites. Perhaps, then, he did not in fact see anyone at all in the building. In one room, we are told, a young girl is looking at her image mirrored in a bowl of water. "Quelques secondes, ou quelques heures, ou quelques années plus tard, la main blanche a brisé le miroir liquide et fait disparaître d'un coup l'image réfléchie . . . Et quand D. H. pousse la porte, la chambre est vide, comme tout le reste de la maison" (Some seconds, or some hours, or some years later, the white hand has broken the liquid mirror and made the reflected image disappear in one stroke . . . And when D. H. pushes the door open the room is empty, like all the rest of the house) (79). Either, then, David H. is just imagining all the women he encounters, or the narrator is giving an account which conflates the time before the first murder, when the old building was inhabited, with the time after, when the rooms are empty. The novel's fifth chapter features a similar scene again: a young girl is sitting in front of a mirror, apparently waiting for the arrival of the murderer. Gradually, however, it turns out that behind her, a dead woman is already lying on a divan, with a pool of blood slowly spreading on the black-and-white checkered floor; the murder, then, has already occurred. But at the end of the chapter, a man in heavy boots comes walking down the hallway, studying photos of all the girls in the building and deciding on one of the keys. The reader expects him to enter that room and kill its inhabitant; but curiously enough, the room he opens is completely dilapidated and empty, except for a painting of a girl in the process of committing suicide. This episode shifts back and forth between no less than three different points in time – the moment after a woman has been murdered, the time of the murderer's arrival, and a time in which the place of the "crime" is no longer even inhabited. "[A]n assassin approaches his victim with a knife which is already on the floor in the room where the victim has already been killed," one critic sums up the temporal paradox inherent in these and similar scenes of *Topologie*.[33]

A final example also occurs in the fifth chapter, in a section entitled "Retour raturé" (Return Erased). The narrator here describes a walk back to his home through the nocturnal city in no less than four different versions. In the first one, he simply walks along a river bank at a steady pace. "Pourtant j'ai dû me coucher très tard; et j'ai dormi longtemps, comme chaque fois" (Yet I must have gone to bed very late; and I slept for a long time, as always), he comments (150). He does not disclose what he did between walking and going to bed "very late," or what is implied by the phrase "as always." In the version following immediately afterwards, he claims he saw some sheets of paper floating in the river along with other debris. "A force de détours, de précautions, de feintes, j'ai dû mettre des heures à retrouver ma porte. Je me suis couché très tard et j'ai dormi longtemps, comme chaque fois" (Due to detours, precautions, ruses, I must have spent hours getting back to my house. I went to bed very late and slept for a long time, as always), he concludes (150). The relevance of the sheets of paper remains unclear, and even more so the "precautions and ruses," which give the reader the impression that the narrator is hiding something and not saying all he could about his nocturnal roams. In the third version the narrator reconfirms that he saw the floating sheets of paper, but now he claims he climbed down to the river, pulled them out of the water and tried to read them, but was unable to do so for lack of light. "Puis je continue ma route à travers la ville morte. Couché fort avant dans la nuit, j'ai dû ensuite dormir très longtemps, comme chaque fois" (Then I continue on my way through the dead city. Having gone to bed very late at night, I must then have slept for a very long time, as always), this version runs, with a telling slip from present to past tense (152). At the same time that the continued variations make the narrator appear

---

[33] Bogue, "Meaning and Ideology," 36.

more and more suspicious, his repeated use of "I must have" also seems to indicate that he suffers from lapses of memory. Finally, in the last version, he pulls the sheets out of the river, brings them close to a street light and reads, "Et maintenant voici le texte: je me réveille . . ." (And now here is the text: I wake up . . .) (152): the narrative switches to the embedded text about a man who is also on his way home, witnesses a knife fight and then sees, or perhaps causes, an explosion. The frame narrative is never concluded, and the reader is left to speculate whether the embedded text perhaps contains the elided moment of the main narrative. If so, it might mean that the narrator deliberately caused an explosion in a building, perhaps to cover up for former crimes, and perhaps the one that was already mentioned in the third chapter. If this is so, the reader is not told, since the text only mentions the narrator's walk and his night of sleep, but not what happened in between: what might have been a relatively linear narration is split up into four alternative versions which cannot be compatibilized with each other.

These examples may suffice to illustrate how *Topologie* organizes narrative time as a variation on and subversion of the hermeneutic temporality of the mystery novel. Instead of moving through detour and delay, false clues and dead ends toward the "correct" account of the moment of crime or disaster, Robbe-Grillet's text is built precisely around the elision of this moment, a temporal dissemination into before and after which makes the very occurrence of the crime appear doubtful. In the absence of any reliable confirmation for the central events of the plot, differing versions proliferate and split narrative time into a myriad of temporal and causal facets which cannot be understood in succession, but only in a self-contradictory simultaneity.

4. "Déjà dit, déjà dit"

The proliferating repetitions of (almost) identical events are foregrounded in *Topologie* through the recurrence of a particular space within the city, that of the theater. According to one critic, the plays performed in the text complement its mystery elements in so far as "the notions of spectacle and discovery . . . oppose each other in the constitution of the novel's order as space (theater) to time (the temporal unravelling of a criminal investigation)."[34] But in this juxtaposition, the theater also brings its own peculiar temporality to bear on the structure of the novel. The space of the theater is characterized by rehearsal or repetition, two terms which are equivalent in French – *répétition* – and whose homonymy the text plays on extensively. Whereas the detective story relies on the kind of "classical" narrative in which, according to Robbe-Grillet, temporality is identical with causality and in which an event A leads to an event B through a causal nexus, theatrical performance comes closer to enacting a postmodern type of narrative temporality by periodically repeating, with slight variations, the same words, the same gestures and the same events.

In *Topologie d'une cité fantôme*, the theater is the space of recursion. This is very clear at the thematic level, since the plays performed at the theater frequently function as *mises en abyme* of the plot. Echoing the constellations of the frame narrative, they also repeatedly blur the boundaries between frame and embedded tale: passages of the text which appear to belong to the framing plot turn out to have been in fact descriptions of events on stage. The initial scene in the "generative cell," for example, which develops into the elaborate legend of the sack of Vanadium and the hermaphrodite god David, ends with the raped woman lamenting her fate as the soldiers sail away on their ship. But then, suddenly, the curtain descends, and applause is heard:

On l'avait deviné: cette paroi absente de la cellule initiale cubique qui constituait le premier tableau de la pièce, ce mur manquant sur le devant de la scène, c'était l'ouverture béante du décor dans la salle à l'italienne de notre grand théâtre municipal, où les fauteuils recouverts d'étoffe écarlate à présent se vident l'un après l'autre . . . La foule des spectateurs endimanchés se dirige dans un piétinement sans hâte vers le vaste foyer aux colonnes de marbre, échangeant des propos convenus sur le jeu des acteurs, sur leurs rôles, sur le destin des personnages, se demandant en particulier ce que devient, pendant ce temps, la jeune prostituée enfermée dans son cachot. (55)

(One had guessed it: that wall missing from the cubic initial cell that constituted the first scene of the piece, this wall missing at the front of the stage was the gaping aperture of the scenery in the Italian-style auditorium of our big municipal theater, where the scarlet-covered seats

[34] Ellison, "Reappearing Man," 100.

are now abandoned one by one . . . The crowd of spectators in Sunday clothes shuffles without haste toward the vast lobby with marble columns, exchanging conventional remarks about the performance of the actors, their roles, the fate of the characters, wondering in particular how the young prostitute is doing in the meantime, locked up in her dungeon.)

The novel's entire first chapter, according to this passage, only occurred on stage – and it matters little at this moment that some of its scenes could hardly have been performed in a theater (as the last sentence reveals), or that the plot continues in the very next paragraph although the play is ostensibly over.

But aside from these metaleptic shifts and overlaps with their thematic echoes and repetitions, the theater in *Topologie* also functions as a comment on the structure of the novel. Dramatic plot does not occur once and is brought to a conclusion as the plot of a mystery novel, *Topologie's* main structural matrix. Rather, the script of a play gives rise to an indefinite number of stagings and rehearsals, none of which can or should be an identical reproduction of the previous one. As opposed to the detective story, which works its way through to the "correct" and definitive version of events, the very existence of theater presupposes that there is no such definitive version, but that plot is always open to modifications and alterations in various re-enactments. Theatrical performance derives its *raison d'être* from the ability of written words to assume ever new shapes and meanings in different stagings and contexts. *Topologie* relies on this ability in its virtually unlimited variations on the elements first presented in the "generative cell," repeating and recombining them, placing them in different contextual frameworks, adding and subtracting elements and features. The analysis of the section titled "Return Erased" already revealed that these procedures lead to a proliferation of text, since the four different versions of the narrator's nocturnal walk led in the end to another text: the one he supposedly found floating in the river. Similarly, the shift from "dress rehearsal" to "première" in the account of the theater murder in the third chapter can be understood to refer not so much to anything that actually occurred at the theater but to the story's rehearsal of itself in repetitions and variations of the same episode. Clearly, *Topologie* in many cases goes beyond theatrical repetition by including versions of events that in fact contradict each other; but the idea of textual rehearsal nevertheless lingers in its structure.

The development of plot as a series of repetitions on the basis of an already articulated repertoire becomes more and more pronounced as the text progresses, and reaches its climax in the last two sections of the novel, "Un autel à double fond" (A Double-Bottomed Altar) and "Coda." In these final pages, the narrative advances at a more and more frantic pace through rapidly shifting events and images that the narrator does not even bother to spell out anymore, referring the reader instead to earlier parts of the text for details. Walking down yet another one of the novel's endless, many-doored hallways, the narrator sees a boy who might be David, "le garçon dont les désirs incestueux puis fratricides se sont révélés au grand jour dès la plus tendre enfance, comme il a été rapporté à plusieurs reprises, ici ou là" (the boy whose incestuous and then fratricidal desires revealed themselves clearly from his earliest childhood, as has been indicated several times here and there) (185–86); incidentally, fratricidal tendencies had not been mentioned before this passage, but the narrator makes even new elements he introduces sound as if they formed part of an already established repertoire. In this case, he cuts himself short by observing, "Inutile de revenir encore une fois sur l'histoire du vaisseau, déjà largement reproduite" (No point in going over the story of the ship again, which has already been covered extensively), probably an allusion to David the hermaphrodite god and the invasion of Vanadium (187). Later, during the performance of a play, a woman sitting next to the narrator is suddenly taken ill, and he carries her to an adjacent room:

Mais la coiffure compliquée de l'inconnue s'est défaite au cours du transport et ses lourds cheveux blonds pendent maintenant jusqu'au sol, ce qui à [sic] l'avantage de nous ramener à une situation déjà répertoriée. . . . Un peu plus tard . . . je marche de nouveau dans la nuit humide et douce, entre les hautes façades alignées dont l'état de délabrement a été signalé déjà, je ne me souviens plus à quel propos . . .   (192–93)

(But the complicated hairdo of the stranger has come undone on the way over, and her heavy blond hair now hangs down to the floor, which has the advantage of bringing us back to a situation that is already part of the repertory. . . . A little later . . . I walk through the humid and mild

night again, between the tall straight façades whose state of disrepair has
already been indicated, I don't remember anymore in what context . . .)

Quite explicitly, the narrator here renounces more detailed explanations because the scene forms part of a narrative inventory
that he claims the reader should already be familiar with,
although his own memory has no sure grasp of the textual past.
Invoking this repertoire of scenes, he drastically abbreviates his
description again soon afterwards, when he arrives at a bridal
store. "Description des vitrines, les costumes en tulle blanc, les
mannequins, la cabine d'essayage, le double fond et son fonction-
nement, etc. Tout ce passage est déjà plus ou moins connu"
(Description of the store windows, the white tulle dresses, the
mannequins, the fitting room, the double bottom and its functioning, etc. This entire passage is already more or less familiar),
he comments laconically (194). But he does not stop at the store
or at "l'avenue bordée de marronniers qui longe la prison, déjà
décrite" (the avenue with the chestnut trees along the prison,
already described) (196). Then the narrator seems to remember an
encounter with a hunter or murderer whose "semelles de crêpe
ne font pas de bruit – déjà dit, je me rappelle . . . Immobile pour
toujours. Il y avait du sang sous la porte entrouverte, déjà dit,
déjà dit" (his rubber soles make no noise – already said, as I recall
. . . Motionless forever. There was blood under the half-open
door, already said, already said) (199), and his narration becomes
ever more frantic as he abbreviates the description of the murder
by saying simply that "le sang s'écoule en ruisselet vermeil, qui
bientôt passera par l'interstice obscur, sous le battant disjoint de
la porte, etc." (the blood flows in a bright red rivulet that will
soon pass through the dark space underneath the badly adjusted
door, etc.) (201). As it draws toward its end, *Topologie* circles
faster and faster through the familiar images and episodes of its
repertoire, dissolving narrative into mere formulas of repetition
such as "etc." or "déjà dit, déjà dit."

Topologie's narrative temporality, then, emerges out of the
fusion of two time patterns. On one hand, the novel relies on the
temporal and causal design of the mystery story, which, in its
retrospective investigation of the crime, drives toward the revelation of a complete causal explanation that reconstitutes the
original temporal sequence of events. But this pattern, as we have

seen, is everywhere distorted and punctured in *Topologie*, which describes a whole series of crimes by juxtaposing the moments that precede them and the moments that follow in such a way that they cannot logically be connected in a linear succession of causal nexi. As the hermeneutic structure of the detective story breaks apart, it comes to resemble more and more the temporal pattern that underlies theatrical rehearsal and performance. Instead of leading to any solution, its repertoire of episodes is repeated again and again with some variations and in different contexts, so that ultimately none of the details which would be essential to a mystery story can be held on to. Thus, "à travers les redites, les contradictions et les manques" (through repetitions, contradictions and omissions) (196), the novel investigates not so much the past as the present, which is constantly leaking away into the various temporal layers of an archaeological structure that resists narrative phrasing. The text concludes by opening even in its final sentence onto a panorama of endless, meaningless successions of future scenes: "Mais de nouveau la vaguelette déferle, emportant tout avec soi: les algues blondes et leur parfum d'iode, les taches de sang, les fines chaussures de bal, le cri des mouettes. Et moi je m'avance, une fois de plus, devant la succession des portes fermées, le long de l'interminable couloir vide, immuablement net et propre" (But the little wave crashes again, taking everything with it: the blond seaweed and its iodine smell, the bloodstains, the delicate dancing shoes, the cry of the seagulls. And again I move along the row of closed doors, down the interminable empty hallway, unalterably clean and tidy) (201).[35] The present as defined in *Topologie* irrupts into and appropriates even the most remote layers of historical temporality, "taking everything with it" only to lapse immediately into yet another re-enactment of the already established narrative repertoire.

This conception of time does not, at first sight, seem to lend itself to the articulation of any cultural or political criticism. And yet, Robbe-Grillet himself has frequently argued that the function

---

[35] Ellison's observation that "[t]he models of topology and generativity are mechanisms that function within a larger textual movement which is constantly exceeding the bounds of its own representation, constantly calling into question the idea that a novel could exist as closed space" aptly characterizes this ending ("Reappearing Man," 108).

of his novels is to expose and deconstruct the myths of bourgeois ideology. In the case of *Topologie d'une cité fantôme*, he relentlessly foregrounds a motif that in his view characterizes Western culture from Antiquity to postmodernity, claiming that

> there is no difference between culture and counter-culture. In *Topologie*, for instance, there's Greek mythology and Hamilton. For me it's the same thing. That is, I don't believe that popular culture is different from high culture. In reality, they deal with the same themes; they are simply spoken differently . . . In particular, take the central theme of *Topologie*, which is the raped virgin. It is really the gimmick which is in our entire civilization, from Greek mythology to the popular novels you can buy in train stations. It is truly the archetype of the novelistic and it belongs to all classes.[36]

But Robbe-Grillet's treatment of such cultural "gimmicks" in *Topologie* and other novels is sufficiently ambiguous to leave some of his readers in doubt as to whether he is not participating in the ideology he pretends to criticize. To begin with, the author's claim that his novels are meant to question and expose bourgeois ideology, a project that one would imagine to be analogous to Roland Barthes' in *Mythologies*, stands in an odd if not irresolvable tension with the text's own emphasis on its self-generation and the purely linguistic nature of its permutations. In addition, the cultural myths that not only *Topologie*, but most of Robbe-Grillet's *oeuvre* revolves around tend to be singularly one-dimensional. The comparison with Barthes' *Mythologies* is instructive in this respect, since Barthes reveals the enormous range of popular myths that a project such as Robbe-Grillet's could address, from preconceived notions about certain types of sports, food, or cosmetics to stereotypes about the writer, the aristocrat, and the historical or colonial Other. But in Robbe-Grillet, the one topic that recurs obsessively and prominently is that of violence – sexual or otherwise – perpetrated against women. Even granting that this kind of violence is an important facet of Western culture, and that Robbe-Grillet combines it with a variety of other targets, this persistent return to the same topic over a literary career that spans four decades cannot but remain striking.

As Susan Suleiman has pointed out, two explanations are usually offered for the emergence of this motif: the justification in

---

[36] Interview with Vicki Mistacco, 39–40.

terms of cultural critique, as Robbe-Grillet himself proposes it, and the argument that these novels are primarily linguistic and narrative experiments in which certain elements arise out of the formal matrix chosen at the outset. She shows persuasively that neither objective leads with any necessity to the thematic configurations that are typical of Robbe-Grillet's novels: cultural critique could aim at any number of elements characteristic of bourgeois ideology, and linguistic experiment could lead to a wide variety of words, motifs and scenes that are generated according to a specific formal principle.[37] As I showed earlier in the case of *Topologie*, the phonological matrix derived from the name "Gradiva" could give rise to a virtually unlimited range of events and stories, even though the text naturalizes the plot that does emerge by suggesting that it was "la série . . . à laquelle d'ailleurs on devait s'attendre" (the sequence . . . that was at any rate to be expected) (49). Similar seemingly casual remarks and subclauses often appear in *Topologie* to indicate that although the reader may not immediately perceive it, there is indeed a structure of narrative causation or "textual generation" that links one episode logically to the other.

Suleiman analyzes this formal concept of self-generation psychoanalytically to suggest that it betrays a misogynist fantasy, an unconscious male resentment against the figure of the mother and a desire to replace maternal procreation by an autonomous generation of identity, which would explain the recurrent violence against women in the novel she analyzes, *Projet pour une révolution à New York*.[38] Leaving aside the question of how satisfactory an interpretation of *Projet* this approach yields, it raises important methodological questions when applied to a text such as *Topologie*, which, as I argued earlier, rejects the psychoanalytical model of explanation through its choice of formal matrix. To be sure, the critic need not always feel bound by the interpretive perspectives the text itself endorses; often, valuable insights are gained precisely by reading literary texts "against the grain." Nevertheless, it is difficult not to hesitate in imposing on the novel a theoretical framework that it is itself clearly aware of

---

[37] Susan Suleiman, "Reading Robbe-Grillet: Sadism and Text in *Projet pour une révolution à New York*," *Romanic Review* 68 (1977): 43–51. On the critique of bourgeois myth in Robbe-Grillet, see also Bogue, "Meaning and Ideology," 34.

[38] Suleiman, "Reading Robbe-Grillet," 59–62.

and designed to resist. Therefore, rather than following Suleiman's model of interpretation, I will focus on the contribution that an analysis of narrative time such as the one I have proposed here can make to the evaluation of Robbe-Grillet's critical project.

Clearly, many of the episodes that make up the narrative inventory of *Topologie d'une cité fantôme* draw in their sensationalism and lurid detail not only on the literary model of the detective story, but also on the repertoire of crime, violence and destruction that sustains the daily news reports in newspapers and on television. Rape, abduction and murder regularly make their appearance in these reports, as do fires, bomb attacks, invasions, earthquakes and other catastrophes. Reading the seemingly random sequence of these cataclysms in *Topologie*, with visits to the theater and descriptions of adolescent girls à la David Hamilton mixed in, in some ways resembles the experience of viewing a sensationalist television news report interrupted by commercials: the reader or viewer is exposed to a labyrinthine and discontinuous accumulation of information from the most diverse places, moments and sources, with no reliable way of telling the important from the trivial. Indeed, one is tempted to imagine Robbe-Grillet's ruined city with its scattered bleeding bodies as the kind of landscape that would be left behind if daily news reports were a faithful reproduction of reality. In its rapid movements from one epoch to another, *Topologie* exploits and heightens the sense of synchronicity that characterizes contemporary mass media by flattening out historical difference into a universal register of catastrophes: the phantom city is carefully constructed as a postmodernist "hyper-space" of sorts in which all temporal moments are simultaneously present and historical distinctions, however ostentatiously they may be foregrounded, make no real difference for the progression of the plot. To the extent that contemporary media also tend to synchronize and amalgamate historical, geographical and cultural differences, as I argued in Chapter 1, *Topologie d'une cité fantôme* participates in the temporal foreshortening that is characteristic of many segments of postmodernist culture.

But the interpretive difficulty lies in deciding whether Robbe-Grillet indeed parodies and criticizes the violent contents and discontinuous time structure of media and mass culture, or whether he turns them into objects of aesthetic pleasure in such a

way that the novel becomes complicit in the ideology that underlies them; by extension, the same question could be asked about
the material that Suleiman focuses on: does Robbe-Grillet's
presentation of violence against women amount to critique or
complicity? Suleiman sees it in the last instance as an endorsement of violence, arguing that the text aims not at distancing the
readers from what it describes but at making them participate in
its sado-erotic scenarios; the de-realizing techniques of the narrative would in this context function as safeguards that allow the
reader to experience the forbidden pleasures of these scenes
without the anxiety or guilt they would produce in real life.[39] I
would argue, however, that, in *Topologie* at least, the temporal
structure of the narrative engages the readers in the narrative
material only to distance them from it all the more brutally as the
plot progresses. The causal gaps and contradictions in the unfolding story, and the incessant repetitions that split many of the
most crucial scenes into series of incompatible versions, prevent
the reader from consuming the novel in the way in which a news
report about a rape or murder can be consumed: not merely a
delay of sadistic pleasure,[40] these narrative strategies end up
dispersing desire to the point where it is no longer fulfillable. If
both contemporary media and Robbe-Grillet's novel create a
virtual space from which the most varied places, moments and
phenomena seem accessible, *Topologie* quickly dispels the sense
that the reader can control and consume these diverse scenarios,
since the narrative present is always lost in its "archaeological"
constructions and reconstructions. One may wish that in his
choice of materials, Robbe-Grillet had taken into account the
broad range of materials that the analyses of Barthes and other
cultural theorists have opened up; but I think one cannot deny
that a novel such as *Topologie* does indeed contribute, through the
configuration of its narrative structure, to the critique of at least
one bourgeois myth: the presence of the present as that time
period which is available for the individual's manipulation and
control.

[39] *Ibid.*, 51–55.
[40] This is Suleiman's argument (*ibid.*, 54).

4

✤✤✤

Print time: text and duration in Beckett's *How It Is*

✤✤✤

The narrator of Robbe-Grillet's *Topologie d'une cité fantôme* wanders down hallways and streets that always seem to give access to too many temporal dimensions, too many historical moments at the same time. Finding himself in buildings and cities that are sometimes antique, sometimes from the nineteenth century, and sometimes contemporary, he reads texts or sees pictures and plays from yet other moments in time that frequently swallow up his own level of reality and turn him from a reader or spectator into a character in the text he reads. As a consequence, his ability to think and exist over time is severely diminished: he remembers imprecisely or not at all and finds himself forced to perform the same actions over and over again. The protagonist of Samuel Beckett's *How It Is* (1964) also finds it difficult to envision his own existence over time, but his problems are of a rather different sort than those of Robbe-Grillet's narrator. If Robbe-Grillet's universe is unstable because it inhabits too many moments in history, Beckett's seems to belong to no history at all and to allow for no narrative development. The story that Beckett's protagonist does finally succeed in telling undermines conventional as well as high-modernist conceptions of the relation between time and identity even more radically than Robbe-Grillet's self-contradictory repetitions – not only because the protagonist in the end denies that anything he said ever happened, but also because the reader cannot even be sure that he is narrating or denying anything at all, since he also claims (and then denies) that he is merely quoting what he hears another voice say. In the complex logical paradox that the ending of the novel sets up, temporal development and narrative voice come to cancel each other out.

But the structure of Beckett's novel differs from Robbe-Grillet's in yet another respect. Not only does the narrator inhabit a universe that is stripped of all temporal coherence, its discontinuity is also brought to bear on the materiality of the printed page. Beckett's text consists of short paragraphs with mutilated syntax and no punctuation or capitalization that alternate with blank spaces of equal length. These spaces translate the narrator's labored breathing and spasmodic outbreaks of speech into the configuration of the page, at the same time that they provide a visual analogue to the disrupted temporality of his narrative. If in Cortázar's *Rayuela* the passage of time came to be dissociated from the numerical sequence of chapters and pages, Beckett's *How It Is* forces narrative time into broken syntax and fractured pages. Under the impact of this linguistic and visual staccato, time turns into a parameter that no longer applies to either the act of narration or the narrated events, but only to the narrative discourse itself as a textual artifact. This radical reduction of time to text implies that narrative can no longer recuperate any temporality or history outside itself, but, as I will argue, precisely its self-referential focus is ultimately symptomatic of a denial of time that goes far beyond Beckett's novel.

In comparison to Cortázar's *Rayuela* and Robbe-Grillet's *Topologie d'une cité fantôme*, Beckett's experiment with time is even more radical because it addresses the dimension of narrative temporality that is perhaps most difficult to account for theoretically, that of duration. To explore some of the details of Beckett's project in *How It Is* with greater precision, I will therefore undertake a brief foray into the narratological treatment of time and specifically that of duration. In terms proposed by Gérard Genette, three parameters define the way in which the time of the story or narrated events relates to the time of narrative discourse, the representation of those events: order, frequency and duration.[1] Order and frequency are relatively easy to define and apply to most types of narration: *order* describes the discrepancies between the succession of events as they are narrated compared

---

[1] Genette formulates his theory of narrative time with these three parameters in *Narrative Discourse: An Essay in Method*, trans. Jane E. Lewin (Ithaca: Cornell University Press, 1980).

to the one in which the reader infers them to have occurred in the story universe, and *frequency* refers to the number of times an event is narrated in relation to the number of times it is inferred to have happened in the fictional world. But *duration*, the length of the narrated story in comparison with the temporal extension of discourse, raises difficulties of analysis that hinge upon the very nature of narrative temporality, and which make a brief theoretical consideration necessary.

1. How long the story?

In his theory of narrative duration, Genette relies on German critic Günther Müller's earlier distinction of *erzählte Zeit* (time of the narrated) and *Erzählzeit* (time of narration).[2] At first sight, this dichotomy seems to align rather comfortably with the familiar narratological distinction of story and discourse, "the time of the thing told and the time of the telling" or "the time of the significate and the time of the signifier."[3] Indeed, a spontaneous definition of *Erzählzeit*, derived from the meaning of the German word itself, would characterize it as "the period of time it takes the narrator to tell his story," understood not as the lived experience of the empirical author, but as the act of narration performed by the narrator of the text.[4] This time period can be measured easily enough if the text itself makes explicit reference to it, or if it locates the act of narration with regard to the narrated events in such a way that its duration can be inferred.[5] For example, Tristram Shandy points out at a certain moment of his autobiography that a year has gone by since he started writing,[6] and Jacques Revel, the narrator of Michel Butor's *L'emploi du temps*, gives precise dates for the entries in his narrative diary

[2] Müller elaborates these concepts mainly in the two essays entitled "Die Bedeutung der Zeit in der Erzählkunst," *Morphologische Poetik*, ed. Elena Müller (Darmstadt: Wissenschaftliche Buchgesellschaft, 1968), 247–268 (first published in 1947), and "Erzählzeit und erzählte Zeit," *ibid.*, 269–86 (originally published in 1948).

[3] Christian Metz, *Film Language: A Semiotics of the Cinema*, trans. Michael Taylor (New York: Oxford University Press, 1974), 18.

[4] See Erhardt Güttgemanns, "Die Funktion der Zeit in der Erzählung," *Linguistica Biblica* 32 (1974): 66–69.

[5] See Jean Ricardou, *Problèmes du nouveau roman* (Paris: Seuil, 1967), 161–70.

[6] Laurence Sterne, *Tristram Shandy*, ed. Howard Anderson (New York: Norton, 1980), 207.

during five successive months. The *Erzählzeit* of Richardson's *Pamela* and *Clarissa* can similarly be defined with a high degree of precision because the heroines interpolate their narrative letters between events that leave them often only minutes and at most a few hours for the activity of writing.

But how can one define the *Erzählzeit* of novels which do not overtly refer to an act of narration and its duration? Novels such as Austen's *Emma* or *Pride and Prejudice* provide no information on the process of narration or the narrator, and neither do most novels by Balzac or Dickens. Lucy Snowe, the narrator of Charlotte Brontë's *Villette*, only alludes once and briefly to the fact that she is writing her account in old age;[7] we learn nothing else about the moment and motif of the narration. Similarly, the narrator of Flaubert's *Madame Bovary* makes an appearance at the beginning of the novel only to vanish afterwards without leaving the reader a clue as to when and how he composed the account of Charles Bovary and his wife. This concealment of the narrative act behind the narrated material, typical of many nineteenth-century novels,[8] leads Genette to observe that

[o]ne of the fictions of literary narrating – perhaps the most powerful one, because it passes unnoticed, so to speak – is that the narrating involves an instantaneous action, without a temporal dimension. Sometimes it is dated, but it is never measured . . . subsequent narrating exists through this paradox: it possesses at the same time a temporal situation (with regard to the past story) and an atemporal essence (since it has no duration proper).[9]

The notion of *Erzählzeit* understood as "time of the telling" seems simply inapplicable to texts whose narration remains outside any specified time frame. But this observation leads to the paradoxical conclusion that these novels lack the dimension of discourse and consist only of story, at least as far as temporality is concerned. One can avoid this narratological absurdity by arguing that the simple bipartition of story and discourse was superseded in the 1980s by a tripartite model proposed by such theoreticians as Mieke Bal, Shlomith Rimmon-Kenan and Gérard Genette himself. Using slightly differing terminologies, all of them suggest a

---

[7] Charlotte Brontë, *Villette*, ed. Mark Lilly (Harmondsworth: Penguin, 1979), 105.
[8] But obviously not of *all* of them: *Wuthering Heights* is an example to the contrary.
[9] Genette, *Narrative Discourse*, 222–23.

subdivision of discourse into discourse and narration, the latter designating all those aspects of narrative discourse which relate it directly to the act and instance of narrating.[10] In such a tripartite schema, it is the dimension of narration, not that of discourse, which is missing in the cases mentioned above.

But this claim leads to another contradiction. As we have seen, "time of narration" is a meaningful concept only in precisely those cases in which it forms part of what is narrated – in other words, in those cases in which it is in fact part of the narrated time of the *story*. Therefore, it should logically be described as a subcategory of story time. If *Erzählzeit* means "time of the telling," it forms part of the narrative signified, not the signifier, since it must be what is told in order to be perceptible at all. As soon as the dimension of narration is introduced into the problem of temporal duration, then, it cancels itself out by merging into the time of the narrated.

Genette avoids these paradoxes by proposing a different interpretation of the term *Erzählzeit*. If *erzählte Zeit* and *Erzählzeit* correspond to story and discourse, the latter must logically be defined as the "time of discourse." But, Genette argues, "no one can measure the duration of a narrative. What we spontaneously call such can be nothing more . . . than the time needed for reading; but it is too obvious that reading time varies according to particular circumstances, and that . . . nothing here allows us to determine a 'normal' speed of execution."[11] This leads him to claim, more sweepingly:

The temporality of written narrative is to some extent conditional or instrumental; produced in time, like everything else, written narrative exists in space and as space, and the time needed for "consuming" it is the time needed for *crossing* or *traversing* it, like a road or a field. The narrative text, like every other text, has no other temporality than what it borrows, metonymically, from its own reading.[12]

The duration of narrative discourse, then, must be understood as

---

[10] Mieke Bal, *Narratology: Introduction to the Theory of Narrative*, trans. Christine van Boheemen (Toronto: University of Toronto Press, 1985), 5–6; Shlomith Rimmon-Kenan, *Narrative Fiction: Contemporary Poetics* (London: Methuen, 1983), 3–4. A useful comparative survey of the different terms employed by the three theoreticians appears in Michael J. Toolan, *Narrative: A Critical Linguistic Introduction* (London and New York: Routledge, 1988), 10–11.

[11] Genette, *Narrative Discourse*, 86.

[12] *Ibid.*, 34.

a kind of *virtual temporality*, realized in the reading process. But since reading time, according to Genette, is inaccessible to analysis, we find ourselves once again in a dead end in our exploration of *Erzählzeit*. If, as time of narration, it merges with the time of the narrated, it falls outside of the scope of the text altogether when it is considered as the time of reading.[13]

Genette adopts neither of these meanings, but follows the suggestion that "written narrative exists in space and as space" to its logical consequences. If *Erzählzeit* is indeed the time of discourse, this implies that it is not properly speaking a temporal dimension at all, but a spatial one. Appropriating the procedure already adopted by Günther Müller, Genette takes as his "textual clock" the number of pages dedicated to a certain span of narrated time. This method does not allow for the computation of absolute narrative duration but provides a measure of *isochrony*, or comparative speed of narrated and discursive time; it thereby becomes possible to assess whether the rate of correspondence between a certain narrated period and a certain length of text varies or remains constant. In Proust's *A la recherche du temps perdu*, for example, Genette observes a "gradual slowing down of the narrative" since at the beginning, relatively large time periods are covered in the space of a few pages whereas toward the end, more and more pages are dedicated to the narration of very short spans of story time.[14] But this procedure also demonstrates the central problem that the study of narrative duration raises: while the concept of story duration is meaningful, discourse duration

[13] One may wonder, however, whether this last claim is entirely accurate. While it is intuitively true that a reader's age, cognitive abilities, linguistic competence, previous reading experience and other individually variable factors make reading time to some extent unpredictable, it is equally plausible that textual factors such as length, syntactical and lexical complexity, abstractness, tightness or looseness of episode connection, and presence or absence of suspense have some systematic impact on the duration of reading. In other words, while reading speed does vary a great deal individually, there also seem to exist some intersubjectively constant factors that one misses if one claims simply that reading time is unanalyzable. Most readers will find a García Márquez novel easier to "devour" than a novel by Samuel Beckett, and this is an important dimension of the narrative temporality of these texts. Since a systematic exploration of such phenomena, however, requires empirical and not only textual study, Genette may be justified in excluding the analysis of reading time from the text-oriented approach that guides not only his but also most other narratological theories.

[14] Genette, *Narrative Discourse*, 92–93.

turns out not to be a truly temporal dimension at all, but rather a spatial one, in the sense of the one-dimensional consecution of sentences across the pages.

Therefore, all the definitions one can give of *Erzählzeit* – the time it takes the narrator to tell the story, the time it takes the reader to actualize the text's virtual duration, or the extension of the narrative text itself – lead to theoretical impasses unless one abrogates the specifically temporal character of discursive duration. In this sense, even the most traditional written narrative texts can be considered spatial and must be "temporalized" through the reading process. But what Genette does not consider – and perhaps cannot, given the structuralist framework of his narratological theory – is that the space of the printed page can itself be mobilized so as to convey a variety of meanings. Typographical experiment is, of course, more frequently deployed in poetry, and is particularly obvious in avant-garde poetry of the early twentieth century, whether it be futurist, imagist, dadaist or surrealist. But it is highly uncommon in the high-modernist novel, with the exception of such generic borderline cases as F. T. Marinetti's *Zang Tumb Tuuum* or Max Ernst's *Une semaine de bonté*. Postmodern novelists from Raymond Federman and Ron Sukenick to Theresa Hak Kyung Cha, by contrast, use the typographical configuration of the page to add dimensions of meaning and possibilities of reading to narrative texts. In some cases, such as Federman's *Double or Nothing*, Christine Brooke-Rose's *Thru* or Cha's *Dictée*, the design of individual pages responds to and visually foregrounds specific elements of the narration. In other cases, the entire text is reconfigured according to a general typographical principle; an example of this kind is Beckett's *How It Is*, whose pages alternate between brief paragraphs of print and blank spaces of approximately equal length. This particular typographical configuration, as I will argue, visually re-creates the concept of time that is at stake in Beckett's text by foregrounding the discontinuity of the narrator's telling as well as that of the story he tells. Through the fracturing of narration and narrative material, the only time that remains in the novel is that of textual articulation itself, unable to contain either narrative voice or event.

2. Text as duration

How It Is consists, like many other Beckett novels, of a prolonged monologue by an unnamed first person-narrator. All the reader finds out for certain about him is that he crawls through the mud and darkness of an undefined, primeval environment, naked, worm-like and all alone. From out of an equally undifferentiated time without any alternations of night and day, he narrates his encounter with another mud-crawler named Pim. This relationship becomes the temporal hinge of his life's story in an insistently foregrounded tripartition: "how it was I quote before Pim with Pim after Pim how it is three parts I say it as I hear it."[15] The text itself is accordingly divided into three sections, which correspond, if only roughly, to the narrator's voyage up until his encounter with Pim, his life with Pim, and the time after Pim has abandoned him. In Part One, the narrator travels east crawling through the mud, occasionally visited by "images," presumably memories from his former "life the other above in the light" (8). Part Two describes his encounter with Pim, whom he makes his victim in elaborate rituals of torture. Himself mute, he develops a code of physical torments to make Pim sing and speak:

table of basic stimuli one sing nails in armpit two speak blade in arse three stop thump on skull four louder pestle on kidney

five softer index in anus six bravo clap athwart arse seven lousy same as three eight encore same as one or two as may be   (69)

But neither these torments nor the questions that he writes on Pim's back with his fingers concerning Pim's past life "above" and "below" bring more than scant illumination. Scenes from life above remain ambiguous: they may be Pim's responses or the narrator's own visual memories, and Pim seems to come up with no recollections from his life below. Possibly this lack of information is the reason why the narrator in Part Three, abandoned by Pim, launches into a philosophical meditation on the entire population he assumes to be co-inhabiting his universe of mud and darkness. All its inhabitants, he imagines, whether there be a total of four, 100,000 or one million, are subject to the same vital

[15] Samuel Beckett, *How It Is* (New York: Grove, 1964), 7. All parenthetical page references to the novel are based on this edition. *How It Is* was first published in French under the title *Comment c'est* in 1961.

pattern: in their nomadic phase, they move ahead crawling until
they encounter their victim, nourishing themselves from a sack
full of canned provisions they find on the way; in the following
phase, they force their victim to sing and speak, but are themselves struck mute; in the third phase, they are abandoned by the
victim, who leaves them his sack of provisions, and motionlessly
lie in the mud waiting for their own tormentor to arrive; life as
victim would then form the fourth part of the cycle. To ensure the
interlocking of these cycles, the phases must be of equal length
for all individuals, and all departures and encounters must occur
at precisely the same moment (112): from the chaos and darkness
of his abandonment in the mud, the narrator creates a cosmic
vision of a universe beating regularly as a clockwork with the
moves and halts of hundreds of thousands of couples and
individuals, all bound by the same rigidly synchronic rhythm
into either a gigantic circular movement or an infinite straight
line (117–24). This horrendous vision of an interminable procession of humans flat on their bellies in the slime, "languidly
wending from left to right straight line eastward" (127), is
disrupted in the narrator's mind by only one detail: the prove-
nance of the sacks, without which none of the individuals could
survive. His inability to account for the system's principle of
subsistence without postulating some metaphysical instance
outside it, "this not one of us" (142, 144), ultimately leads him to
the denial of the vision as a whole, to "a solution more simple by
far and by far more radical / a formulation that would eliminate
him completely and so admit him to that peace at least while
rendering me in the same breath sole responsible for this unqua-
lifiable murmur" (144). As the narrator confesses that this entire
system was just his invention, the fictional universe collapses,
leaving only his voice. But is it indeed *his* voice? Up until the last
pages of the monologue, the narrator insists that he in fact only
quotes what he hears another voice say, that all he says is mere
repetition, "murmurs in the mud" of words not his own. But his
final denial includes this other voice: in the end, then, the narrator
does seem to find his own voice, though only to tell the readers
that nothing he told them ever happened.[16]

---

[16] We shall see later, however, in what ways even the apparent self-identity of the
narrator's voice in his final denial is undermined (Section 3, "Time Against
Voice").

If such a text cannot but raise intricate questions concerning the problem of narrative voice, it is equally complex in its temporal structuring:

> here then part one how it was before Pim we follow I quote the natural order more or less my life last state last version what remains bits and scraps I hear it my life natural order more or less I learn it I quote a given moment long past vast stretch of time on from there that moment and following not all a selection natural order vast tracts of time (7)

This paragraph, one of the first of the novel, already alludes to narrative order ("natural order"), frequency ("last state last version") and duration ("vast tracts of time") with verbal motifs which will recur insistently throughout the text. But if all three temporal parameters are touched upon, the problem of narrative duration nonetheless most markedly shapes the form of *How It Is*. This claim may seem paradoxical at first, since the text provides no criteria for judging the objective temporal duration of either the events narrated or the act of narration: how long ago the narrator came to leave "life above in the light," when he met Pim, how long he stayed with him, how much time has passed since, and how long his narration lasts – all these are questions without relevance in a universe in which there is neither day, night nor year (the very words seem to repulse the narrator every time he is forced to pronounce them), and in which time scales are as relative as in the biblical reminder that to the Lord, a thousand years are like a day:[17]

> question old question if yes or no this upheaval daily if daily ah to have to hear that word to have to murmur it this upheaval yes or no if daily it so heaves me up and out of my swill

> and the day so near its end at last if it is not compact of a thousand days good old question terrible always for the head and universally apropos which is a great beauty (39)

But instead of temporal bearings that mimetically represent "real" time, *How It Is* relies on a *textual* structure of duration that informs both the novel's content and its form.

This structure emerges most obviously in the printed appearance of the text. All three parts of the novel consist of short

---

[17] Susan D. Brienza, "*How It Is*: Midget Grammar," *Samuel Beckett's New Worlds: Style in Metafiction* (Norman: University of Oklahoma Press, 1987), 94.

paragraphs without punctuation or capitalization which are separated from each other by blank spaces: instead of rendering a
continuous flow of speech, the novel alternates between words
and silence, text and blanks. If the text, extending from the past
tense of its initial words, "how it was I quote," to the present tense
of its final ones, "end of quotation . . . how it is," might be
construed as a narrative bridge between past and present which
merges them into an unbroken temporal flow, the typographical
configuration of the page denies such continuity. The seemingly
even progression of time, symbolized by the symmetrical tripartition into three chapters, is belied by the fragmentation of the text
into visually isolated paragraphs which are frequently not even
linked by syntactic or logical devices.[18] Temporal progression
does not congeal into a smooth flow of sentences in *How It Is*, but
instead gives rise to brief spasmodic utterances interrupted by
pauses; this alternation represents in very visual form the narrator's repeated observation that he can only hear the voice he
claims to be quoting "when the panting stops," that is, when a
temporary halt in the noise of his own breathing allows him to
perceive a voice not his own. "[S]uddenly afar the step the voice
nothing then suddenly something something then suddenly
nothing suddenly afar the silence," is the narrator's characteriz-
ation of this rhythm (13).[19] In the systolic and diastolic alternation
of bursts of speech and silence, text and blank, the reader is forced
to listen to the "breath" and rhythm of narrative discourse.[20]

Erzählzeit, the time of discourse, here obviously has the spatial,
printed dimension Genette describes; but the spatial arrangement
immediately translates into a temporal rhythm, a measure of
duration quite unlike the counting of pages per narrated time
period proposed by Genette. Discursive duration in *How It Is* is
not presented as a persistence of the same, but rather as a
patterned alternation of differences: speech does not simply

[18] See Hugh Kenner's discussion of syntax in *How It Is* in his "Shades of Syntax,"
Samuel Beckett: A Collection of Criticism, ed. Ruby Cohn (New York: McGraw-
Hill, 1975), 30–31.
[19] Judith Dearlove comments on this sentence in "The Voice and Its Words: *How
It Is* in Beckett's Canon," *Critical Essays on Samuel Beckett*, ed. Patrick A.
MacCarthy (Boston: Hall, 1986), 107.
[20] William Hutchings, in his analysis of the digestive metaphors that inform the
novel, calls its rhythm "peristaltic" ("'Shat into Grace' Or, A Tale of a Turd:
Why It Is How It Is in Samuel Beckett's *How It Is*," *Papers on Language and
Literature* 21.1 (1984): 67.

continue forever and ever as it still did in *The Unnamable*, but periods of narrative articulation and periods of silence must be read and measured against each other. "[U]nder the ideal observer's lamps sudden flurry of mouth and adjacent all the lower brief dart of rosy tongue a few beads of froth then sudden straight line lips gone no trace of mucus gums clenched arch to arch he suspects nothing but where am I flown then sudden same again then then where do I go from then to then and in between" (95–96): this detailed description of the narrating act on the part of the narrator himself emphasizes its discontinuous movement "from then to then and in between" that creates the duration of narrative discourse in the novel.

In the absence of durational indicators in the text, then, it is its printed arrangement which provides a measure of speed and rhythm. But the reverse formulation may be even more important: the printed configuration will seem arbitrary *unless* it is understood as a medium of narrative temporality. The "virtual time" of narrative I discussed earlier is here given a very concrete realization not so much in the reading process as in the spatial design of the page. In some sense one might describe this innovative strategy as a shift of temporality from story to discourse, a phrase one critic has used to describe the foregrounding of the composition and narration process in postmodern novels.[21] But more importantly, this strategy effects a fundamental change in the functioning of narrative discourse, which in novels such as *How It Is* exploits the spatiality of the printed page precisely to convey temporality.

This innovation may become even clearer when we consider that the printed configuration, a device available only to *written* narrative, is here used insistently to convey the *orality* of the narration, the very breath with which it is uttered: "Through the visual typography, paradoxically, Beckett emphasizes the oral lyricism of his fiction. Though most of the verses . . . endure for longer than a breath, the reader is forced to breathe as guided by the verses."[22] In fact, *How It Is* does everything to discourage the

21 Philippe Le Touzé, "Aspects de l'esthétique du temps chez quelques 'romanciers de Minuit'," *Passage du temps, ordre de la transition*, ed. Jean Bessière (Paris: Presses Universitaires de France, 1985), 191.
22 Ruby Cohn, *Back to Beckett* (Princeton: Princeton University Press, 1973), 229; see also Brienza, "Midget Grammar," 118; Victor Sage, "Innovation and

reader from thinking of it as a written narrative, since the way in which the narrator's existential situation is described physically excludes the possibility of his producing a written text. Unlike Malone, who after all still owned a notebook and pencil and had a bed to sit on or lie in, this narrator crawls naked through the mud, with no possessions other than a sack of cans and a can opener, and no human contact other than his victims and torturers (if they exist). This makes it inconceivable that his story should ever have been recorded.[23] The only act of writing mentioned in the novel is that of Kram the witness and Krim the scribe, two characters who appear in Part Two and seem to be observing Pim and the narrator, "keeping the record a little aloof sitting standing it's not said yes or no samples extracts" (80). But it is unclear whether these characters are even part of the narrator's own reality, since they might be figures from one of Pim's stories. Even if they are not, they could not possibly record the words of a narrator who throughout most of the novel claims he is mute. Furthermore, if the narrator is indeed only quoting word by word what he hears another voice say, Krim and Kram belong to the universe of the other voice, not his own; and if, on the contrary, his final disclaimer of the entire story is authentic, witness and scribe are only figments of his imagination.[24] I

Continuity in *How It Is*," *Beckett the Shape Changer*, ed. Katharine Worth (London: Routledge, 1975), 95.

[23] Frederik N. Smith also compares *How It Is* to *Malone Dies* in "Fiction as Composing Process: *How It Is*," *Samuel Beckett: Humanistic Perspectives*, ed. Morris Beja, S. E. Gontarski and Pierre Astier (N.p.: Ohio State University Press, 1983), 106–21, and observes that whereas both novels focus on the process of composition, *Malone Dies* emphasizes the "writing situation" and *How It Is* the "mental and imaginative operations of the writer." But Smith takes this to imply that "in *How It Is*. . . Beckett retreats from the page, or rather goes behind it, attempting to catch the flux of the writing process at the moment it is occurring" (*ibid.*, 108; see also Hugh Kenner, *Samuel Beckett: A Critical Study*, new edn (Berkeley: University of California Press, 1973), 200, and Cohn, *Back to Beckett*, 227). I would disagree with this interpretation in so far as *How It Is*, unlike *Malone Dies*, revolves not primarily around a writing process, but a process of oral narration, conveyed through a printed configuration that is foregrounded rather than overcome. Smith seems to make a similar point later when he notes that "the absence of punctuation and the minimalization of grammatical connectives enable us to track the evolution of . . . thought without being reminded that what we are reading is in fact *written* discourse" (*ibid.*, 114); original emphasis.

[24] Concerning this last possibility, Francis Doherty notes: "The circle closes in infinite circularity: a voice murmuring creating a world of observers who note the murmurs which are the substance of the fictional work" ("Breath-Clock Breath: *How It Is*," *Samuel Beckett* [London: Hutchinson University Library,

mention these details not to push a "logical" analysis of the text, which may be inappropriate given its many paradoxes and inconsistencies, but to point out precisely one of these paradoxes: how much this *written* text insists on its own *oral* character – and its very peculiar oral character at that (a disembodied voice quoted by another, embodied but mute "voice"). In other words, the text insists on being read as a temporal process by making it logically impossible to think of it as recorded in writing: its printed words aim at making the reader forget the spatiality of print and to experience the temporality of the voice.[25]

Speaking throughout most of the novel with a voice "not his own," the narrator himself experiences this temporality not unlike the way in which a reader might perceive it: with the desire to end it soon, on one hand, and the anxiety of making it last, on the other. Like the Unnamable, the narrator of *How It Is* considers the telling of his story a chore to be fulfilled as quickly as possible: both are anxious to utter the quantity of speech dictated to them by unknown voices so that the end may deliver them.[26] Duration is undesirable to them, a necessary evil that keeps off the longed-for ending, as is revealed in *How It Is* by the narrator's self-exhortations to get on "quickly": "but first quick make an end of life in common end at last of part two leaving only last at last" (96); "never anything of all this little quick then the little that is left add it quick before Bom before he comes . . . the little that is left add it quick how it was after Pim before Bom how it is/quick then end at last of part two" (98); "Pim quick after Pim before he vanishes never was only me me Pim how it

1971], 128). Dearlove believes that Krim and Kram are the "authors" of the text we read but considers them unreliable ("The Voice and Its Words," 113). She does not discuss the ambiguity as to what diegetic level these characters belong to, or the contradictions that arise when one tries to solve this ambiguity. See also the discussion of Krim and Kram's books in Howard Harper's "*How It Is*," *Samuel Beckett and the Art of Rhetoric*, ed. Edouard Morot-Sir, Howard Harper and Douglas McMillan III (Chapel Hill: North Carolina Studies in the Romance Languages and Literatures, 1976), 261–63.

[25] Paul St-Pierre analyzes the relationship between speech and writing in *Comment c'est* in his article, "*Comment c'est* de Beckett: production et déception du sens," *Revue des lettres modernes* 605–610 (1981): 106–09. On the relationship between the spatiality of print and the temporality of the speaking voice, see also Walter Ong, "A Dialectic of Aural and Objective Correlatives," *Essays in Criticism* 8 (1958): 166–81, and Garrett Stewart's *Reading Voices: Literature and the Phonotext* (Berkeley: University of California Press, 1990).

[26] Dearlove, "The Voice and Its Words," 108.

was before me with me after me how it is quick" (105). Aware that for reasons beyond his control, he is forced to tell all three parts of his story, that he cannot omit anything, the narrator attempts instead to shorten the time of discourse by speeding up his performance, not unlike a reader who might attempt to shorten the duration of a long novel by reading more quickly.

But at other moments, the narrator of *How It Is* follows just the opposite impulse, that of making the narration last, stretching out each incident as long as possible. In these moments, story becomes identical with vital duration, with the time of life left to the narrator, and he seems desperately intent on prolonging his life by dwelling on its story so as to "last a moment," a phrase repeated over and over in some sections of the novel:

what to begin with drink to begin with I turn over on my face that lasts a good moment I last with that a moment in the end the mouth opens the tongue comes out lolls in the mud that lasts a good moment they are good moments perhaps the best difficult to choose . . .

. . . it's I who fall asleep again stop drinking and sleep again . . . I sleep that's my night present formulation I have no other I wake from sleep how much nearer to the last that of men of beasts too I wake ask myself how much nearer I quote on last a moment with that it's another of my resources   (27–28)

Similar passages with extensive descriptions of trivial activities occur on many other pages of the novel (see 26, 31, 32, 33, 36), where what is being told has no importance since its only function is to prolong the duration of discourse.

The narrator's attitude toward his own storytelling, therefore, is contradictory: he sometimes attempts to prolong his story so as to make his life last, and at other moments seems intent only on finishing it as fast as possible. Obviously, the activity of story-telling mediates the experience of temporality for the narrator and indeed becomes identical with it. From the beginning, his very existence is defined through its relation with the story he tells. On one hand, the narrator exists before and outside the story that is imposed upon him by the unknown voice, and he can slow it down or speed it up at will; on the other hand, his very existence depends on his story, to the point where the time of his life and the time of his story coincide, and he has no existence outside his narration. Hence the prolongation of discourse through the telling of trivial detail can in fact become the prolongation of his own life time: in *How It Is,* narrative discourse *is* (existential) duration.[27]

This does obviously not mean that narrative here mimetically *represents* lived duration through the story it tells. On the contrary, two of the phrases most frequently repeated by the narrator, "vast stretches of time" and "vast tracts of time," typically allude to the incommensurability between the "real" time period the story is supposed to cover, and the duration of this story itself: "I quote a given moment long past vast stretch of time on from there *that moment and following not all a selection* natural order vast tracts of time" (7); "passing time is told to me and time past vast tracts of time the panting stops and *scraps of an enormous tale* as heard so murmured to this mud" (27); "it's then I hear it my life here a life somewhere said to have been mine still mine and still in store *bits and scraps strung together* vast stretch of time an old tale my old life" (133 – emphasis mine; see also 22, 25, 34, 58, 106, 107, 108). These insistent reminders that the story consists only of selected bits and pieces that cannot measure up to "objective" time sever any mimetic relation between discursive duration and the duration of concrete, "real" events. Narrative, as a consequence, comes to be experienced as temporality itself, detached from the incidents which may or may not come to fill it.

The narrator's ambiguous attitude toward storytelling and the voice he claims to be quoting, as well as his insistence that he does not relate events in "real time," dissociate his story from both narration and narrative material: the story told in *How It Is* is not the expression of a narrator in control of his material, but is merely told *through* him,[28] and it is not told for the sake of its content, but its content is invented for the sake of dilating its form. The justification of its existence is therefore precisely its temporal duration. Displaced from its source and only arbitrarily

---

[27] The identification of storytelling with existential duration is, of course, as old at least as the *1001 Nights.* Perhaps the most comprehensive recent exploration of this analogy is Peter Brooks' *Reading for the Plot: Design and Intention in Narrative* (New York: Random House, 1985), especially Chapters 1, 2 and 4.

[28] Gerald Bruns calls it a "[n]arrative without narration" in "The Storyteller and the Problem of Language in Samuel Beckett's Fiction," *Modern Poetry and the Idea of Language: A Critical and Historical Study* (New Haven: Yale University Press, 1974), 183.

connected to its content, the story told through bursts of speech and spells of silence exists as nothing more than an articulation of temporal duration.

Marjorie Perloff's reading of the novel as a "truncated, tick-ertape version of Proust" adds a further dimension to this analysis.[29] Focusing in particular on the "bits and scraps" of the past that visit the narrator's mind in Part One, Perloff argues that *How It Is* echoes and parodies the working of involuntary memory in *A la recherche du temps perdu*. But unlike Marcel's memories, which are triggered by specific moments of sensual perception, the images of the past in Beckett come and go arbitrarily and therefore cannot give the protagonist a more coherent experience of temporal existence: "The past cannot be recaptured; it can only be glimpsed at random and unpredictable intervals."[30] This leads to a temporal shuttling between past and present moments similar to the linguistic alternation of the text between speech and silence. Not only is it impossible to recapture the past, but the present itself eludes the protagonist's grasp: as a flickering of presence and absence, words and silence, past and present, the self's experience of the present in Beckett is as discontinuous as that of the past in Proust.

This discontinuity between past and present and the incoherence of the narrator's memories from life "above" invalidate any allegorizing approach to temporality in *How It Is* such as the one proposed by Eric Levy, who suggests that the novel is

a monumental effort to recapture time itself . . . the attempt to reclaim time as a genuine succession giving form and meaning to experience. The elaborate story of before, with, and after Pim, with its attempt to establish past, present, and future, constitutes an agonising failure to rise from the mud of lost time or no time and improvise true succession. . . .

---

[29] Marjorie Perloff, " 'The Space of a Door': Beckett and the Poetry of Absence," *The Poetics of Indeterminacy: Rimbaud to Cage* (n.p.: Northwestern University Press, 1983), 229. For a detailed analysis of the "images," see James Knowlson and John Pilling, *"How It Is," Frescoes of the Skull: The Later Prose and Drama of Samuel Beckett* (London: Calder, 1979), 64–68.

[30] "'The Space of a Door'," 234. In "Beckett's Sociability," Leo Bersani and Ulysse Dutoit even suggest that the memories that surge up in *How It Is* are in fact not those of one individual, but are circulated among all the inhabitants of the mud universe; fragments of the same life are passed on along the chain of tormentors and victims under the endlessly repeated injunction to remember and speak as if it were for the first time (*Raritan* 12.1 [1992]: 3–4). This interpretation takes an additional step away from a Proustian conception of memory.

[The narrator's] need to narrate a history or story is the need to order time, to have a time to order.[31]

Beckett reveals, according to Levy, "that temporality is just another empty, structural hypothesis necessary to give human experience significance and meaning."[32] This observation comes dangerously close to paradox, for it is hard to see why time would be "empty" and merely "structural" if it does in fact succeed in conveying meaning and significance to human life. What meaning this might be, however, is not easy to say: certainly the procession of crawling torturers and victims can hardly be understood as a promising allegory of how time bestows meaning on human life.[33]

But more importantly, Levy's claim that the three chapters of the novel allegorically stand in for past, present and future imposes a linear concept of time on the novel which the text itself resists. The narrator himself never draws this analogy, but only characterizes the three parts of his narrative as corresponding to his life "before, with and after Pim." Both the periods before and with Pim lie in the past from his viewpoint, whereas "after Pim" refers to the present. The narrator's ostensible tripartition of his life, then, is in fact overlaid by the bipartition expressed in the first sentence of the novel: "how it is" and "how it was," present and past. In addition, the narrator's claim that after having been abandoned by Pim, he is now awaiting his own torturer, Bom, whose arrival would form the fourth part of the cycle, invalidates the alignment of the novel's structure with past, present and future. Susan Brienza even argues that the entire monologue is spoken at the moment of this fourth part, the phase in which the narrator would have become Bom's victim and would hence be forced to produce speech; in this view, all of "before, with and after Pim" would be past. This hypothesis has its own problems,[34]

---

[31] Eric P. Levy, "*How It Is*: An Allegory of Time and Personal Identity," *Beckett and the Voice of Species: A Study of the Prose Fiction* (Totowa: Gill, 1980), 92.
[32] *Ibid.*, 84.
[33] I am leaving aside the important methodological problem of reading allegorically a novel by an author who insistently warns, "No symbols where none intended" (Addenda to *Watt*; quoted in Perloff, "'The Space of a Door'," 215).
[34] Brienza, "Midget Grammar," 89. Most notably, her claim conflicts with the narrator's statement that the story of his life emerges between Pim's departure and Bom's arrival (133); but there is also a great disparity between Pim the victim's almost complete amnesia concerning his "life below" and the narrator's detailed recall of his that militates against conceiving of the latter as a

but it certainly makes one wary of accepting the narrator's tripartition of the story as a reliable guide to the temporal structure of the novel, especially when one considers that the narrator himself frequently transgresses the boundaries he sets and mixes accounts of different phases of his life "before, with and after Pim."[35] As Marjorie Perloff observes, "[t]he neat tripartite structure of *How It Is* is thus an empty container, within which 'bits and scraps' coalesce for a moment and then separate to form new configurations."[36]

But if the text does not simply allegorize past, present and future, its insistence on tripartition nevertheless requires some explanation. "[D]ivide into three a single eternity for the sake of clarity," the narrator explains his own procedure (24) and thereby points to the structuring of duration as a sequence of alternating phases that the tripartition allows him. Time presents itself to him originally as an unbounded duration, an "eternity" unsuitable for narrative representation. Hence he does what at a larger scale entire cultures do in their structuring of time through a calendar: set a moment that becomes the zero-point of the temporal coordinate system, so that time becomes binary, divisible into *before* and *after*. Duration, still infinite, is placed in relation to a boundary, a beginning and/or end,[37] and the flux of past, present and future is converted into the successive durational phases of

victim, given the complete analogy that the narrator himself stipulates between all torturers and all victims.

[35] Ruby Cohn, "Comment c'est par le bout," *Samuel Beckett: The Comic Gamut* (New Brunswick: Rutgers University Press, 1962), 183; Cohn, *Back to Beckett* 236–37, 239; Smith, "Fiction as Composing Process," 112; see also Brienza, "Midget Grammar," 109–10.

[36] "'The Space of a Door'," 233.

[37] See Brienza, "Midget Grammar," 109–110; Alan Singer, "The Need of the Present: *How It Is* with the Subject in Beckett's Novel," *A Metaphorics of Fiction: Discontinuity and Discourse in the Modern Novel* (Tallahassee: Florida State University Press, 1983), 125–27. H. Porter Abbott analyzes in detail Beckett's "aesthetic of recommencement" with its play between *commencer* and *comment c'est* ("begin" and "how it is" in the French text) in "Beginning Again: The Post-Narrative Art of *Texts for Nothing* and *How It Is*," *The Cambridge Companion to Beckett*, ed. John Pilling (Cambridge: Cambridge University Press, 1994): 112ff. For a detailed discussion of the problem of temporal duration vs. temporal succession, one of the most persistent ones in the history of the philosophy of time, see Cornelius A. Benjamin's essay, "Ideas of Time in the History of Philosophy," *The Voices of Time*, ed. J. T. Fraser, 2nd edn (Amherst: University of Massachusetts Press, 1981), 3–30, and Friedrich Kümmel's "Time as Succession and the Problem of Duration," trans. Francesco Gaona, *ibid.*, 31–55.

before, with and after. In the macrostructure of the novel, then, duration is organized as phases of patterned alternation not unlike the ones I pointed out earlier in its microstructure.

In the universe of *How It Is*, Pim becomes the temporal hinge that makes duration susceptible to narrative representation:[38] he is appropriately characterized by the narrator as a being with "a chronometer and a voice" from his first mention in Part One.[39] During a moment of deep silence after one of Pim's songs, in which "finally vast stretch of time a distant ticking" becomes audible, the narrator discovers that Pim possesses a watch and begins to listen avidly to its sound (58). He describes it twice in successive paragraphs, once as a wristwatch and once as a chain-watch, in part obviously to draw attention to its fictionality,[40] but also to emphasize the only crucial feature of this timepiece in the darkness of the mud world: the intermittent sound which marks time. "I finally have the watch to my ear the hand the fist it's preferable I drink deep of the seconds delicious moments and vistas" (59), he remarks after he has twisted Pim's arm so that he can hold the watch close to his ear. But he must soon return it to its former position, and the interlude of "objectively" measured time ends:

from it to me now part three from way off out on the right in the mud to me abandoned the distant ticking I derive no more profit from it none whatever no more pleasure count no more the unforgiving seconds measure no more durations and frequencies take my pulse no more ninety ninety-five

it keeps me company that's all its ticking now and then but break it throw it away let it run down and stop no something stops me it stops I shake my arm it starts no more about this watch (59)

The analogy these paragraphs establish between Pim and his watch turns the disappearance of the latter, which "keeps [the narrator] company," into a foreshadowing of Pim's departure ("part three . . . abandoned")[41] and equates Pim's presence with the existence of measurable time. But it is also a measure of the narrator's own life, the beat of his pulse, and when the watch

[38] Singer, "The Need of the Present," 125.
[39] Cohn, "Comment c'est," 201.
[40] Dearlove, "The Voice and Its Words," 111; see also Doherty, "Breath-Clock Breath," 126.
[41] Doherty, "Breath-Clock Breath," 126.

stops ticking, the deliberate ambiguity of the narrator's "stop no something stops me it stops" signals the amalgamation of the watch as object, time as a physical phenomenon, and the narrator's life: it is impossible to tell in the syntax of the paragraph whether the narrator stops the watch, it stops him, or time stops. The ticking of the watch and the beating of the pulse, binary rhythms both, are temporarily fused in the narrator's "breath-clock breath" (19). The abrupt ending of the incident is immediately followed by the narrator's account of how he gave Pim his name: quite literally, Pim himself replaces the watch as that device which allows the narrator to structure time in patterns of alternation.

3. Time against voice

I have so far discussed the temporal structure of *How It Is* without paying more than marginal attention to the questions of narrative voice the novel raises, as if the story were told by a more or less reliable narrator. But this is of course not the case. The story the narrator tells in *How It Is* is disauthenticated in three ways: first, through his insistence that what the reader hears is only the "last version" or "present formulation" of his life's story, implying that other versions might follow; second, through his assertion that he is in fact not telling his own story at all, but merely quoting the text he hears another voice pronounce; third, through his final confession that the entire story, including the foreign voice, was all just invented by him and him alone:

all these calculations yes explanations yes the whole story from beginning to end yes completely false yes

that wasn't how it was no not at all no how then no answer how was it then no answer HOW WAS IT screams good

there was something yes but nothing of all that no all balls from start to finish yes this voice quaqua yes all balls yes only one voice here yes mine yes when the panting stops yes (144–45)[42]

---

[42] There is an even earlier denial toward the end of Part Two: "can't go on we're talking of me not Pim Pim is finished he has finished me now part three not Pim my voice not his saying this these words can't go on and Pim that Pim never was and Bom whose coming I await to finish be finished have finished me too that Bom will never be no Pim no Bom and this voice quaqua of us all never was only one voice my voice never any other" (86–87).

The intricate problems of narrative voice that this triple dis-authentication raises are a focal point of much criticism of the novel. The final disavowal has generally been interpreted as a resolution of the ambiguities that the pretense of quotation had created, even if this resolution literally leaves the readers with no text at all: in spite of the authoritativeness the title of the novel seems to convey, they never do find out "how it is."[43] This reading, I would argue, is correct and yet oversimplifies both the nature of the "quotation" and of the ending in that it avoids the final crux of the text: the reader is left with an irresolvable ambiguity which *opposes* narrative voice and narrative time. In the end, voice and time logically exclude each other, but the novel nevertheless forces them together in a paradox of identity, so that neither the story *nor* its denial are finally validated as definitive.

The problem with the narrator's claim that everything he says is merely quoted begins with the very words "I quote" and "I say it as I hear it," repeated over and over throughout the text. When the narrator declares, "I say it as I hear it every word always" (42), does the quotation also include the very sentence he is pronouncing at that moment? Does he hear the other voice say, "I quote"? If so, this would open up the rather vertiginous possibility of the other voice being itself only a repetition and quotation of yet another voice *it* hears, which could itself be read as yet another quotation, and so forth.[44] One may reject this possibility as absurd, but in that case the words, "I say it as I hear it *every word always*" (emphasis mine) are not literally true, and one must instead assume that the narrator is some-

[43] Perloff, "'The Space of a Door'," 244; see also Bruns, "The Storyteller," 177–82; Cohn, *Back to Beckett*, 240; Dearlove, "The Voice and Its Words," 106–08; Doherty, "Breath-Clock Breath," 119–20; Raymond Federman, Review of *How It Is*, *Samuel Beckett: The Critical Heritage*, ed. Lawrence Grover and Raymond Federman (London: Routledge, 1979), 231; Susan Schurman, "*How It Is*," *The Solipsistic Novels of Samuel Beckett* (Cologne: Pohl-Rugenheim, 1987), 139–45; Smith, "Fiction as Composing Process," 117. The exception is Alan Singer, whose analysis of the narrating instance in *How It Is* shows that "[t]he subject of rational discourse in Beckett's novels exists virtually as an absent cause denoted by a narrative structure for which the word 'effect' no longer accords the certainty of definition" ("The Need of the Present," 120).

[44] Bersani and Dutoit brilliantly analyze this regression in terms of its implications for the origin of language and the ability to speak ("Beckett's Sociability," 5–6).

times quoting and sometimes commenting on the act of quotation in his own voice. Where, however, does his own voice begin and end?

The problem is aggravated by other passages in which the narrator seems to be commenting on or correcting the material he quotes:

. . . you begin again all over more or less in the same place or in another as when another image above in the light you come to in hospital in the dark

the same as which which place it's not said or I don't hear it's one or the other the same more or less . . .   (22; emphasis mine)

The narrator here seems to be quoting the "image" or visual memory from the other voice and then adding the request for more specific information in his own voice. But then who provides the subsequent answer? The narrator or the quoted voice? The latter is logically impossible since the quoted voice could not answer a question asked by the narrator; the former implies that the text may in fact contain many contributions in the narrator's own voice, but that they cannot be told apart from the quotations. In the last section of the novel, the narrator even resorts, apparently, to correcting the version of the story he has "quoted" to us:

when according to me [the voice] said Bem speaking of how it was before the journey part one and Bom speaking of how it will be after the abandon part three and last it said in reality

it said in reality in the one case as in the other either Bem solely or solely Bom

or it said in reality now Bem now Bom through carelessness or inadvertence not realizing that it varied I personify it it personifies itself

or finally it passed prepensely from the one to the other according as it spoke of how it was before the journey or of how it will be after the abandon through ignorance not realizing that Bem and Bom could only be one and the same   (113)

Here the narrator has clearly moved quite far away from mere quotation and is rewriting the story he claimed he was only repeating. If in the first two parts of the novel the use of the first person constantly tempted the reader to conflate the "I" of the story and the "I" of the discourse, the subject of the utterance and the subject of the act of uttering,[45] the distinction between the two is quite transparent in some passages toward the end of Part Three. In the very act of pretending to quote, in the process of uttering the words, "I quote," then, the narrator in fact affirms that he is *not* quoting all of the time, that he does, after all, possess a voice and a text of his own.[46]

This dissociation between the narrator's and the "foreign" voice culminates in the passage quoted at the beginning of this section, in which the narrator denies that he ever heard any but his own voice at all, and that the existence of any other voice was merely a figment of his imagination. This denial seems to resolve the peculiarities of the narration – but only up until the novel's last sentence: "good good end at last of part three and last that's how it was end of quotation after Pim how it is" (147). This final sentence must necessarily leave the reader nonplussed; what can the phrase "end of quotation" mean after the narrator just spent three pages claiming that he never quoted anything at all? Just when it looked as if the novel's ambiguities had been resolved, the text lapses again into self-referential paradox: was the denial of quotation after all itself part of the quotation? If so, has the narrator's own voice been heard at all? If not, what could account for the passages in which the narrator seemed to be correcting or commenting on the other voice?

The novel does not answer these questions, but it is important to raise them because they show that the text does not proceed from a story told by a self-alienated and somehow displaced "double" voice to a self-present, unitary voice whose denial of the story is the final, if devastating, touchstone of truth for the novel. Rather, the quotation structure and its disavowal are from the beginning implicit in each other: the very words which affirm that everything is quoted in *How It Is* reveal that *not* everything is quoted, and the final denial that anything was quoted is immediately followed by a phrase that seems to indicate that everything was quoted after all. The novel therefore cannot be read as a progression from one to the other, but must be understood as a

---

[45] In Emile Benveniste's terms, the difference between *sujet de l'énoncé* and *sujet de l'énonciation* (*Problèmes de linguistique générale*, vol. 1. [Paris: Gallimard, 1966], 258–66).

[46] St-Pierre also comments on this simultaneous affirmation and negation of the quotation structure ("*Comment c'est*," 93–100).

flickering, an alternation of both, not unlike those perspectival drawings of cubes which look solid one moment and hollow the next: both readings logically exclude each other and yet are simultaneously present.

The logical paradox that informs the structure of *How It Is* pits narrative time and narrative voice against each other at the same time that it inextricably entangles one with the other. In one reading, the "plot" can be understood as a temporal development, but the identity of the narrating instance remains uncertain even at the end of the novel. In the other reading, the final passages re-establish a unitary, self-present voice – but this occurs, eerily enough, at the expense of narrative itself, since this voice, no sooner found, invalidates the events that had been related. The negation leaves the readers with absolutely nothing that they can affirm about the narrator's present or past. All one knows at the end is that he lies on his belly in the mud and darkness, talking to himself (see 146). If the narrative voice becomes "self-identical" and "self-present" at the end, then, this identity and presence must be read in quotation marks because it goes hand in hand with an elimination of the very categories of character and time. The central "I" of the novel therefore leads a precarious, flickering existence in between a temporal dimension which subverts his identity because it is ambiguously attributable to himself or another "I," and a denial of this temporality that erases the other "I" and his own identity at the same time.

Phrased more generally, the paradoxes in the narrative logic of *How It Is* can be understood to arise from the perception that temporality is necessary to the constitution of identity as that which lasts, but simultaneously disperses and annihilates the very concept of identity, since it is precisely the force that brings about change.[47] Beckett considers this paradox in his essay on the

[47] The only critic who explicitly discusses this contradiction between voice and time is, again, Alan Singer, although he argues that the very *assertion* of a "master voice" creates this tension, whereas I would argue that the paradox only emerges fully with the *denial* of this voice at the end. Singer observes: "While the narrator of *How It Is* meticulously orders the details of his life before Pim, with Pim, and after Pim, he nonetheless passionately protests that the words so ordered are not his own . . . Beckett's narrator scrupulously ascribes the cause of his speech to a higher cause in relation to which he is the obedient effect. The resultant transposition of cause and effect carries the force of a logical contradiction that disturbs the teleological certainty of the tripartite plot structure (the movement toward and away from Pim, but always centered on

notion of time in Proust. As Steven Connor has observed, the essay argues against the simplistic notion that the self can somehow be distinguished from the time it inhabits, and the idea that its "solid essence" is merely carried along by the flow of time "like a vessel in a stream."[48] It shows that self and time are on the contrary inextricably entangled with each other:

> There is no escape from the hours and the days. Neither from to-morrow nor from yesterday. There is no escape from yesterday because yesterday has deformed us, or been deformed by us. The mood is of no importance. Deformation has taken place. Yesterday is not a milestone that has been passed, but a daystone on the beaten track of the years, and irremediably part of us, within us, heavy and dangerous. We are not merely more weary because of yesterday, we are other, no longer what we were before the calamity of yesterday.[49]

Beckett sums up this view of time as a process of relentless transformation in the striking metaphor of the individual as "the seat of a constant process of decantation, decantation from the vessel containing the fluid of future time, sluggish, pale and monochrome, to the vessel containing the fluid of past time, agitated and multicoloured by the phenomena of its hours."[50] Whereas time is in one sense only an arbitrary condition or "accident" of existence, it is in another sense impossible even to conceive of selfhood in other than temporal terms, since time is necessary to bring it into being.[51] But this temporal condition also implies that for the largest part of our existence, we live alienated from what Beckett calls "the essence of ourselves, the best of our

the narrator's being). After all, the narrator cannot be both cause and effect within the same hierarchy of priorities" ("The Need of the Present," 126–27); later, he shows that "the narrator's hypothesis of the prior – that is, timeless – voice appears as a deliberate compensation for the contradictions that the experience of real time must breed in any human life. This 'master voice' suggests a causality that brings an unstable heterogeneity neatly under the sign of a privileged homogeneity" (*ibid.*, 127–28), a homogeneity which collapses at the end (*ibid.*, 129). Thus, Singer argues, "in the narrative form of *How It Is*, Beckett gives us the play between two kinds of knowledge – a knowledge revealed by the reduction of differences and assimilable to the form of linear causality, will, expression, monadic subjectivity – and a knowledge proliferated in difference and apparently disunified, unwilled and unexpressive" (*ibid.*, 131). Needless to say, my own analysis has close affinities with this reading.

48 Steven Connor, *Samuel Beckett: Repetition, Theory and Text* (Oxford: Blackwell, 1988), 45.

49 Samuel Beckett, *Proust* (New York: Grove, 1957), 2–3.

50 *Ibid.*, 4–5.

51 Connor, *Samuel Beckett*, 45.

many selves" – precisely those moments in time which, due to the numbing of our perception by habit, we do not remember, and which are hence stored away in an inaccessible part of our temporal existence.[52] In Proust, Beckett points out, only the accidental triggering of "involuntary memory" opens up these hidden moments to individual consciousness, which implies that coherent identity may ultimately depend on a series of coincidences.[53]

Still, as long as these coincidences do occur, the lost time of the past can be recaptured, and Marcel's search for identity is in the end successful. But the narrator of *How It Is* lives in a universe in which coincidence has become almost inconceivable, and even more so the prospect that a mere accident might give the individual access to his own forgotten but rich and varied past. Indeed, it is not certain that the narrator has any past to recall; the images that occasionally visit him from what seem to be his childhood and youth may be fantasies rather than memories, and, due to the ambiguous diegetic structure of the text, might at any rate not be his but those of the "other voice." Memory, in so far as it can still be said to exist in this world, provides no sure foundation for identity. Moreover, as I have shown, it is not only the past that is no longer susceptible to recuperation, but also the narrator's present. Since what appears to be his own account of his situation is first attributed to another source and then rejected as mere invention, there is no way of grasping even the present moment in the world of the ironically titled *How It Is*. Or, to put it somewhat differently, the only way of attempting to grasp it at all is to rely on quotation, on scraps of discourse pronounced by unknown voices out of nowhere. If Fredric Jameson characterizes the posthistorical predicament of the late twentieth century by claiming that "we are condemned to seek History by way of our . . . simulacra of that history, which itself remains forever out of reach,"[54] Beckett takes this reflection one step further by creating a fictional universe in which even the present is accessible only

---

[52] Beckett, *Proust*, 18.

[53] *Ibid.*, 19–21. In "Time and Habit," Chapter 4 of his *Samuel Beckett and the Pessimistic Tradition* (New Brunswick: Rutgers University Press, 1976), Steven J. Rosen gives a detailed analysis of Beckett's philosophy of time and particularly his relationship to Proust in this regard.

[54] *Postmodernism, or, the Cultural Logic of Late Capitalism* (Durham, NC: Duke University Press, 1991), 25.

by way of such simulacra. The "other voice" that is both origin and double of the narrator's discourse functions as such a simulacrum of the present, of "how it is," not unlike the merged voices of Proteus and Menelaus that tell the story of their loosening grasp of time in John Barth's "Menelaiad." In both texts, the elaborate play with quotation and self-quotation, the doubling-up of the narrative voice, and the narrator's problematic relation to memory and history put not only the experience of the past but also that of the present in question.

In both cases, narrative stages its own increasing dissociation from any imagined or inferred time dimension – whether it be that of the story told or that of the storyteller – and focuses instead on the temporality of the text itself. *How It Is* does so more emphatically since it lacks the obvious intertextual links that still connect the "Menelaiad" to history, even if it is primarily literary history. This retreat of narrative from signifying time in *How It Is* leads to a text that uses a wide range of strategies – from the narrator's concern with the temporal organization of his life, the tripartition of the text, and the handling of narrative voice to the typographical configuration of the page – to foreground that narrative time is not measured out by physical or psychological events but by words. By focusing on this basic characteristic of narrative and renouncing what Barthes once called the "referential illusion" of "true time,"[55] *How It Is* marks a moment in the evolution of the novel in which narrative seems to give up its function of mediating, through its form, the experience of temporality.

But one could argue that precisely through this renunciation, *How It Is* and other postmodernist texts do in fact work through and participate in a reconceptualization of time that goes far beyond literature. The crisis of narrative time that takes place in the pages of Beckett's novel is one of a whole range of crises in the representation of time that have taken place in various cultural fields, discourses and disciplines since the 1960s, and whose contours I have outlined in Chapter 1. In this context, the specific contribution of *How It Is* lies in the way in which it places time at the intersection of two different media, oral narration and

[55] "An Introduction to the Structural Analysis of Narrative," trans. Lionel Duisit, *New Literary History* 6 (1975): 252.

the printed book, so that print seems to represent the voice, but the voice – through the situation in which it claims to be speaking – denies the possibility of any script. Since it also, in the end, implicitly disavows this denial, the printed page finally remains an ambiguous surface which both means time (in its graphic configuration) and rejects time as a viable parameter for organizing experience (through the words spelled out on it). This self-consciousness about the book and its association with time inserts itself into a historical moment in which not only time as a social category but also its relationship to a variety of older, newer and emergent media – print, radio, film, television – becomes a central cultural concern in many Western societies, as the work of, for example, Marshall McLuhan shows. If McLuhan argues that "the 'content' of any medium is always another medium,"[56] Beckett's text both confirms and problematizes this relationship. In *How It Is*, time becomes the intersection where two media collide which are forced to be a message because they are no longer able to mean one.

[56] *Understanding Media: The Extensions of Man* (Cambridge, MA: MIT Press, 1994), 8.

III

Posthistories

❖❖❖

5

Δt: time's assembly in *Gravity's Rainbow*

❖❖❖

"Will Postwar be nothing but 'events,' newly created one moment to the next? No links? Is it the end of history?" one character wonders near the end of World War II in Thomas Pynchon's novel *Gravity's Rainbow*.[1] This concern over the viability of history as an organizing parameter emerges as one of the novel's central issues throughout its more than 700 pages, its multiplicity of plots, scores of characters, and the innumerable connections and disjunctions that structure its enormous variety of elements. Due to its unusual complexity, *Gravity's Rainbow* has often been characterized as an encyclopedia, a data bank, or a cosmic web, descriptions that emphasize the extent to which the novel functions as a textual space or cognitive field whose tightly woven symmetries and correspondences promise coherence, but ultimately defy attempts at ordering them into a meaningful pattern.[2] As a narrative text, however, *Gravity's Rainbow* operates also and primarily as a temporal construct that makes information only gradually available and molds it according to genre conventions that prompt the reader to ask certain questions at the expense of others, and to select specific types of information to answer these questions. The analysis I am proposing here therefore focuses on the ways in which *Gravity's Rainbow* suggests a

---

[1] *Gravity's Rainbow* (New York: Viking, 1973), 56. All future page references to *Gravity's Rainbow* will be given parenthetically and refer to the same edition.

[2] Edward Mendelson, "Gravity's Encyclopedia," *Thomas Pynchon's Gravity's Rainbow*, ed. Harold Bloom (New York: Chelsea House, 1986), *passim*; Steven Weisenburger, "The End of History? Thomas Pynchon and the Uses of the Past," *Critical Essays on Thomas Pynchon*, ed. Richard Pearce (Boston: Hall, 1981), 141; N. Katherine Hayles, "Caught in the Web: Cosmology and the Point of (No) Return in Pynchon's *Gravity's Rainbow*," *The Cosmic Web: Scientific Field Models & Literary Strategies in the 20th Century* (Ithaca: Cornell University Press, 1984), 168–69.

set of narrative problems with a temporal or historical dimension together with a variety of theories on how to solve them; the successes and also, quite often, the failures of these theories to account for the questions the plot raises map the functioning of historical causality and narrative time in the novel. Most of its protagonists find themselves in quintessentially posthistorical scenarios in which past and future no longer lend themselves to the construction of a coherent narrative about the present, and see themselves forced to reflect in a highly self-conscious manner about problems of causation and storytelling; often, they end up shuttling back and forth between visions of the world as a conspiratorial web with no escape, or as a meaningless playfield of pure chance. Through the divergent theories and narratives that these characters construct about themselves and the events they are involved in, *Gravity's Rainbow* explores problems of narrative in an age in which the individual human's understanding of time and chance has to confront the causalities of molecular chemistry as well as those of global economic and political transactions. How does one experience and narrate time after the end of history? Not only the characters but also the readers of *Gravity's Rainbow* must confront this question with all its implications for conceptions of the self, the social environment and historical knowledge.

1. Pointsman's dilemma

The events of *Gravity's Rainbow* occur during an interval of approximately ten months from mid-December 1944 to mid-September 1945, and are set against the background of the final phases of World War II: London during the *Blitzkrieg* and the German "Zone" after the cessation of hostilities.[3] But the temporal sequence of these events is undercut by a time reversal in the first and last scenes: *Gravity's Rainbow* starts out at the moment just after a V-2 rocket seems to have struck London, and ends in the description of a rocket launching. Or almost: just when it seems as if the launch of a 00000, the V-2's successor, will conclude the narrative, it turns out that the entire plot of the

---

[3] A detailed chronology of all the novel's major events is given in Steven Weisenburger's "The Chronology of Episodes in *Gravity's Rainbow*," *Pynchon Notes* 14 (1984): 50–59.

novel has only taken place on the screen of a Los Angeles movie theater that is about to be hit by an incoming rocket. There is just the last moment left, the infinitesimal Δt before impact in which the text invites the readers to join in the singing of a hymn with the words, "Now everybody – " (760), interrupted by perhaps a song and perhaps by death, but certainly the end of the novel. From the moment just after an explosion to the moment just before, *Gravity's Rainbow* seems to describe a time-reversed curve: the novel "begins – almost – with the words: 'It is too late.' It ends – not quite – with the words: 'there is time,'" Louis Mackey observes.[4] The narrative structure of *Gravity's Rainbow* is shaped by this tension between temporal progression and causal inversion, movements it constantly juxtaposes so as to open up alternative fictional universes.

The novel's opening chapter presents a protagonist who is cut off from history in so far as he can barely remember the past and fears there may be no future: American Lieutenant Tyrone Slothrop, working in London during the Blitz, is obsessed with the idea that not only one but *all* of the incoming rockets may have his name written on them. Under the constant threat of death, reinforced by this personal paranoia, and with the past a mere haze in his mind, Slothrop attempts to save a few moments from his disappearing time by keeping a "journal" of sorts of his multiple short-lived love affairs: every day, he pastes colored paper stars with the names of his latest lovers and the date on a map of London in his office, marking the sites where he happened to meet them. This is the initial scenario of *Gravity's Rainbow*: the past out of mind, the future uncertain, and the present a configuration of paper stars on a map.

It is impossible to summarize the plot that develops from this initial constellation, or even to speak of any central "plot" of the novel in the conventional sense; with its mix of disparate genres, its overlapping, competing and contradicting themes, metaphors and incidents, its several hundred characters and multiple strands of plot, *Gravity's Rainbow* defies the readers' ability to classify and synthesize. As Katherine Hayles has pointed out, the

---

[4] "Paranoia, Pynchon, and Preterition," *Thomas Pynchon's Gravity's Rainbow*, ed. Harold Bloom (New York: Chelsea House, 1986), 67; see also Peter L. Cooper, *Signs and Symptoms: Thomas Pynchon and the Contemporary World* (Berkeley: University of California Press, 1983), 214.

abundance of information tends to blur the distinction of figure and ground and to make it impossible for the reader to decide what is central and what marginal, what is crucial information and what accidental detail.[5] But certain foci of importance and narrative questions nevertheless do gradually emerge from the profusion of detail. One way of sorting and processing the information conveyed by the text is to ask what it contributes to the solution of these problems. *Gravity's Rainbow* is, after all, a novel with a good deal of suspense, and its narrative tension depends on the readers' recognition of storytelling "knots" and the ways in which they might possibly be untied: this search for solutions and answers structures the reading of the novel as a temporal experience.

In the first two of the novel's four long chapters, three central complexes of narrative questions (besides dozens of minor ones) emerge. The first one revolves around American officer Tyrone Slothrop and his map of sexual adventures. Unbeknownst to him but not to Allied Intelligence Services, this map corresponds point for point to that of the German V-2 attacks on London, but it pre-dates the strikes by anywhere between a few hours and ten days. Certain documents and clues indicate that Slothrop was subjected to a sustained Pavlovian conditioning process in his early childhood that might account for his strange interaction with the German rockets. Naturally, this unusual phenomenon is of the highest interest to various branches of the Defense Department and diverse Secret Services. At the initiative of British Intelligence, Slothrop is sent away from London to the Côte d'Azur, "accidentally" stripped of all of his identification papers and personal possessions, and then trained in German rocket technology, presumably in preparation for some secret mission. But when Slothrop becomes aware of the reasons for the Secret Service's intense interest in him, he escapes to the post-war German "Zone" to continue investigations on his own, which quickly turn into a quest for his own identity. One of the main narrative riddles of *Gravity's Rainbow*, then, is the figure of the American Slothrop, and his secret connection to the V-2 rockets.

In the course of his training in rocket technology, Slothrop encounters certain abnormalities that develop into further narra-

---

[5] "Caught in the Web," 174–75.

tive enigmas: an unexplained device, the "S-Gerät," shows up on one of the parts lists he studies. It appears in connection with an unknown material called Imipolex G, and both are classified as confidential and go unmentioned in any other descriptions and materials lists related to the V-2. The "plot" here begins to take on a distinct spy-novel twist: the "accidental" appearance and sudden disappearance of a beautiful but mysterious woman, Katje Borgesius (whom the reader already knows to be affiliated with various Secret Services), the discovery of confidential documents about a mystery device that is presumably a clue to the 00000 rocket, the Nazis' latest and most dangerous weapon, and the gradually accumulating clues to a conspiracy that uses Slothrop as its tool, engage the reader's hermeneutic impulse. Slothrop himself, more and more secretive about his discoveries and ever more cunning in diverting possible enemies from his activities, grows from the pathological case study he was in London into a masterful secret agent. His gradual implication in the search for the mysterious 00000 rocket and the interests and conspiracies surrounding it forms the second complex of questions that organizes the plot.

Slothrop's quest leads him as well as the reader to the third and maybe most important narrative "knot." Slothrop is characterized from the beginning of the novel as a person prone to paranoid delusions: during his work in London, he not only has a natural fear of the rocket strikes, but in fact suspects that the *Blitzkrieg* itself might be a complex maneuver on the part of unknown powers to get rid of him. Unwilling though the readers may initially be to lend credence to this extravagant interpretation of events, they are gradually given more and more hard evidence that some conspiracy is indeed afoot. The presence of some secret complex of power is aptly symbolized by a giant octopus on the Côte d'Azur from whose attack Slothrop saves Katje Borgesius, an incident that is itself engineered by the British Secret Service so as to put Borgesius in touch with Slothrop. As the novel lays out more and more historical detail concerning the involvement of certain corporations in the chemical industry with not only the Nazi regime, but simultaneously with the Allied governments, the reader cannot help but suspect that some gigantic international conspiracy may indeed be manipulating global political developments as well as the lives of individuals.

World War II itself, in this view, may not ultimately be a political conflict at all, but a confrontation engineered by transnational business corporations to promote their interest in the rapid development of certain technologies. Not only Slothrop, but two other protagonists of the novel, the German Herero Enzian and the Russian Intelligence Officer Tchitcherine, have periodic blinding visions of the global functioning of this conspiracy. None of these characters is by himself particularly reliable (Slothrop is paranoid from the start, while Enzian and Tchitcherine are avid drug users), but the startling similarity of their insights cannot but leave the reader with the growing suspicion that their fears may not be as unfounded as they appear. The third narrative problem the novel poses, then, is whether there is indeed an international conspiracy of ruthless business corporations, and if so, what their goals and the exact extent of their powers are. One may admit, by the sheer force of the historically accurate detail included in the novel, that "The Firm" – that is, primarily the German industrial conglomerate IG Farben and its international counterparts – controls international politics to some degree and may not hesitate to instigate world wars when that is in its interest. But it is less clear whether "They" are indeed the only power that moves global politics, and to what extent They are also able to control the minute detail of individuals' lives. Several of the novel's characters wonder whether it is possible to operate a "counterforce" under these circumstances, or whether any revolutionary impulse would be infiltrated and subverted from the start. But perhaps most importantly, the constant insinuations of global conspiracy in *Gravity's Rainbow* raise the question of whether chance or contingency are still conceivable at all in this world, and if so, what their role in shaping (post-)historical developments might be. With these questions, the text moves beyond the level of the individual characters (Slothrop, Borgesius, Blicero, Prentice, Mexico, Tchitcherine, Enzian) to the much more general level of global developments in science, technology and politics, and the extent to which these innovations give rise to a completely determined and causally defined universe, or on the contrary open up a more contingent one.

At the same time, the question of the role of temporality and causation not only in historical understanding but in narrative form emerges in full force. The reader must take into account not only the events narrated in *Gravity's Rainbow*, but also the implications of its narrative structure, and the role it assigns to causation and contingency. The text itself proposes several scientific and philosophical theories to explain the function of chance and causation in a posthistorical context; the importance of these theories lies not so much in their inherent plausibility or implausibility as in the kind of narrative structure they suggest when they are "bent back" onto the plot itself so as to account for its gaps and contradictions. Understood as reflections of the text on itself, they provide a basis for analyzing what narrative and temporal form *Gravity's Rainbow* offers to an age in which causality has become questionable and larger time perspectives difficult to envision. Through this analysis, a fourth problem emerges regarding the activity of reading itself; since none of the theories proposed by characters in the novel accounts satisfactorily for its various plots, the reader is left with the task of producing a meta-model, of which the interpretation that follows might count as one example. This meta-reading is not necessarily more successful than those in the novel itself, but it adds a level of observation that does help to foreground the way in which *Gravity's Rainbow* responds to a postmodernist understanding of time and history.

Four different interpretations of the relation between time and causality are proposed explicitly in the novel. Pointsman, a Pavlovian behaviorist in PISCES (Psychological Intelligence Schemes for the Expedition of Surrender), the psychological department of British Intelligence that first discovers and investigates Slothrop's strange connection with the V-2, advocates the most traditional view of causality: the reduction of all processes to the sequence of stimulus and response. His strongest opponent in the same outfit is Roger Mexico, a statistician who believes that notions such as cause and effect have become obsolete, and that contemporary science must rely on different concepts, those of frequency and probability, to make progress. A third perspective emerges in the course of a spiritist seance in which the ghost of Walter Rathenau, one of Germany's chief industrialists and its foreign minister during World War I, is conjured up. Rathenau, speaking from beyond death, suggests that causality may be a concept of some use in the world of the living, but really is just part of a tactic designed to mislead investigative minds: the truth, he claims, lies in the notions of "synthesis" and "control." Lastly, Leni Pökler, wife of one of the German technicians who work on the 00000, attempts to convince her husband that events must be understood simultaneously, not in sequence, and as "metaphors" or "signs and symptoms" of each other rather than as causes and effects. Each of these suggestions reflects fundamental changes in twentieth-century reasoning about causality, but each of them also has different implications for the questions identified above as those which structure the progression of the text.

If the novel's first few scenes place the reader at a moment when history seems to have shrunk to an insubstantial present in between a forgotten past and a doomed future, its first sentence, "A screaming comes across the sky," already points to the temporal loops and inversions which become possible in such a "time out of joint." The sentence refers to the fall of a V-2 rocket on London, and although the particular bomb described here explodes only in SOE officer Pirate Prentice's dream, it points to one of the V-2's real peculiarities: since this rocket travels faster than the speed of sound, the noise of its final approach to the target can only be heard after it has already detonated on the ground. The perception of a screaming sound therefore ominously signals "too-lateness" as soon as the text has started.[6]

This characteristic of the V-2 bombardment foreshadows the much stranger and much more disturbing temporal inversion implicit in the correspondence between statistician Roger Mexico's map of V-2 detonations and the record Tyrone Slothrop keeps of his love adventures. Not only do both maps follow the same general statistical distribution, but the sites they mark correspond point for point. Since Slothrop's stars regularly predate Mexico's points, his sexual activity literally seems to predict the arrival of the V-2s. The exact replication in time of an apparently random pattern cannot but raise the question whether there is any causal connection between the V-2 and Slothrop's love life, and what it might consist of.[7] All the specialists in Roger

[6] Mackey, "Paranoia," 67.
[7] In *Writing Pynchon: Strategies in Fictional Analysis* (Urbana: University of Illinois Press, 1990), Alec McHoul and David Wills observe:

A common 'finding' about *Gravity's Rainbow* is that it reverses standard narrative sequentiality. The sight of the V2 falling precedes the sound of its

Mexico's department propose some solution to this problem in keeping with their varied scientific and philosophical agendas; but the central confrontation occurs between the probabilist Mexico and the Pavlovian Pointsman. In one of the most frequently quoted scenes of the novel, Mexico claims that " 'there's a feeling about that cause-and-effect may have been taken as far as it will go. That for science to carry on at all, it must look for a less narrow, a less . . . sterile set of assumptions. The next great breakthrough may come when we have the courage to junk cause-and-effect entirely, and strike off at some other angle' " (89).[8] This alternative approach is obviously probability theory, which has come to replace deterministic notions of cause and effect in almost all branches of twentieth-century science.[9] Pointsman, by contrast, holds on to the older, determinist and behaviorist theory of stimulus and response, arguing that " 'Pavlov believed that the ideal, the end we all struggle toward in science, is the true mechanical explanation. [. . .] His faith ultimately lay in a pure physiological basis for the life of the psyche. No effect without cause, and a clear train of linkages' " (89). Whereas for Pointsman all phenomena must be analyzed in binary terms, as zeroes and ones, "to Mexico belongs the domain *between* zero and one – the middle Pointsman has excluded from his persuasion – the probabilities" (55; original emphasis).

In many interpretations of the novel, Mexico has been cast as Pynchon's spokesperson, the scientist who overcomes simplistic

arrival. Slothrop's erection precedes the mysterious stimulus (perhaps). Many readings are motivated, that is, by an odd reversal of what Barthes calls 'the post hoc ergo propter hoc' fallacy. To this extent *Gravity's Rainbow* has been taken as a sometime reversal of standard narrative syntax. But, and this is the rub, nothing comes of the reversed chain. There can be no outcome; it is literally impossible to reach back before the Zero or forward into the indefinite Void. No future or past history, no definite origin or destination can be guaranteed. The telos has been cancelled. In its place there are only possibilities . . .   (56)

This observation is accurate, but it leaves open the question why causal inversion is the device used to create these possibilities, and how they are organized into something enough like a plot or "narrative syntax" that the reader can at least attempt to understand the novel in its temporal and causal dimension.

[8] Since Pynchon uses ellipsis abundantly in his text, I will mark my own ellipses with square brackets to distinguish them from his.

[9] For a brief survey, see Norbert Wiener, *The Human Use of Human Beings: Cybernetics and Society* (New York: Da Capo, 1950), 7–12. A more detailed and technical account is Mario Bunge's *Causality and Modern Science*, 3rd edn (New York: Dover, 1979), especially 3–30 and 333–53.

binary models of the world. Pointsman, by contrast, with his
eagerness to experiment on a human subject, his immoral treatment of Slothrop and his ultimate disastrous failure (exasperated
with the riddle of Slothrop's sexuality, he sends out a team to
have him castrated, but the two end up emasculating another
American instead) is the very essence of reductive science that
destroys what it sets out to analyze.[10] This reading seems to be
supported by the fact that Mexico, in his relation with Jessica
Swanlake, emerges as one of the very few characters in the novel
who are capable of genuine emotional engagement.[11] But one
must be cautious of identifying Pynchon's or the narrator's view
too hastily with either one of the two philosophies.[12] First of all, it
is noteworthy that the confrontation between Pointsman and
Mexico is itself presented in starkly binary terms: Mexico is the
"Antipointsman" (55) whereas Pointsman functions as "Anti-
mexico" (89), an opposition that leaves no room between the two
poles. Secondly, although Mexico's statistical approach may yield
interesting results for large-scale phenomena, it does not offer
any solution for the riddle of Slothrop's sexuality: Slothrop is a
"statistical oddity" to him that he has no explanation for, to the
point where "he feels the foundations of that discipline [statistics]
trembling a bit now, deeper than oddity ought to drive" (85).
When he finds out toward the end that Slothrop was under the
surveillance of the chemical industry complex IG Farben for
many years before the War, and begins to suspect the intricacy of
the conspiracy against Slothrop, his violent but pointless reaction
is to storm the headquarters of IG-affiliate ICI and urinate all

[10] Cooper, *Signs and Symptoms*, 120–22; Mark Richard Siegel, *Pynchon: Creative Paranoia in* Gravity's Rainbow (Port Washington: Kennikat, 1978), 76–78 and 105; John O. Stark, *Pynchon's Fictions: Thomas Pynchon and the Literature of Information* (Athens: Ohio University Press, 1980), 55–56; David Seed, *The Fictional Labyrinths of Thomas Pynchon* (Houndmills: Macmillan, 1988), 177. In his essay "Antipointsman/Antimexico: Some Mathematical Imagery in *Gravity's Rainbow*," *Critique* 16.2 (1974): 73–90, Lance Ozier provides a detailed comparison of the two characters and their philosophies.

[11] Ozier, "Antipointsman/Antimexico," 80; Seed, *Fictional Labyrinths*, 177; Michael Seidel, "The Satiric Plots of *Gravity's Rainbow*," *Pynchon: A Collection of Critical Essays*, ed. Edward Mendelson (Englewood Cliffs: Prentice-Hall, 1978), 210–11.

[12] Kathryn Hume, in *Pynchon's Mythography: An Approach to* Gravity's Rainbow (Carbondale: Southern Illinois University Press, 1987), recognizes that to side with Mexico against Pointsman is to accept just the kind of binarism that Mexico's philosophy discourages (119–21).

over the assembled members of the managing board. Soon afterwards, he breaks up an industry magnate's formal dinner party by initiating a verbal orgy of nauseating food descriptions, in another act of sincere but impotent rebellion. As sympathetic a figure as Mexico may be, then, his methods do not offer any solution to the problems raised by the narrative.[13]

Thirdly, although Pointsman fails miserably in the end, his theory concerning Slothrop turns out to be much closer to the truth than anyone else's. He surmises that the regularity of correspondence between Slothrop's sex acts and the dropping of the V-2 is in fact due to an enchainment of stimulus and response. The problem he runs into, obviously, is that the response seems to precede the stimulus, which leads him to postulate that Slothrop's response is not actually to the rocket itself, but to something that precedes its arrival. He and other specialists in the field know that as a young child, Tyrone Slothrop was the subject of Pavlovian conditioning experiments at the hands of German chemist Laszlo Jamf. But the "mystery stimulus" Slothrop was conditioned with is unknown, and Pointsman suspects that it might be the key to the riddle of his connection with the V-2.

These peculiar circumstances point toward a familiar temporal scenario. The fact that the inexplicable event which occurs in the present is Slothrop's apparently abnormal sexual behavior, and that the explanation for this behavior may lie in his early childhood, in events that have long disappeared from his conscious memory, give the Pavlovian configuration of the narrative problem a distinctly Freudian twist. Critics of the novel who have simply discarded Pointsman's approach as a simplistic enchainment of cause and effect, obsolete in the eyes of the more advanced scientists in the novel, have generally overlooked how complex Pavlovian theory becomes in Pointsman's hands.[14] Once the original stimulus-response sequence is considered over longer periods of time, Pointsman believes, certain intricate inversions and reversions occur that preclude any simple linear

[13] Michael Bérubé points out in addition that although Pointsman's scientific approach may be outdated, it succeeds as a tool for manipulating a whole set of characters (*Marginal Forces/Cultural Centers: Tolson, Pynchon, and the Politics of the Canon* [Ithaca: Cornell University Press, 1992], 234).

[14] An exception is Thomas H. Schaub in *Pynchon: The Voice of Ambiguity* (Urbana: University of Illinois Press, 1981), who gives a very detailed account of Pavlovianism in the novel (88–94).

progression from cause to effect. The conditioned subject continues to evolve after the original period of conditioning: in the "equivalent" phase, stronger stimuli no longer evoke a stronger response, but exactly the same as weak stimuli; at the "paradoxical" stage, strong stimuli are followed by weak responses, and vice versa; and in the "ultraparadoxical" phase, the subject shows no reaction to the stimulus anymore at all, but will search for it when it is absent (90). At this stage, of course, the idea of simple binary oppositions is seriously in jeopardy (49). The process of deconditioning offers further temporal complications. As Pointsman and his colleagues point out, the end of the deconditioning process is not signalled simply by the absence of response in the presence of the stimulus; rather, this moment needs to be followed by a " '*silent extinction beyond the zero'* " (85; original emphasis). Hence, if Jamf deliberately deconditioned the child Tyrone to the point of zero response only, the question arises whether "a conditioned reflex [can] survive in a man, dormant, over 20 or 30 years?" (85). If so, the Pavlovians argue, it might provide an explanation for Slothrop's present behavior patterns.

If an incomplete deconditioning process in early childhood leads to a resurfacing of the conditioned response later in life and thereby to deviant behavior, Slothrop's development begins to resemble a psychoanalytic case history in its temporal structure. Pointsman and his Pavlovians gradually turn into Freudians who search in the past for a repressed trauma that they assume manifests itself through a delayed reaction in present pathological symptoms. This psychoanalytical principle of "Nachträglichkeit" offers itself as a promise of solution to the riddles posed by the beginning of *Gravity's Rainbow*.[15] The text insinuates that if the reasons and nature of Slothrop's conditioning process were known, the puzzle of his connection to the V-2s might turn out to be solvable. This expectation is reinforced by ever more explicitly Freudian allusions. Slothrop, on his way to the Zone, discovers documents showing that Dr. Jamf had entered into business relations with Slothrop's father. As he reads these papers relating to his past,

---

[15] Hanjo Berressem briefly alludes to the concept of "belatedness" in *Pynchon's Poetics: Interfacing Theory and Text* (Urbana: University of Illinois Press, 1993), 125, but does not develop its implications.

[h]e is also getting a hardon, for no immediate reason. And there's that *smell* again, a smell from before his conscious memory begins, a soft and chemical smell, threatening, haunting, not a smell to be found out in the world – *it is the breath of the Forbidden Wing* . . . essence of all the still figures waiting for him inside, daring him to enter and find a secret he cannot survive.
Once something was done to him, in a room, while he lay helpless.
. . .   (285; original emphasis)

The resurgence of memories, the encounter of secrets and forbidden zones, and the sexual reaction all suggest, if rather imprecisely, some Freudian scenario and the sexual trauma of a "primal scene." But the partial revelation of this scene inverts psychoanalytical causality:

A smell, a forbidden room, at the bottom edge of his memory. He can't see it, can't make it out. Doesn't want to. It is allied with the Worst Thing.
He knows what the smell has to be: though according to these papers it would have been too early for it, though he has never come across any of the stuff among the daytime coordinates of his life, still, down here, back here in the warm dark, among early shapes where the clocks and calendars don't mean too much, he knows that what's haunting him now will prove to be the smell of Imipolex G.   (286)

The traumatic "Worst Thing," hard to reconcile with a simple conditioning process, still points to a psychoanalytic scenario. But if this trauma and Slothrop's adult sexuality are associated with Imipolex G, a causal paradox arises: according to *Gravity's Rainbow*, Imipolex was invented in 1939 (249) – at least fifteen years *after* Slothrop's early childhood.[16] Instead of uncovering a childhood scene as the prime cause of Slothrop's unusual sexuality, therefore, the Freudian plot leads back to another causal loop. If the "symptom" in this case history is the inversion of stimulus and response in Slothrop's reaction to the rockets, the childhood scenario, instead of providing an aetiology of the symptom, simply repeats the same inversion. The past in the world of *Gravity's Rainbow*, therefore, turns out to hold no hidden reasons or prime causes, but only repetitions of the present.[17]

[16] Hume, *Pynchon's Mythography*, 7.
[17] One function of this and other causal inversions in the novel is satire: both the psychoanalytical thriller and the spy novel are satirically subverted through the

But even if Imipolex *were* the substance Slothrop was conditioned with, this association would raise more questions about the correspondence of his sexual map and the V-2 strikes than it could answer. According to the information the novel provides, Imipolex was not a substance routinely used in the V-2s, but only in the rocket that carries Blicero's lover Gottfried to his death.[18] Even if it had been, however, how could Slothrop have responded to it days *before* these rockets arrived in London? In an alternative hypothesis, one might assume that Imipolex was implanted in Slothrop's genitals: the text stresses that Imipolex is "the first plastic that is actually *erectile*" and can be made to stiffen under an electronic impulse (699; original emphasis); therefore, it might react to the electronic impulses that accompany the launching of a rocket. Such a theory would be no more esoteric than many others the novel invites its readers to accept, but it still does not explain why the two maps correspond point for point, since the electronic signal would presumably have reached Slothrop wherever he happened to be at the moment of the launch, not at the site where the rocket ultimately landed.[19] Also, this theory does not allow for time spans up to ten days between one of Slothrop's adventures and the explosion of a rocket. Neither is the problem eliminated by those critics who have pointed out that the novel raises some doubt as to how real Slothrop's love affairs are by suggesting that at least some might have been mere fantasies.[20] Even if *all* of them were, the temporal and causal problem is left intact: how can Slothrop's dated map of fantasized sex scenes "re-create" the map of the V-2 strikes before the fact?[21] The mystery substance Imipolex, while it

unsolvable logical loops; on satire in *Gravity's Rainbow*, see Seidel, "Satiric Plots," esp. 193–203.

[18] Molly Hite, *Ideas of Order in the Novels of Thomas Pynchon* (Columbus: Ohio State University Press, 1983), 116. Interestingly, Gottfried himself also seems to have been conditioned with the substance in early childhood; just before his death, the text suggests that his experience is a mirror inversion of Slothrop's traumatic scenario: "The soft smell of Imipolex, wrapping him absolutely, is a smell he knows. It doesn't frighten him. It was in the room when he fell asleep so long ago, so deep in sweet paralyzed childhood . . . it was there as he began to dream. Now it is time to wake, into the breath of what was always real. Come, wake. All is well" (754).

[19] Hite, *Ideas of Order*, 116.

[20] Brian McHale, "Modernist Reading, Postmodern Text: The Case of 'Gravity's Rainbow'," *Constructing Postmodernism* (London: Routledge, 1992), 71–73.

[21] See Hite, *Ideas of Order*, 116–17.

creates an indirect link between Slothrop and the rocket, falls far short of providing any coherent explanation of this phenomenon, and instead produces yet another, similarly structured causal paradox.

Therefore, if Pointsman's insistence on mechanic connections of cause and effect remains unsatisfactory, it is not because the narrated events are better accounted for by other theories. On the contrary, everything the novel offers in the way of "reliable fact" – the Pavlovians' knowledge of the "infant Tyrone" case, the documents Slothrop discovers, and his own half-memories – confirm that Pointsman is probably not far from the truth when he suspects a connection between Slothrop's sexual reaction to the rocket and his conditioning at the hands of Jamf. In fact his hypothesis concerning Slothrop works remarkably well – except for the problem of time, which Pointsman is unable to solve.[22] The Pavlovian paradigm of cause and effect seems to allow the reader to untie at least some of the narrative knots rather smoothly, but time is the one factor that resists this strategy of naturalization, since there is no way of aligning the temporality of *Gravity's Rainbow* with Pointsman's model of causality.

2. Between molecule and management

The reason for this impasse is articulated by one of the other voices in the novel that opposes mechanistic causality: that of the dead Walther Rathenau. The dead, through spiritist seances and occasional supernatural occurrences, make their presence felt throughout *Gravity's Rainbow*. Their presence points to a compression of time through which past and present come to co-exist simultaneously as consciousnesses inside and outside of linear time appear side by side.[23] Conjured up before an assembly of Nazi business managers through medium Peter Sachsa, Rathenau quite explicitly rejects causal modes of reasoning:

"All talk of cause and effect is secular history, and secular history is a diversionary tactic. Useful to you, gentlemen, but no longer so to us here. If you want the truth – I know I presume – you must look into the technology of these matters. Even into the hearts of certain molecules – it

---

[22] See Schaub, *Pynchon*, 93.
[23] *Ibid.*, 50; Hite, *Ideas of Order*, 122.

is they after all which dictate temperatures, pressures, rates of flow, costs, profits, the shapes of towers. . . .

"You must ask two questions. First, what is the real nature of synthesis? And then: what is the real nature of control?"   (167)

This denunciation of causality as a mere diversion comes at the end of a long speech on the history and development of the synthetic dye industry in general, and that of the international conglomerate IG Farben in particular. The crucial causative forces in the new age of chemical synthesis, Rathenau argues, can no longer be found at the human scale, but in the microscopic universe of atoms and molecules. As elementary building blocks of nature, they determine the structure and properties of all known substances, and their manipulation and alteration makes possible the creation of entirely new ones, whether these be drugs, plastics, nylon or nerve gases. John Barth's question, "What snowflake triggers the avalanche?" in his short story "Two Meditations," which I discussed in Chapter 1, raises the same question Rathenau is concerned with here.[24] In an age which has discovered the enormous difference that the presence or absence of an electron can make, questions of causality can no longer be answered in terms of human agency. "Causality is linked to a conventional scale of reality," Claude Richard argues.[25] "If microscopic causes can be known only by their macroscopic effects, if causes escape the possibility of representation, what remains is only awareness and representation of, at best, betweenness."[26]

But Rathenau alludes to even more crucial problems. Once chemical – and presumably other kinds of – technology have come into being, he suggests, they develop a temporal dynamic of their own that is no longer subject to the control of human intention. Historically, World War I triggered a technological explosion in the development of the German and later the international synthetic-dye industry, a fact Pynchon does not fail to emphasize in his fictionalization of the IG Farben.[27] But according to

---

[24] See Claude Richard, "Causality and Mimesis in Contemporary Fiction," *SubStance* 40 (1983): 89–90.

[25] *Ibid.*, 90.

[26] *Ibid.*, 87.

[27] Joseph Borkin, *The Crime and Punishment of I.G. Farben* (New York: Free Press, 1978), 4–37; Gottfried Plumpe, *Die I.G. Farbenindustrie AG: Wirtschaft, Technik*

Gravity's Rainbow, the force of the new technologies might have become such by the 1930s that World War II is not ultimately a political venture, but an event triggered with the deliberate intent of accelerating certain technological developments. Enzian, for example, the leader of the German-Herero "Schwarzkommando" ("Black Commando"), gradually begins to suspect that

this War was never political at all, the politics was all theatre, all just to keep the people distracted . . . secretly, it was being dictated instead by the needs of technology . . . by a conspiracy between human beings and techniques, by something that needed the energy-burst of war, crying, "Money be damned, the very life of [insert name of Nation][28] is at stake" [. . .] The real crises were crises of allocation and priority, not among firms – it was only staged to look that way – but among the different Technologies, Plastics, Electronics, Aircraft, and their needs which are understood only by the ruling elite . . .   (521)

This suspicion leads Enzian to envision "distribution networks we were never taught, routes of power our teachers never imagined, or were encouraged to avoid" (521). Once science has discovered the possibility of changing the face of the globe as well as the metabolism of individual organisms through molecular manipulations that are able to create entirely new materials and substances, no nation or individual will remain unaffected. But the nature of these effects cannot be controlled by single agents.[29] Neither Rathenau nor Enzian are referring to possible unwanted side-effects of new technologies; rather, they maintain that even the desired effects are already beyond human control. Once crucial historical events take place at the scale of atoms, man and molecule enter into a complex dynamic that cannot be defined in terms of conventional causality.

Rathenau mentions yet another dimension of the new technological age he helped to bring about, that of "control." This term, which recurs frequently in *Gravity's Rainbow*, describes the other face of chemical synthesis: the power of the business corporation.

und Politik 1904–1945 (Berlin: Duncker, 1990), 63–106; Khachig Tölölyan, "War as Background in *Gravity's Rainbow*," *Approaches to Gravity's Rainbow*, ed. Charles Clerc (Columbus: Ohio State University Press, 1983), 54–58; Robert McLaughlin, "IG Farben and the War against Nature in *Gravity's Rainbow*," *Germany and German Thought in American Literature and Cultural Criticism*, ed. Peter Freese (Essen: Blaue Eule, 1990), 320–21.

[28] These brackets are Pynchon's.
[29] Hite, *Ideas of Order*, 104; Hume, *Pynchon's Mythography*, 104–07.

At least three of the novel's central figures – Slothrop, Enzian and Tchitcherine – have intermittent or permanent visions of an all-encompassing network of corporate power that regulates not only global political developments but also the most minute details of their own lives. Such visions may be partly due to their drug-induced paranoias; but obviously, their drug-dependence is itself ironic testimony to the power of the chemical industry over their private mental processes. Even apart from their personal conjectures, however, the novel gives the reader ample evidence to confirm some of their worst suspicions. Rather than to the power of the atom, "control" refers to a kind of causality that has shifted beyond the agency of the individual to the complex needs and goals of "The Firm," the international business cartel with its innumerable branches and departments. This corporate octopus, the novel indicates, masters Pavlovian conditioning just as well as the frequencies and probabilities of advanced statistics, and hence leaves individuals like Tyrone Slothrop, caught between molecule and management, with little space or time for the exercise of independent reasoning or free will. In the age of atomic forces and corporate power, cause and effect belong to an obsolete, anthropocentric notion of the universe, good only for "diversionary tactics."

This shift of causality outside of the sphere of human agency is crucial for the narrative structure of *Gravity's Rainbow*, but nevertheless leaves some important questions open. Obviously, it provides a striking explanation for Slothrop's predicament: on one hand, the chemical reactions of his own body obey to impulses that are controlled by outside forces, to the point where even the most intimate and personal area of his life, his sexuality, lies beyond his own reach; on the other hand, his work in London, his stay on the Côte d'Azur, and even his escape to Germany are clearly engineered and supervised by institutions which range from the British Secret Service to the corporate world of ICI Chemicals and its partner IG Farben. His encounter with Katje Borgesius, the theft of his papers and personal possessions, and his training in rocket technology are all planned, and Slothrop surmises as much. But it turns out that the clues about the mysterious "S-Gerät" and Imipolex G were also planted so as to make him go off to the Zone: when Slothrop believes he is escaping the powers that play with him, the reader knows it is not so. Pointsman's surveillance team only loses his track when he is already in Switzerland, and as a conversation between ICI manager Clive Mossmoon and British politician Sir Marcus later in the text reveals, control did not even end there: Slothrop was quite deliberately sent into the Zone to ferret out and destroy the Herero *Schwarzkommando* ("We sent him out to destroy the blacks, and it's obvious now he won't do the job," Sir Marcus comments [615]).

But while such tight control looks at first sight like a confirmation of Slothrop's paranoias as well as of the Firm's absolute power, this "logical" explanation of the novel's events turns out to be quite enigmatic upon closer analysis. Why would the British need Slothrop to find the *Schwarzkommando*? When he first runs into Enzian and his troops on the train to Nordhausen, they are already being followed and closely monitored by the American major Duane Marvy and his Technical Intelligence unit. Why would the Americans not deal with the Hereros, or at least communicate their whereabouts to their British allies? It may be clear why Slothrop would necessarily encounter the *Schwarzkommando* sooner or later, since both he and they look for witnesses and clues concerning the 00000; but how and for what reason would Slothrop have destroyed them? His general racial prejudice against Blacks seems hardly enough to accomplish this.[30] If, as the novel has us believe, an Allied conspiracy exists to use Slothrop for such purposes, this plot is an extraordinarily inept and complicated means of achieving goals that the Allied forces could accomplish in any number of much more straightforward ways.

The same irrationality attaches to the construction of the mystery weapon, the 00000 rocket. Although Slothrop never discovers what the *S-Gerät* and Imipolex G were ultimately used for, the *Schwarzkommando* does find out, and through it so does the reader. As it turns out, the 00000 was a rocket specially designed with the help of a whole army of technicians to carry a human, SS officer Blicero's adolescent lover Gottfried, in its trajectory. In the last days of the War, Gottfried, cloaked in a sensually exciting Imipolex shroud and attached to the rocket by

[30] See Lawrence Wolfley, "Repression's Rainbow: The Presence of Norman O. Brown in Pynchon's Big Novel," *Critical Essays on Thomas Pynchon*, ed. Richard Pearce (Boston: Hall, 1981), 110–11.

means of the *S-Gerät*, was launched from the Lüneburg Heath –
not in the direction of any conceivable enemy target, however,
but due North, to the symbolic region of death. In other words,
the secret Nazi super-weapon, the revelation of whose purpose is
delayed until the very end of the novel, turns out to serve no
strategic purpose either in terms of Nazi Germany's goals or,
more importantly, in terms of what the international business
cartel might intend. What makes this climax of the novel so
strange is not that the 00000 turns out to be a symbol of the
reckless sacrifice of human life – given the Firm's systematic
exploitation of human beings, this comes as no surprise – but that
it is difficult to construe any practical purpose for this sacrifice.
According to the information the novel provides, Blicero is one of
the prime representatives of the Firm: he has no trouble commanding the very elite of German rocket technicians to work on
the project and to impose the utmost secrecy on them. And yet
the project he invests all these resources, manpower and creative
design into is one that satisfies nothing but his personal fantasies.

A strange discrepancy here emerges between the idea that
science, politics, business and individuals are all controlled by
the designs of an institutional network, and the impression that
the Firm's resources can at random be turned over to the
arbitrary use of compulsive individuals like Blicero. There are, I
would argue, two ways of resolving this tension. The first one
would be to assume, as Yves Petillon does, that the launch of the
00000 prefigures the manned space travel of the 1960s, which
might have been much on Pynchon's mind in the early 1970s.
The novel indeed refers to space travel repeatedly, and the
historical connection between German military technology and
American space exploration through figures such as Wernher
von Braun (who is quoted in one of the novel's epigraphs) is
notorious.[31] Blicero's project, then, erratic as it might have
seemed at the end of World War II, could be construed as just
another step in the Firm's long-term development of key technologies. As the reader knows by historical hindsight, this development was later no longer fueled by actual war but by the Cold
War, which would explain the abrupt transition, on the novel's

[31] Pierre-Yves Petillon, "Thomas Pynchon and Aleatory Space," trans. Margaret S. Langford, *Pynchon Notes* 15 (1984): 31, 38–41.

last page, from the 00000 launch to the rocket about to hit a Los Angeles movie theater. In this reading, the Firm emerges from the novel as the undisputed master of long-term temporal perspectives, which all the individuals involved with it have long lost, restricted as they are to an ever more time-compressed idea of the "present."

What may seem erratic and contingent in the individual's perspective, according to this interpretation, would be quite planned and systematic from the Firm's viewpoint. But another reading of the 00000 would suggest that They are in fact not in complete control, and that Their large-scale designs do leave room for contingency and free will. The conversation between Mossmoon and Sir Marcus seems to imply something like this, since obviously the Firm's handling of Slothrop has in some way been unsuccessful. When Mossmoon anxiously asks, " 'Are we going to fail?,' " Sir Marcus serenely responds, " 'We're all going to fail [. . .] but the Operation won't' " (616). Although Sir Marcus seems to confirm the ultimate power of the Firm, his remark also opens up the possibility that Blicero might have been another failure. If so, the Firm contains elements that become subversive with no deliberate intention of being so – a Counterforce from within.

3. Parallel and series

So far, two objections to the idea of causality have emerged from the novel: first, the inclusion of certain forms of contingency into twentieth-century science, which leads to the formulation of scientific laws and observations in terms of probability rather than causal determinacy; and second, the shift of causal forces from the scale of individual volition and agency to the realm of the atom on one hand, and to the realm of supranational forms of organization on the other. But *Gravity's Rainbow* proposes yet another critique of causality, formulated by Leni Pökler, wife of one of the rocket technicians. Although she uses much the same vocabulary as Walther Rathenau, her critique addresses neither scientific nor socio-political changes so much as the problem of representation. Her viewpoint emerges in the course of a confrontation which, just as the one between Pointsman and Mexico, pits an advocate of conventionally understood causality against an alternative approach.[32] Leni calls her husband Franz a "cause-and-effect" man who rejects astrology because he cannot conceive of any causal relationship between stars and human lives: "'There is no way for changes out there to produce changes here,'" he argues (159). Leni resists this argument: "'Not produce [. . .] not cause. It all goes along together. Parallel, not series. Metaphor. Signs and symptoms. Mapping on to different coordinate systems, I don't know . . .'" (159). And when they both watch Fritz Lang's film *Die Frau im Mond*, Leni reflects, "Real flight and dreams of flight go together. Both are part of the same movement. Not A before B, but all together . . ." (159). This, to her, is "the moment, and its possibilities." Pökler the technician comments, somewhat disdainfully, "'Try to design anything that way and have it work'" (159).[33]

Pökler may be right as far as technology is concerned, but Leni's critique addresses the relationship between representation, imagination and reality, which is important not only for the understanding of messages, dreams and hallucinations experienced by the characters in the novel, but also for narrative as such as a particular mode of representation. By substituting representation for temporality, Leni's theory of causality denies the relevance of succession and sequence for sense-making. In her theory, events can come to refer to each other regardless of their temporal relation or the contingencies that separate them. This view captures a crucial dimension of the narrative configuration

[32] Stark, *Pynchon's Fictions*, 58–59. Susan Strehle, in her reading of *Gravity's Rainbow*, opposes the "realists" to the "actualists" among its characters, after Heisenberg's distinction of the actual as the kind of reality that pertains at the subatomic level (*Fiction in the Quantum Universe* [Chapel Hill: University of North Carolina Press, 1992], 6–7). Realist characters, Slothrop foremost among them, believe in linear temporality and causal coherence, whereas for the actualists, "time is not a causal chain directed at death, transcendence, or salvation but a succession of coincidental moments to be celebrated for their own sake," a "game of chance" (54). Her discussion of this opposition in Pynchon's novel (52–57) makes it clear that she believes in actualism as the adequate response to twentieth-century realities; such an endorsement, in my view, oversimplifies Pynchon's conceptualization of the relationship between causality and contingency.

[33] A perspective similar to Leni's is articulated earlier in the novel by one of the spirits who communicates with medium Carroll Eventyr: "'[. . .] you had taken on a greater, and more harmful, illusion. The illusion of control. That A could do B. But that was false. Completely. No one can *do*. Things only happen, A and B are unreal, are names for parts that ought to be inseparable. . . .'" (30; original emphasis).

of *Gravity's Rainbow*, namely, its endless chain of analogies, substitutions and mirrorings of characters and events. Several critics have pointed out that the Pöklers' own child, Ilse, is the product of such a metaphorical substitution, since she is conceived after Pökler watched a rape in a film starring the actress Greta Erdmann. Just as Erdmann becomes pregnant with her daughter Bianca as a consequence of this rape, Leni conceives Ilse in Pökler's re-enactment of the scene.[34] Similarly, during some of the spiritist seances, medium Carroll Eventyr begins to perceive himself as an analogue of his "control" Peter Sachsa, and starts to wonder whether the analogy also extends to Sachsa's lover, Leni Pökler, and his own mistress, Nora Dodson-Truck. SS officer Blicero explicitly establishes mirror analogies between his blond lover Gottfried in Holland, and his black catamite Enzian in Southwest Africa; the simultaneous presence of his Dutch mistress Katje Borgesius even leads him to surmise that he must have overlooked her black female analogue in Africa. But Gottfried, the boy for whom the "Schwarzgerät" (Black Device) is invented, is also a metaphorical double of Slothrop, who is referred to in Jamf's documents as "Schwarzknabe" (Black Boy), a doubling reinforced by the connection of both figures with the polymer Imipolex. "Schwarzknabe" and "Schwarzvater" (Black Father), Slothrop's father, are also inversions of "Blicero" Weissmann himself. On the other hand, "Schwarzknabe" Slothrop and Gottfried at the same time invert and duplicate Greta Erdmann's daughter Bianca, the "White One," whose lover Slothrop briefly becomes. A similar black and white doubling links Enzian and his Russian half-brother, Tchitcherine. And indeed, it is, as various critics have pointed out, very easy to extend the list of analogies and link practically every character in the novel with at least a few of the others.[35]

And not only characters metaphorically stand in for each other.

---

[34] Joseph W. Slade, *Thomas Pynchon* (New York: Lang, 1990), 204–05; Schaub, *Pynchon*, 44; Hayles, "Caught in the Web," 181; Bérubé, *Marginal Forces/Cultural Centers*, 240–41.

[35] Hume, *Pynchon's Mythography*, 108–18. Commenting on the possibility of these virtually unlimited pairings, McHoul and Wills observe that in *Gravity's Rainbow*, "characters cannot be kept separate as persons in any obvious way . . . . characters are not based on the idea of separate and unique biological, psychological, or social personages" (*Writing Pynchon*, 33). See also Kathryn Hume's "Repetition and the Construction of Character in *Gravity's Rainbow*," *Critique: Studies in Contemporary Fiction* 33 (1992): 243–54, and, for a more

Pointsman, for example, meditates on the mirror inversion of sound and detonation that occurs with the movement from V-1s to V-2s. The extermination of the Dodoes on the Isle of Mauritius, in which Katje Borgesius' ancestor, Frans van der Groov, was centrally involved, is metaphorically replicated by the genocide of the Hereros in Südwest at the hands of the Germans, and the "final solution" for Jews and homosexuals in the concentration camps of the Third Reich.[36] Enzian, at the end of the novel, will probably replicate Gottfried's death by launching himself in the 00001. In a more humorous mode, Slothrop's dive after his mouth harp into the toilet bowl of the Roseland Ballroom in 1939 is echoed by his trip into the shadowy territory of the Zone where six years, one transatlantic move and 600 pages later, the very same mouth harp turns up again, apparently by sheer coincidence.[37] The attempt of some Black Americans to rape him at the beginning of this 1939 dive ironically inverts Weissmann's sodomization of Enzian. And so on, and so forth: there is literally no end to the "Kute Korrespondences" one can establish in the text (590).

But this abundance of metaphors and correspondences is precisely what makes Leni Pökler's approach to causality unhelpful. In contrast to Roger Mexico's probability theory, which explains too little, her metaphorical understanding accounts for too much. While it allows the reader to establish infinite series of substitutions between persons and events, it precludes any genuine historical or narrative interpretation. In a sense, her approach has the same effect as Slothrop's paranoia, since it is able to connect anything with everything. Nevertheless, this understanding in some cases allows one to give more specific answers to the narrative questions the novel raises. Particularly with regard to Slothrop's relation to the rocket, a metaphorical reading practically imposes itself: his map of London, covered with colored paper stars, and Mexico's map of rocket landing sites attract the attention of various Secret Services precisely *because* they appear to be substitutable for each other. Not only do these two maps metaphorically superimpose love and death,

conventional analysis of character in the novel, Siegel, *Pynchon: Creative Paranoia*, 44–72.
[36] Petillon, "Thomas Pynchon and Aleatory Space," 5–6.
[37] See Schaub, *Pynchon*, 124.

they also suggest the hidden identity of Slothrop and the V-2. The starred map is the first image of Slothrop the reader sees, and it shows him as quite literally "scattered all over the map," a figure of spatial dispersal rather than a coherent human identity. His assigned task in London is to visit the sites where a V-2 has struck and to gather what technical intelligence he can from the left-over fragments, a mission that might be understood as another metaphor of his own dispersal. This construction out of fragments is repeated later in the novel when "Blicero" Weissmann designs and builds the 00000 by assigning partial tasks to each of his engineers, keeping the complete design secret from all of them. And, of course, all the seekers and hunters of the rocket in the Zone (diverse Intelligence Services, the *Schwarzkommando*, and Slothrop himself) are forced to piece together the fragmentary hints and clues they are able to glean from rocket launch sites or the technicians and eyewitnesses they apprehend. According to the metaphor, this would indicate that at least part of what is at stake in these reiterated efforts to put together the parts of the rocket is the definition of Slothrop's identity. But whereas the reader of *Gravity's Rainbow* finds out the secret of the 00000, and the *Schwarzkommando* presumably even succeeds in constructing another one, Slothrop's own quest never attains its goal. He never does find out the meaning of the *S-Gerät*,[38] and his abortive quest ends up dissolving rather than establishing his identity. Toward the end of the novel, Slothrop simply turns into space, a site of crossings: "At last, lying one afternoon spread-eagled at his ease in the sun, at the edge of one of the ancient Plague towns he becomes a cross himself, a crossroads, a living intersection where the judges have come to set up a gibbet for a common criminal who is to be hanged at noon" (625). In confirmation of Leni's views, this metamorphosis into a spatial intersection implies access to a different, ahistorical temporality, which is typical of certain

crossroads, where you can sit and listen in to traffic from the Other Side, hearing about the future (no serial time over there: events are all there in the same eternal moment and so certain messages don't always "make sense" back here: they lack historical structure, they sound fanciful, or insane). (624)

---

[38] See Wolfley, "Repression's Rainbow," 100.

Slothrop's metamorphosis into an ahistorical site of spatial crossings harkens back to his initial representation as a constellation of
paper stars on a map, since he has now turned from the map into
the space it represents. This concretization of the initial metaphor
becomes even clearer in his final dissolution of identity, which
scatters and disperses Slothrop throughout the Zone:

> There is also the story about Tyrone Slothrop, who was sent into the
> Zone to be present at his own assembly – perhaps, heavily paranoid
> voices have whispered, *his time's assembly* – and there ought to be a
> punch line to it, but there isn't. The plan went wrong. He is being broken
> down instead, and scattered.   (738; original emphasis)

At the end of this process, Slothrop is "[s]cattered all over the
Zone. It's doubtful if he can ever be 'found' again, in the
conventional sense of 'positively identified and detained'" (712).
Only his friend, the sailor Pig Bodine, can still approach him as a
whole human being, and finally he becomes impossible to
perceive or conceive of for anyone.

This scattering of the novel's central character has sometimes
been read as a narrative translation of the thermodynamic
concept of entropy, an interpretation which I will discuss in more
detail later on. But if we stick for now to Leni Pökler's philosophy
of "metaphors" and "signs and symptoms," which understands
events not serially but in parallel, we must hold against the
notion of Slothrop's gradual dispersal the observation that the
text presents him as a disseminated distribution in space to begin
with. If Slothrop is scattered throughout the Zone at the end, he
was scattered all over London at the start. In this perspective,
narrative progression through time in *Gravity's Rainbow* functions
not so much as entropic disintegration than as the gradual
literalization of a metaphor that informs the text from its beginning.

Slothrop's identity, therefore, has no firm ground anywhere in
the novel. It defines itself through the shift from a represented,
metaphorical dispersal to an "actual" fragmentation which nevertheless obeys the same metaphor and retrospectively confirms its
validity. Neither the end nor the beginning of the text offers us a
more literal definition of the protagonist, who in between
assumes a whole series of disguises and fake identities that do
nothing to stabilize his flickering individuality: British journalist

Ian Scuffling, "Rocketman," German actor Max Schlepzig, Russian secret agent, mythological German pig hero Plechazunga. In a way, the protagonist of *Gravity's Rainbow* consists of a series of representational mirages, none of which emerges in the end as more basic than the others. Leni's philosophy of "signs and symptoms" is extremely well suited to describe this process. And if Roger Mexico's as well as Walther Rathenau's views rely on twentieth-century innovations of thought that complicate or block the notion of causality, so does Leni Pökler's. Her resistance to cause and effect is based on the blurring of the distinction between the sign and what it designates, the postmodernist conviction that there is no reality more "real" than the sign system it is represented by. Hence representations can "cause" real events just as real events give rise to representations: the malicious song about Rathenau Leni and her friends sang as schoolchildren was followed by his assassination (163), for example, and film director Gerhard von Göll is convinced that his film about black German rocket troops brought the *Schwarzkommando* into being (388). Moreover, if both Mexico's and Slothrop's maps refer to no reality beyond themselves, or if they create the realities they designate, the question of whether any cause-and-effect relationship exists between them loses its urgency. Representation then exists in a temporality of its own which is not dependent on the time laws of the "real" world.

4. Δt

Through the philosophies some of its characters articulate, *Gravity's Rainbow* shows the concept of causality to be beleaguered from various sides. Three main complexes of ideas, as we have seen, stand against linear causality understood as a progression from cause to effect or stimulus to response: first, the idea that the natural sciences themselves no longer adhere to a mechanistic view of causality; secondly, the observation that, in at least one reading of contemporary history, the causal forces that affect the life of the human individual are no longer individual agents, but have shifted to the microscopic scale of molecules, atomic and subatomic particles on one hand, and to the macroscopic scale of global networks of commerce, communication and transportation, on the other; thirdly, the notion that in an age of "hyper-real" forms of representation, and an intense awareness of the role symbolic systems play in our under-standing of the world, causality is undermined through the blurring of borders between the real and the represented.[39] Confronted with these fundamental shifts in the configuration of what was once the "common-sense" world, the protagonists of *Gravity's Rainbow* tend to react paranoiacally, countering the impossibility of understanding the causal connections that struc-ture their world with (perhaps) exaggerated visions of total coherence.[40] Several critics have pointed out the clearly pseudo-religious nature of this paranoia, which, just as if the universe were ruled by God, allows for no accident or coincidence but leads to "the discovery that *everything is connected*" (703; original emphasis).[41] The conviction not only that the world is carefully plotted even in its most minute details, but that this plot is specifically directed against the paranoiac himself, alternates with phases in which the conspiracy falls apart and leaves nothing but randomness in its wake:

> If there is something comforting – religious, if you want – about paranoia, there is still also anti-paranoia, where nothing is connected to anything, a condition not many of us can bear for long. Well right now Slothrop feels himself sliding onto the anti-paranoid part of his cycle, feels the whole city [of Berlin] around him going back roofless, vulner-able, uncentered as he is, and only pasteboard images now of the Listening Enemy left between him and the wet sky.
>
> Either They have put him here for a reason, or he's just here. He isn't sure that he wouldn't, actually, rather have that *reason*. . . .
>
> (434; original emphasis)

Finding themselves in a universe in which common-sense causality has been replaced by regularities and forces beyond the perception and control of the individual, the characters of *Gravity's Rainbow* vacillate between visions of complete coherence

---

[39] See, for example, Jean Baudrillard, *Simulations*, trans. Paul Foss, Paul Patton and Philip Beitchman (New York: Semiotext(e), 1983), 2–4.

[40] Schaub, *Pynchon*, 88.

[41] Mackey, "Paranoia," 53–57; Petillon, "Thomas Pynchon and Aleatory Space," 7–29; Scott Sanders, "Pynchon's Paranoid History," *Mindful Pleasures: Essays on Thomas Pynchon*, ed. George Levine and David Leverenz (Boston: Little, 1976), 139–48. For an excellent analysis of paranoia, reading and the institution of literature in *Gravity's Rainbow*, see Leo Bersani's "Pynchon, Paranoia, and Literature," *Representations* 25 (1989): 99–118.

and total contingency – an all-encompassing, if threatening, meaning, and the freedom of utter meaninglessness.

This vacillation is intimately related to the temporal structuring of the novel's universe. It is a commonplace of Pynchon criticism that all of this author's fictions describe worlds shaped by the second law of thermodynamics: subject to the inexorable increase of entropy, these fictional universes foreground their own gradual disintegration, the dissolution of highly organized patterns into random accumulations of facts and events. In *Gravity's Rainbow*, as has often been pointed out, the force of entropy is pitted against the evolutionary power of organic life: an early scene of the novel, for example, describes Pirate Prentice's rooftop garden, in which an accumulation of garbage from several decades has decomposed into a soil so fertile that Prentice is able to grow bananas in the midst of a London winter.[42] But this thrust towards fertility and higher forms of organization in *Gravity's Rainbow* is overwhelmed by a sense of the growing impact of the inorganic on the organic. Walther Rathenau's speech, for example, characterizes the West's recently acquired ability to synthesize new materials and substances as a mere "'impersonation of life'": "'The real movement is not from death to any rebirth. It is from death to death-transfigured. The best you can do is to polymerize a few dead molecules. But polymerizing is not resurrection'" (166). And Rathenau warns that the seemingly "organic" growth of the new industry is "'only another illusion. [. . .] The more dynamic it seems to you, the more deep and dead, in reality, it grows'" (167). World War II is the last and clearest symptom of this gradual encroachment of the inanimate upon the organic, since, in the view of at least some of the protagonists, it sacrifices human life to the advance of technology.

Entropy is the physical law that gives time direction; as opposed to the Newtonian laws of physics, all of which were time-reversible, the second law of thermodynamics defines the direction of time as going from lesser to greater disorder, and thereby distinguishes the past from the future.[43] In the structure

[42] Hayles, "Caught in the Web," 171–72; Alan J. Friedman, "Science and Technology," *Approaches to Gravity's Rainbow*, ed. Charles Clerc (Columbus: Ohio State University Press, 1983), 85–86.
[43] Alan J. Friedman and Manfred Puetz discuss the relationship between entropy, statistics and biology in detail in "Science as Metaphor: Thomas Pynchon and

of the novel, some critics have argued, the force of entropy reveals itself in the scattering of the protagonist and the disintegration of clear narrative progression especially in the last chapter, which incorporates an increasing number of disjointed episodes and characters with ever more tenuous relations to the central story line.[44] Slothrop himself disintegrates not only spatially but also temporally, in accordance with the so-called "Mondaugen's Law" (named after one of the German rocket engineers), which relates individuality to "temporal bandwidth":

"Temporal bandwidth" is the width of your present, your *now*. It is the familiar "Δt" considered as a dependent variable. The more you dwell in the past and in the future, the thicker your bandwidth, the more solid your persona. But the narrower your sense of Now, the more tenuous you are. It may get to where you're having trouble remembering what you were doing five minutes ago, or even – as Slothrop now – what you're doing *here* [. . .]   (509; original emphasis)

Due to his weakening time sense, Slothrop loses track of his own motivations and the causal structure of his past and present course of action. Since he becomes increasingly unable to conceive of himself as a historical being, he ultimately makes himself invisible to those around him.[45] The loss of agency and causation at an individual human scale is thereby associated explicitly with a shift in the experience of time, a theme that I will explore in greater depth in the next chapter on Christine Brooke-Rose's

---

Gravity's Rainbow," *Critical Essays on Thomas Pynchon*, ed. Richard Pearce (Boston: Hall, 1981), 69–72, and interpret the conflict between determinists and statisticians in the novel from this angle (73–77).

[44] William M. Plater, *The Grim Phoenix: Reconstructing Thomas Pynchon* (Bloomington: Indiana University Press, 1978), 51–53; Hite, *Ideas of Order*, 104; see also Schaub, *Pynchon*, 145. An exception is Siegel, who reads Slothrop's disintegration as the achievement of an "unthinking peace with nature" (*Pynchon: Creative Paranoia*, 70); "Slothrop's disintegration can be seen as a total transcendence of his human state – he . . . crosses over into the realm of the spirit where there are no borders between subject and object" (*ibid.*, 88). Deborah L. Madsen also interprets Slothrop's end in positive terms as a liberation from conspiracy and attainment of transcendence in *The Postmodernist Allegories of Thomas Pynchon* (Leicester: Leicester University Press, 1991), 102. Leo Bersani views the disintegration with moderate optimism, since according to him it offers at least some possibilities for escaping from the Firm's control ("Pynchon, Paranoia, and Literature," 113–15).

[45] Bénédicte Chorier, in "Thomas Pynchon: la fin de l'histoire?," *Revue Française d'Etudes Américaines* 43 (1990), also sees Slothrop's temporal disintegration as a sign that he finally escapes history, confirming that he is the "historical monster" that Pointsman took him for even at the beginning (15).

novel *Out*. When the temporal experience of the individual restricts itself to an increasingly narrow present, causal connections, which are defined through time, lose their meaning and can only be perceived as mere effects, or "signs and symptoms."[46]

Slothrop's temporal "shrinking" toward the end seems to form part of his general disintegration.[47] But if Slothrop was, as I argued earlier, already dispersed spatially at the beginning of the novel, the same applies to his sense of time. Slothrop may be losing "temporal bandwidth" in the Zone, but it is not very wide to start with: even while he is still in London, he has already lost his sense of past and future. For example, when he receives word of his unexpected reassignment to the Political Warfare Executive's Testing Programme – the beginning of his involvement with various Secret Services – he is not particularly surprised or concerned: "Once upon a time Slothrop cared. No kidding. He thinks he did, anyway. A lot of stuff prior to 1944 is getting blurry now. He can remember the first Blitz only as a long spell of good luck" (21). The map he keeps of his love adventures, "daily, boobishly conscientious" (23), turns out to be a rather desperate attempt to arrest this hemorrhaging of memory and expectation: "At its best, it does celebrate a flow, a passing from which – among the sudden demolitions from the sky, mysterious orders arriving out of the dark laborings of nights that for himself are only idle – he can save a moment here or there" (23). Ironically, then, the spatial configuration he traces on the map with his paper stars is a record of time, a historical rather than geographical document.[48] Already at this moment, Slothrop is living time symbolically; when the end of the novel converts him into what the initial map represents, a spatial figure of dispersal, he loses time definitively.[49] Slothrop's attempt to regain time through its figuration on a map is therefore doomed to failure from the start: in the course of the novel, he only becomes what in

<hr/>

[46] See Siegel, *Pynchon: Creative Paranoia*, 107.
[47] See Cooper, *Signs and Symptoms*, 150.
[48] So is Mexico's map of the V-2 strikes (Schaub, *Pynchon*, 15). Molly Hite also analyzes the parabolic trajectory of the rocket underlying the "rainbow" of the novel's title as a temporal pattern "transmuted into space" (*Ideas of Order*, 101).
[49] As Schaub suggests, Roger Mexico's map "represents the transformation of literal, consecutive experience into abstract, timeless meaning" (*Pynchon*, 15): this is also true of Slothrop's.

a sense he is from the beginning – trapped and dispersed in an acausal hyper-present.

Nevertheless, the hypothesis of a "narrative entropy" in *Gravity's Rainbow* is not entirely invalid. The text clearly offers no solutions in the traditional or even modernist sense, and the readers' hope that they will know definitively by the end of the novel how all its events and strands of plot fit together is rudely disappointed. In addition, the narrative emphasizes the irreversibility of time by systematically foreclosing all possibilities of returning to the past. There is no question that Slothrop will ever be able to recover his papers and return to the United States; he cannot clear up his childhood trauma because the man who inflicted it on him, Laszlo Jamf, is dead; neither is he able to ascertain what became of the only real friend he has in the novel, Tantivy Mucker-Maffick, who disappeared along with Slothrop's possessions and identification papers in southern France and was later – maybe falsely – reported to have died; none of the people who sympathize with him and who try to find him in the Zone, such as Pirate Prentice, Roger Mexico and Katje Borgesius, can ever catch up with him again; and he returns to the ship where he had his love affair with the adolescent Bianca Erdmann only to find her hanged. As the novel progresses and Slothrop loses temporal perspective, the possibility of recovering the original thrust and goal of his investigation also vanishes gradually; searching desperately after clues for the 00000, he is not even aware of having reached a "holy center" when he comes to Peenemünde in the company of one of the very engineers who helped design the secret rocket, Klaus Närrisch; neither does he question Närrisch about the project. And although Slothrop personally meets Miklos Thanatz, an eye witness of the final launch, he never gets to hear his story. There is certainly a sense, then, in which Slothrop's development demonstrates the functioning of entropy and the impossibility of quest: "Slothrop begins as a realist, chasing a deterministic version of the past, and ends as a surrealist, renouncing connections and forgetting the past."[50]

But the reader's quest is ultimately not identical with Slothrop's, and where Slothrop fails, the reader may not. The

---

[50] Strehle, *Fiction in the Quantum Universe*, 30.

reader *does*, for example, find out about the particulars of Blicero's
final launch when the *Schwarzkommando* catches up with Thanatz
and has him give a detailed account of the event. The narrator
does not fail to remind *the readers* of Peenemünde's importance,
and they do find out what Närrisch knows about the rocket, since
the narrator reveals his thoughts. Also, the reader does meet up
again with most of the characters Slothrop has left behind for
good. The reader's problem is therefore not so much that the
quest for meaning simply falls apart as that the narrative
provides more and more information concerning the central
questions of the plot, and yet never answers them – or answers
them in such a way that further explanations seem to be required.
We already saw that the "revelation" of Slothrop's childhood
trauma not only turned out to be a chronological impossibility,
but also did nothing to clear up his relation to the rocket. The
same is true of the other narrative riddles. Through Greta
Erdmann's account, for example, it becomes clear that the device
called *S-Gerät* must be Gottfried's physical connection to the
00000, and that his shroud was made out of Imipolex G, a
material that sexually arouses those that touch it. But as I
mentioned, this final human sacrifice itself seems to call for
further explanation, especially with regard to the intentions of the
rocket cartel that might have backed it. It points to the most
important question that remains unanswered: whether there is
such a rocket cartel at all, or whether the world is ultimately run
by the whims of ruthless megalomaniacs like von Göll and sadist
psychopaths like Blicero who, along with desperate expatriates
like the Herero and paranoiacs such as Slothrop and Tchitcherine,
latch on to technological developments like the 00000 as a
repository of their personal obsessions, fears and fantasies. Seen
in this light, the Zone may finally turn out to be a scenario of
utter randomness. Admittedly, transnational corporations like
Shell and IG Farben might have collaborated regardless of
loyalties to different nation states at war; admittedly, they might
have performed inhumane experiments on individuals like
Slothrop, and kept an eye on them throughout their lifetime. But
this neither proves that these corporations hold absolute power
over the world, nor that they can control individuals whenever
they choose to. It may show nothing more than that they are able
occasionally to manipulate and deform personalities like Slothrop

and Blicero, who develop conspicuously abnormal behavior patterns when they are left to their own devices.

Therefore, although *Gravity's Rainbow* provides a wealth of information regarding the solution of its narrative riddles, it also systematically precludes definitive answers. Some solutions that the text proposes turn out merely to repeat the structure of the problem. In other cases, answers seem gradually to emerge without ever assuming final shape, so that one might describe them in Leni Pökler's words "as Δt approaching zero, eternally approaching, the slices of time growing thinner and thinner, a succession of rooms each with walls more silver, transparent, as the pure light of the zero comes nearer . . ." (159). The paradox of both narrative procedures lies in the fact that although time is the medium that brings about a certain degree of coherence, it is also precisely the "last slice" of time, the Δt, that resists causal construction and harbors the possibility of contingency. Blicero's launch of the 00000, the central symbolic event of the novel, demonstrates this double-edged procedure. Chronologically speaking, the launch occurs about midway through the novel, in April or May of 1945.[51] But at that time, the firing is not mentioned because the narrative focuses on Slothrop, who is staying in southern France and then begins his trip to the Zone. Instead, the text slowly builds up to this climax over hundreds of pages. Engineers such as Franz Pökler are introduced as they work on parts of the rocket prior to the launch. Other groups and individuals seek to reconstruct the event after it is over, digging rocket fragments out of the ground, studying secret documents, and interrogating anyone they can find with a connection to the project. After Enzian, the leader of the *Schwarzkommando*, has found out from Thanatz that the rocket was in fact designed for a human sacrifice, he decides to sacrifice himself in similar manner, and at the end the *Schwarzkommando* is hauling rocket parts towards Peenemünde to put together the 00001. But this is the last we see of them: Enzian's launching of the 00001 is replaced by Blicero's in the narrative, in an analeptic move that takes us from September back to the spring of 45, so that the firing of the 00000 becomes a launch into the past for the reader. The novel slowly approaches Enzian's future self-sacrifice only to replace it

[51] Weisenburger, "Chronology," 60–61 n. 1.

212

at the last minute by Gottfried's in a leap back into the past: the reader is not allowed to escape from the ∆t of the present, which resists continuity with past and future, and hence narrative coherence.

The resistance of time to causal construction also underlies one of the novel's most important metaphors: that of film, the "moving pictures." Apart from the possibility, suggested on the last page, that the entire text might in fact be a movie plot, allusions to films also pervade it throughout.[52] As Friedman points out, the illusion of continuous movement in film is created through our inability to perceive the infinitesimal moment between individual frames; this moment is explicitly likened to the ∆t of calculus used to predict the flight of rockets:[53]

Three hundred years ago mathematicians were learning to break the cannonball's rise and fall into stairsteps of range and height, ∆x and ∆y, allowing them to grow smaller and smaller, approaching zero as armies of eternally shrinking midgets galloped upstairs and down again, the patter of their diminishing feet growing finer, smoothing out into continuous sound. This analytic legacy has been handed down intact – it brought the technicians at Peenemünde to peer at the Askania films of Rocket flights, frame by frame, ∆x by ∆y, flightless themselves . . . film and calculus, both pornographies of flight.   (567)

Elsewhere, the text emphasizes the same "rapid flashing of successive stills to counterfeit movement," which structures even human experience in the case of, for example, the engineer Franz Pökler (407). Leni Pökler wonders how her husband is able to follow movie plots, since he periodically falls asleep during screenings: "How did he connect together the fragments he saw while his eyes were open?" (159). And later, when Pökler works on the secret 00000 project, his superior Blicero comes up with an ingenious strategy to ensure his continued loyalty: once a year, Pökler is allowed to spend a few days with his daughter, herself

[52] For detailed discussions of film in *Gravity's Rainbow*, see David Cowart's essay "Making the Unreal Reel" in his *Thomas Pynchon: The Art of Allusion* (Carbondale: Southern Illinois University Press, 1980), 31–62; Charles Clerc's essay, "Film in *Gravity's Rainbow*" in *Approaches to Gravity's Rainbow*, ed. Charles Clerc (Columbus: Ohio State University Press, 1983), 103–51; and Thomas Moore's "*Gravity's Rainbow* as the Incredible Moving Film," Chapter 2 of his *The Style of Connectedness: Gravity's Rainbow and Thomas Pynchon* (Columbia: University of Missouri Press, 1987).

[53] "Science and Technology," 74; see Slade, *Thomas Pynchon*, 201–08; Hayles, "Caught in the Web," 180; Schaub, *Pynchon*, 46.

conceived during the re-enactment of a movie scene, who had disappeared in a labor camp with her mother years before. But although the gradually maturing girls Pökler meets over the years look sufficiently like each other that they might indeed be one and the same person, they also have pronounced enough differences in physical features that they could be different individuals. Pökler is continuously plagued by doubt whether the girl he is talking to is in fact his daughter, or even the same person that visited him the year before, and suspects that Weissmann might be sending him different camp inmates every year. Caught in the Δt between the frames of a film, with only one glimpse per year of his daughter's life, Pökler is unable to establish the continuity of motion that is the essence of the moving picture.[54] He is literally forced to live inside Δt, with no access to temporal and causal continuity or narrative coherence.

The end of the novel leaves the reader in the same time gap when the "film" about Gottfried's launching in the 00000 breaks with the word "*Now* – " (760; original emphasis). This deictic time signal, pointing the readers to the future just ahead which would have brought final illumination, traps them instead in the present "reality" of impending doom: "And it is just here, just at this dark and silent frame, that the pointed tip of the Rocket, falling nearly a mile per second, absolutely and forever without sound, reaches its last unmeasurable gap above the roof of this old theatre, the last delta-t" (760). The novel's very last words, "Now everybody – " (760) repeat the image of the definitively ripping strip of film; they suspend the readers in the final Δt in which the next frame will never come,[55] without any way of knowing whether the images add up to a coherent whole, or whether they were just a random assembly of individual shots with no more than some "Kute Korrespondences" to connect them.

Gravity's Rainbow, as I mentioned at the beginning, is set at a historical juncture, and the novel suggests that the insulation of the present from past and future, as well as the opening of boundaries and collapse of political establishments that charac-

---

[54] Slade, *Thomas Pynchon*, 204–05; Siegel, *Pynchon: Creative Paranoia*, 27–28; Cooper, *Signs and Symptoms*, 150–51; Schaub, *Pynchon*, 47; Moore, *Style of Connectedness*, 39; Bérubé, *Marginal Forces/Cultural Centers*, 252–53.
[55] Slade, *Thomas Pynchon*, 207.

terize the Zone after the War, might offer the chance of a new beginning.[56] If not a time reversal, it might nevertheless be a historical reversal, the chance to turn towards the historical "fork in the road America never took": "It seems to Tyrone Slothrop that there might be a route back – [. . .] maybe for a little while all the fences are down, one road as good as another, the whole space of the Zone cleared, depolarized, and somewhere inside the waste of it a single set of coordinates from which to proceed, without elect, without preterite, without even nationality to fuck it up . . ." (556). But the characters who find themselves at this juncture are only rarely optimistic about the opportunities it presents; for some, like Pointsman, history seems to disintegrate into disjointed "events," whereas for others, such as Slothrop himself, Enzian or Mexico, it brings on the contrary the revelation that their personal lives as well as their larger social and political environment may long have been engineered by global forces about whose institutional shape they can only speculate. Through these characters and the events that befall them, *Gravity's Rainbow* continuously questions whether in fact the historical moment it is concerned with is a juncture of any kind at all; it might, so the text suggests, be just the beginning of another phase of global domination by the Firm. On the other hand, the irrationality of achieved goals and the failure of quests in the novel might indicate that no deterministic or even explanatory principle is available anymore. Given over to chance, history no longer leaves any room for meaningful individual action, but only for statistical calculation. In either case, individuals, caught in a present which allows no long-term temporal perspectives for either the past or the future, are condemned to the interpretation of "signs and symptoms" rather than the analysis of cause and effect.[57]

What kind of narrative is still possible in such a universe? *Gravity's Rainbow* answers this question through its narrative

---

[56] Plater, *Grim Phoenix*, 60–61.

[57] Molly Hite interprets the novel in its entirety as an "ultimately futile project of trying to exhaust a historical period, and in this way to discover the antecedents of a present-day situation" (*Ideas of Order*, 139); the project remains futile because no agreement emerges from the text on what World War II means for the present, or for that matter, what actually happened during the period *Gravity's Rainbow* describes (*ibid.*, 101; see also Judith Chambers, *Thomas Pynchon* [New York: Twayne, 1992], 133). Although Hite doesn't use the term, her reading describes very accurately the "posthistorical" awareness that I analyzed earlier.

structure, which operates according to two principles. On one hand, the novel builds up tight causal structures on the basis of incidents that are either temporally and causally impossible (like Slothrop's conditioning to Imipolex), or that could be radically contingent (such as the correspondence of Slothrop's sexual map with that of the V-2 strikes). Narrative logic, in other words, rests upon an illogical foundation that ultimately precludes definitive inferences about the fictional world. On the other hand, the plot of *Gravity's Rainbow* can be characterized as a chain of apparent coincidences inching closer and closer to the final Δt that will bring coherence, but which is over and again replaced by yet another Δt, even closer to meaning, but still not quite there: this asymptotic temporality holds out the promise of coherence and always seems on the point of fulfilling it, but never answers the reader's questions completely. Both the premises and the telos of narrative, therefore, remain indeterminate in Pynchon's novel.

But arguably, this narrative organization does not have the same implications for the readers of *Gravity's Rainbow* as for its characters. Neither group has access to an interpretive model that would account satisfactorily for the complexities and contradictions of the plot; but for the readers, the distinction between the historical and the fictional is operative in a way that is by definition impossible for the characters. Readers cannot help but bring to bear certain facets of their historical knowledge upon the text that force them to distinguish between places and events that did play a role in World War II (Peenemünde, the V-2s, the *Blitzkrieg*, the involvement of the chemical industry with the Nazi regime, and the connections of German military research with later developments in space technology) and those that are pure invention (such as the *Schwarzkommando*, Squalidozzi's Argentine anarchists, Imipolex and the 00000). Pynchon's mixture of the historically accurate and the wildly fantastic may not prevent the readers from expecting and searching for narrative coherence in the novel; but it does make a difference when coherence cannot be established, since the readers can then fall back on their historical knowledge to construct an alternative story line and metaphorical meanings that might explain the inconsistencies of the plot (for example, Enzian's *Schwarzkommando* as an allusion to the SS with its black uniforms, Gottfried as a prefiguration of the first astronauts, or Slothrop's conditioning as a comment on the political implications of psychoanalysis). This explanatory approach is obviously not available to the characters within the novel, for many of whom the unintelligibility of the world that surrounds them leads to paranoia, psychic disintegration or permanent exile.

Nevertheless, it would clearly be inaccurate to claim that the characters' posthistorical predicament is simply superseded by the historical information that is accessible to readers. History cannot be called upon, for example, to explain the connection between Slothrop and the V-2s or to answer the question whether there is a global business cartel that triggers world wars and manipulates individuals. Rather, the incorporation of historical material into a novel that often flaunts its fictionality and indulges in the most extravagant forms of hyperbole in the end problematizes historical knowledge and the explanatory models it might offer. If historical information cannot fully account for the complexity of *Gravity's Rainbow*, the novel by contrast succeeds in defamiliarizing and "post-historicizing" what readers think they know about the twentieth century. Not only the combination of fact and fantasy, but the manipulation of diegetic levels contributes to this defamiliarization, as the first and last scenes of the novel show. I discussed these two scenes at the beginning of the chapter to emphasize the way in which they foreground temporal and causal inversion, since the first scene describes a city already struck by a rocket, whereas the last one is interrupted by an approaching missile. But neither of these scenes logically forms part of the main plot: the initial attack turns out to take place only in Pirate Prentice's dream and is therefore an embedded narrative;[58] the final one, by contrast, belongs to a frame narrative that is only hinted at, in which the entire plot of *Gravity's Rainbow* turns into a film being shown at a movie theater in Los Angeles. This frame story takes the reader out of the plot of the novel to a narrative level at which only a few moments are left, in a last fictionalization of the readers' own predicament: in an age of rapidly shrinking temporal horizons, they only have a thin slice of time, a "Δt" to assemble and live their own history. This final scenario might have been triggered by Cold War fears of imminent annihilation that were very much

---

[58] McHale, "Modernist Reading, Postmodern Text," 61–62.

a part of American political culture at the time *Gravity's Rainbow* was published. But two decades later, it continues to provide a compelling metaphor of the "posthistorical condition," social temporality sped up to the point where long-term developments have become difficult to envision. Through its encyclopedic format, its complex combinations of fact and fantasy, its subtle manipulations of diegetic levels and the paradoxes and indeterminacies of its temporal and causal structure, *Gravity's Rainbow* succeeds in looking back at the twentieth century from a moment in which historical reasoning has become a precarious undertaking; it succeeds, in other words, in posthistoricizing history.

6

Effect predicts cause: Brooke-Rose's *Out*

Pynchon's posthistorical scenario is set in the aftermath of a real historical catastrophe in the recent past; Christine Brooke-Rose's *Out* (1964) creates a similar scenario in a fictional future. *Gravity's Rainbow* abounds in the encyclopedic detail of multiple strands of plot which make it difficult for readers as well as characters to understand the temporal development and causal coherence of events; *Out* limits itself to a minimalist inventory of characters and scenes which are replayed again and again with alterations that make it impossible to infer which events, if any, make up the plot. But both novels explore the possibilities of knowledge, language and narrative in a context in which the past has become uncertain and causal reasoning inadequate. *Out* finally pushes this analysis further than *Gravity's Rainbow*, which in its narrative structure still relies on the reader's expectation that the plot will cohere at some point, although that moment in fact never arrives. *Out* does almost without any plot at all, and challenges the readers to find their way through a universe of disembodied voices, perceptual sequences of discontinuous shapes and colors, and linguistic fragments from various scientific as well as everyday types of discourse. All these elements combine and recombine in a text which offers only the present up for narrative understanding, but presents it in a variety of alternative versions.

The protagonist of *Out* is a sick white man looking for work in a Europe whose political and social configuration has changed beyond recognition. The old nation-states have disappeared; instead, Europe is now called Afro-Eurasia and co-exists with such other geopolitical blocks as Chinese Europe, Sino-America, and Seatoarea. All over the globe, racial barriers have been inverted: since the Whites, now referred to as the "Colorless,"

219

have fallen prey to a radiation disease against which the other races are immune, political power has been taken over by the "Melanian" races, who discriminate against the Whites much as those had discriminated against them before. Afro-Eurasia in particular is governed by an African ethnicity, the Asswati, who, in an officially "multiracial" and non-segregating state, live the feudal lifestyle of a privileged elite whereas the mass of impoverished and often unemployed Colorless barely eke out a living in huge "Settlements," agglomerations of shacks many of which are inhabited by two families at a time.

At the beginning of the novel, the protagonist is unemployed and has given up his mandatory daily visits to the Labor Exchange, where the state administers "unemployment benefits" to him in the shape of daily rations of stimulants. His wife, Lilly, works as a domestic servant for an Asswati lady, Mrs. Mgulu, who shows a great deal of concern over the well-being of her employees and especially that of Lilly, her former nanny. To help Lilly out, she asks the protagonist to present himself for a job interview with the head gardener at her estate. This interview is replayed in several versions; in some of them, the protagonist is instructed regarding his new tasks, whereas in others, a quarrel breaks out between him and the head gardener regarding their differing national and perhaps racial pasts. Unsuccessful in the interview, the protagonist returns to the Labor Exchange, where Mrs. Mgulu has in the meantime intervened on his behalf, claiming that the incident with the head gardener was merely a "misunderstanding." After a series of further bureaucratic obstacles are overcome, Mrs. Mgulu asks him to introduce himself to her Managing Agent, Mr. Swaminathan.

Mr. Swaminathan seems at first hostile toward the protagonist, but then puts him to work, and he begins to do varied construction jobs around the estate. During one of them, however, the protagonist falls off a ladder and is found unconscious by Mrs. Mgulu. On other occasions, Mrs. Mgulu finds him ill-adjusted and reproaches him with living too much in the past. Finally, she sends him in for a special psychiatric treatment called "psychoscopy." The events after his visit to the hospital are none too clear, but for a while he is out of work, and then is apparently working in Mrs. Mgulu's garden again. Some of the last scenes repeat incidents that had already been narrated in the first chapter; at the very end, he burns leaves in the garden with a fire that comes to stand in for his own disintegration.

At one level, this plot explores the social construction and functioning of racial difference, through its inversion of the usual power and discrimination patterns. It shows how a biological fact, the Colorless' susceptibility to a non-contagious disease, is constructed as a sign of mental and cultural inferiority and thereby leads to a complete reorganization of social and political power relationships. Read with this focus, *Out* is obviously meant to expose the hypocrisy of a society that claims to be pluralistic, but in fact discriminates against one ethnicity in everything from access to jobs and housing to medical care. Discrimination is justified by the elite in subtle but persistent shifts of argument from well-grounded concern over the "malady" to simple prejudice. This socio-political scenario remains unremittingly bleak throughout the novel, since there seems to be very little room for the Colorless, firmly held in place by omnipresent and overpowering bureaucracies, to change their lot.

But the novel's narrative concern is broader than the analysis of racism, since *Out* investigates the possibilities of knowledge in a context in which historical time is no longer available. Since the upheaval commonly referred to as "the displacement," the Colorless have been deprived of everything that ties them to the past: their places of residence, professions and nationalities. The political apparatus systematically encourages them to live only in the present, obviously in the interest of making them forget a past in which they held power. But the protagonist repeatedly complains about the difficulty of living in the present when there is no past and future. Himself only an instance of perception without a name that functions much like a camera lens, he experiences this present as a discontinuous sequence of voices, shapes and colors.[1] Only through the kinds of patterns he perceives and the

---

[1] The absence of any reference to the protagonist by either name, first- or third-person pronoun is clearly inspired by Robbe-Grillet's novel *La Jalousie*: see Ellen G. Friedman and Miriam Fuchs, "Conversation with Christine Brooke-Rose," *Utterly Other Discourse: The Texts of Christine Brooke-Rose*, ed. Ellen G. Friedman and Richard Martin (Normal: Dalkey Archive Press, 1995), 30; Christine Brooke-Rose, "Illicitations," *Review of Contemporary Fiction* 9.3 (1989): 102; and Brian McHale, "'I draw the line as rule between one solar system and another': The Postmodernism(s) of Christine Brooke-Rose," *Utterly Other Discourse*, 193.

terminology he uses to describe them does he betray that he may once have been a chemist or a doctor. But scientific and medical modes of explanation have become impossible in their old form; since time is no longer a dimension available to thought in this society displaced from its past, causal understanding has also become inaccessible: what the protagonist perceives is a series of movements and patterns, phenomena apparently without motivation or intent, caused by nothing and leading to nothing, repeating themselves again and again in different versions none of which can ultimately be considered authoritative. His difficulties in coping with the loss of time finally lead his Asswati employer to send him in for "psychoscopy," a highly condensed version of psychoanalysis that in the end confirms that the past is inaccessible and unusable, since the doctors rely on the maxim that aetiology is created in the process of diagnosis. But again and again, the protagonist asks superiors, doctors and friends, "Is there a story?," a question which reveals that his job search is really an exploration of the possibilities of narrative in the absence of historical time. *Out*, then, analyzes the relation between causality and narrative in a posthistorical context through the predicament of the Colorless characters, through the relationship between observation and scientific induction in the protagonist's perceptions, through the question of aetiology in a futuristic version of psychoanalysis, and finally through the main character's search for a story that might make his perceptions and experiences coalesce into a meaningful whole.

1. After the displacement

Out begins, not with its first sentence, but with a reproduction of three index cards from the files of a resettlement camp, a labor exchange and a state hospital. All three are obviously meant to describe the novel's protagonist, but most of the entries on the cards only characterize him through what he once was but no longer is: his "ex-nationality," we find out, is "Ukayan"; his "ex-occupation" is variously "humanist," "Ph.D.," "psychopath" and "gardener"; and he seems to have been re-trained as either a "fitter" or an "odd-job man." No name is given on any of the cards, and the only items that would allow one to identify the protagonist unambiguously are multi-digit file numbers, arbitrary bureaucratic designations without meaning outside the filing system they refer to. More substantial information seems to be reserved to other documents that the cards can only point to (a D.P.I., a letter from Mrs. Mgulu, a "biogram"). These index cards at first sight evoke a Kafkaesque or Orwellian dystopia of universalized and inhumane bureaucracy; but such bureaucracies rely on an individual's having a past and present that *can* be established, categorized and filed; the index cards *Out* begins with, however, are inconsistent with each other and seem to have only a tenuous hold on that history, since they attempt to seize it through categories such as nationality or occupation that have themselves become obsolete. By contrast, the one parameter that does matter in the new society, race, does not appear among the filing categories – presumably because only the Colorless would be assigned to resettlement camps and labor exchanges in the first place.

For the bureaucratic apparatuses in *Out*, such categories are, at any rate, pure filing conveniences without any real information value. On several occasions, tired or bored officials simply shrug off inconsistencies between their files and the real persons they are confronted with by uttering the standard phrase, " 'Well, it all comes to the same thing in the end' " (39, 50, 62, 100, 167).[2] On at least one occasion, the protagonist aggressively turns this phrase back on an official to question the institution's right even to interrogate him about a past that obviously has no further relevance in the present. But this brief rebellion against bureaucracy is of no avail to him in his persistent struggle with the loss of history that has befallen him and his entire race. The cataclysm that ousted white Europeans from their superior position in the international social, economic and cultural scale is not spelled out in detail in the novel; the reader only finds out that it was related to the Whites' susceptibility to a fatal radiation disease possibly related to nuclear warfare, and that as a consequence, radical socio-political changes propelled the Africans and the Chinese to the top and reshuffled the nation-states into four or five large power blocks. This "displacement" is touted as the beginning of "an age of international and interracial enlightenment" by the

---

[2] All quotations from *Out* refer to *The Christine Brooke-Rose Omnibus: Four Novels: Out, Such, Between, Thru* (Manchester: Carcanet, 1986). Future references will be given parenthetically in the text.

class now ruling. But for the Colorless, it constitutes the temporal watershed at which their histories, nationalities, professions and family relationships became insignificant and, in fact, everything that constituted their identities except their race.

In the new society, identity for all members of the underclass is defined by negatives: they are no longer white, but "Colorless"; after the demise of the European nation-state, they are classified as "ex-French" (48), "ex-Ukayan" (44, 47) or "ex-Uessessarian" (190), and so, as "ex-Europeans" (158) they are expected to bury their "ex-differences" (36, 176). Yet at the same time, they are not allowed ever to forget their useless past, since officials and bureaucrats of all descriptions ceaselessly question them about their "[e]x-nationality" and "[e]x-occupation" (50). As a consequence, the Colorless in general and the protagonist in particular find themselves lost in a posthistorical wasteland in which the past is irrelevant, the future bleak, and the present difficult to hold on to: "It's because of there being no past, and no future . . . it's so difficult, living in the present," the protagonist complains to his Asswati employer (124; see also 133). Indeed, the Colorless are being encouraged to mind only the present with slogans and catch phrases that Lilly, the protagonist's wife, angrily reprimands him with when he, in her view, immerses himself too much in the past: "Why now? Why not now? You know the past proves nothing. There's no such thing as the past, save in the privacy of concupiscence. That's an article of faith. So stop fretting about how it might have been" (118). Mrs. Mgulu's Managing Agent similarly instructs him that "[t]here is no such thing as history, except in the privacy of concupiscence. That is an article of faith" (91). The protagonist, however, resists this ideology, challenging Lilly and one of their neighbors, Mrs. Ned, to explain to him why he is constantly being asked for his former occupation if indeed the past proves nothing. Mrs. Ned sees it as a quaint habit of the privileged elite:

It's their little weakness, they fed on our past you see, and drained us of its strength, and we feed on their present. Now they deny the past, but need to ask as a matter of form, it flatters them, it's a relic that they adhere to. We must allow them their little weaknesses.   (119)

In her view, interrogatories regarding a past that has no relevance for the present function as instruments of domination by means of which the Colorless lower class is subjugated and humiliated. In the society that *Out* describes, this seems to be the only public use left for historical thinking.

It does, however, continue to have its uses in the private domain. As the phrase "There is no such thing as the past, *save in the privacy of concupiscence*" already indicates, history, in *Out*'s futuristic society, has become a substitute for sexual intimacy. Personal memories are erotically arousing: twice in the novel, the protagonist goes to bed with his wife only to indulge in reminiscences about their past in terms that leave no doubt about the erotic nature of memory. "Come to bed, Lilly. I want to make love," he requests (91); what follows is not the description of a sexual act, however, but a dialogue that calls up scenes from the time of their first acquaintance. "You're forgetting me. Tickle my memory a little too," Lilly complains so as to make her husband retell what she did during those encounters (93), and insists again, "No, you titillate me now" later (94); phrases such as "Don't stop, don't stop," "Aaaah," and "Go on, go on" (94) further reinforce the sense that memory is sexually arousing to the point of orgasm. The past turns into an erotic stimulant, and memory parallels desire; but since it is banned from articulation in the public sphere, the association of the past with sexual taboo also effectively prevents it from exerting any influence outside the intimacy of the individual couple.

And not even intimacy guarantees that the past evoked in these moments is in fact an authentic one. The protagonist, for example, is associated with a first name only in these memories; but this name at one time seems to be "Bill," at other times "Charlie" or "George" (92–93), so that the reader is in the end no closer to his "real" identity in these intimate moments than in the public sphere of files and index cards. Even more obviously, Lilly insists at one point that the story of the past be retold a certain way not for reasons of accuracy but aesthetics, claiming that it is "prettier" than her husband's present version (172). *Out*, therefore, does not contrast a public domain of lies and deception about the past with the authenticity of the individual's "titillation" of memory (see 94, 171). Both types of manipulation of the past turn out to be highly unreliable, neither of them a touchstone of truth.

Even where the past might be accessible, it does not offer any reassurance as to the shape and meaning of the present, as is suggested by the one character in *Out* who rejects as nonsense the idea that there is no past: Joan Dkimba, a schoolmate of Lilly's who, though Colorless, has moved up into the ruling elite by marrying an Asswati politician. In a long monologue during a visit to Lilly's shack, Joan emerges as a vain and opportunistic person who professes loyalty to her race but shows no sensitivity to or even awareness of her friend's desperate economic situation. She mindlessly repeats many of the slogans and indoctrinations with which the ruling class obviously deludes itself into believing it is doing the best it can. But when one of her commonplaces about the uses of "ancient wisdom" prompts a remark from the protagonist regarding the non-existence of the past, she contradicts him with some impatience: "Of course the past exists. Whatever next? We must face facts . . . I can't stand not knowing where I stand, if you know what I mean" (151). But she insists at the same time that old books and films make her feel uncomfortable and depressed because their meaning is too ambiguous and indeterminate: "[W]hat view are we being urged to take? Well, it's impossible to tell, I mean, it's unnerving, isn't it. No. I like to know where I stand" (152). Joan's view, although it acknowledges the existence of the past, confirms its irrelevance for the present: it is useless in practice because it does not assign a clearly defined stance to the observer. Interestingly, Joan associates the past with such fields as art and diplomacy, which require advanced interpretive skills from the observer or participant; the present, by contrast, holds no hidden meanings for her, mapped out and deciphered as it is through the ideological slogans that shape her world view. Joan Dkimba is clearly not a character with whom the text makes it easy to agree or sympathize: her blindness to the misery before her very eyes, and her supercilious and opportunistic identification with the ideology of the racist elite disqualify her as a reliable source of information. But precisely her incessant, self-congratulatory flow of speech reveals that the upper class lives in a posthistory of its own, in which not the existence but the relevance of the past is systematically questioned. Although this skepticism is obviously ideologically motivated, Joan articulates a real problem that the protagonist, in his hankering after the lost past, generally overlooks: even if the past *were* accessible, there is no guarantee that it would really serve to define and explain the present. The past might well turn out to be too multiple, too ambiguous and too self-contradictory to illuminate the genesis of the present – an observation that is reflected in the very structure of the novel, which never allows the reader to establish univocal causal connections from one episode to the next. Since the past is not linked to the present by any linear causal chain, its occasional and fragmentary recuperation might not increase but on the contrary diminish the coherence of the present.

The Whites' loss of history, the Melanians' historical skepticism, and the relegation of memory to the zone of sexual taboo all contribute to the emergence of a quite literally posthistorical society in *Out*. The end of history for this society seems to be clearly demarcated by the set of events that all characters refer to as "the displacement." But this term itself undergoes strange shifts of context which gradually make one doubt whether it actually refers to any definable set of historical occurrences. "Since the beginning there has been a displacement from cause to effect," the narratorial voice observes cryptically at one point (174), suggesting that perhaps *any* temporal or causal sequence should be envisioned as displacement rather than as concatenation. The same peculiar phrase recurs in a conversation between the protagonist and his neighbor, Mrs. Ned. When Lilly's husband complains about the constant interrogatories regarding the past that he has to undergo at the Labor Exchange and exclaims, "What were you before the displacement! What displacement for heaven's sake?," Mrs. Ned answers calmly, "The displacement from cause to effect" (119). She repeats the same words a little later when the two exchange what passes for childhood memories in their society:

– Did you ever find your trauma?
– Not really. It got lost, in the displacement, you know.
– What displacement?
– The displacement from cause to effect.
– From birth to death.
– From nothing to something.
– From red to sickly white. Then black.
– From infra-red to ultra-violet.
– You're beautiful. You're wonderful. (120–21)

In this dialogue, the displacement no longer refers simply to the political upheaval that turned the Colorless from social agents into medical patients. Lilly's husband views it as the inexorable human displacement from life to death ("From birth to death"), aggravated for the Colorless through the radiation disease ("From red to sickly white. Then black"). But Mrs. Ned's brief replies suggest a different interpretation; she views the displacement as a process of emergence ("From nothing to something") and as a passage through the whole range of the visible between the two extremes of the color spectrum that remain invisible to the human eye ("From infra-red to ultra-violet"). In very minimalist form, both Lilly's husband and Mrs. Ned here suggest various patterns of narrative development from a beginning to an end, but Mrs. Ned's last remark reveals why this development must be a displacement rather than a causal chain: in the passage from infra-red to ultra-violet, beginning and ending are invisible to the human observer. In more subtle ways, this invisibility also afflicts the protagonist, who cannot observe his own birth or death, or the onset and ultimate outcome of his disease. The "displacement," in other words, is as much a metaphor as a historical event in the world of *Out*, since it comes to refer to the general epistemological trauma that its posthistorical characters suffer from: their inability to perceive first causes and last effects. This inability has very serious consequences for the nature of knowledge and storytelling, which are explored through the way in which the protagonist observes his environment and translates these observations into words.

2. What the microscope might reveal

Events in *Out* are usually presented as they appear to the eyes and ears of the protagonist, which function much like a camera lens and tape recorder in their systematic avoidance of any reference to the protagonist himself as the perceiving medium. Although this "impersonal" viewpoint is adapted from Alain Robbe-Grillet's novel *La Jalousie*, its effect is quite different in *Out*. The incessant repetitions and recombinations of perceptual elements in *La Jalousie* can be interpreted as symptoms of the husband's obsessive concern with the most minute details of his wife's daily life and what they might imply for her marital fidelity, an interpretation that may not do justice to the complexity of Robbe-Grillet's intentions, but does allow one to account for many of that novel's otherwise strange features. The observations of *Out*'s protagonist are so much more discontinuous and surreal, however, that it becomes very difficult to explain them in terms of a psychological rationale. The parallel that imposes itself is in fact not so much with *La Jalousie* as with Faulkner's Benjy in *The Sound and the Fury*, who, just as the protagonist of *Out*, is incapable of understanding himself as agent and events as causally related to each other. Phrases such as "the gruel was not brought but come to, arrived at. Sooner or later movement, which is necessary but not inevitable, will lead to attainment. Yet, frequently, the gruel is brought" in *Out* (16) are closer in the structure of perception they describe to Benjy's "Then the bowl was empty. It went away. 'He's hungry tonight.' Caddy said. The bowl came back" than to the observations of Robbe-Grillet's focal character.[3] Like Benjy, the protagonist of *Out* cannot perceive or articulate reasons, motives or causes, but only sequences of effects; whereas this inability was still a symptom of mental illness in Faulkner, however, it has become the normal state of affairs in Brooke-Rose's posthistorical world. The peculiar disjunctiveness of perceptions in *Out* does not seem due to illness so much as to a world whose basic functional parameters have changed so radically that conventional reasoning cannot account for them anymore.

Nevertheless, some personal features are still discernible in the protagonist's mode of perceiving the world. Most obviously, phrases, images and metaphors from medicine and chemistry recur so frequently that one cannot help but assume that he used to be a doctor or scientist of some sort, a hypothesis that at least sometimes seems to be confirmed by the sparse information the reader receives about his life before the displacement. But equally striking is the protagonist's habit of perceiving parts rather than wholes, abstract configurations of shape and color rather than concrete objects, and visual metaphors whose point of reference is either given much later or not at all. As a consequence, much of *Out* reads like a succession of strange, hallucinatory visions, sequences of shapes and colors described with the utmost preci-

[3] William Faulkner, *The Sound and the Fury* (New York: Modern Library, 1956), 86.

sion, but which do not seem to add up to anything the reader can readily identify. This narrative strategy makes for the fantastic, science-fiction-like atmosphere that pervades *Out* even in the description of what turn out to be quite common, everyday occurrences. The following scene, for example, occurs near the beginning of the novel:

The spider is advancing with sparkling teeth bared in a wide flattened grin that blares white as it catches the luminosity of the white winter sky. Nearer and nearer it smoothly advances, apparently stretching across the whole width of the drive, broadening as the drive broadens, approaching with an engulfing threat to the wrought-iron gates until suddenly the gates dwarf it with their own tall fangs that close slowly behind it as it passes through. A pale blue face floats in a blue glass globe above the wide metallic grin. Beyond it, outlined against more light, more glass and moving fronds, a cavern-blue chin-line curved like a madonna's and pale blue teeth flashing in wide mauve lips under a wide mauve hat of falling plumes, all of it cut, swiftly, by a shaft of light reflected in the glass, and then away, only a purple blob in a moving bubble of quickly shifting blue and green. The number of the vehicle is 24.81.632. There is no numerical significance in such a number. Beyond the vertical bars of the closed wrought-iron gates there is the thick network of the first plane-trees on either side of – oh hell. The number of the vehicle is, the number of the vehicle, the number of the vehicle is gone. The number of the vehicle is insignificant.

(42)

This paragraph contains one version of a very simple scene, repeated several times in the novel: Mrs. Mgulu's limousine approaches the gates of her estate, and as it passes by, the protagonist catches a fleeting glimpse of her face ("chin-line curved like a madonna's") and elegant pink hat behind the car windows, which are tinted for protection against the sun and therefore make everything inside appear blue or purple. But this explanation is only given in one of the subsequent repetitions of the scene ("It was the glass that was blue of course, making the hat look purple and the face cave-blue and the wide mouth mauve in the avenue of the mind. The hat inside the vehicle must be pink" [53]). Here, if it were not for the last few sentences, it would be hard even to know that there is a car involved in the scene at all. Because the protagonist had mentally compared the intertwined branches of the trees that line the driveway to a cobweb just before, the appearance of the limousine prompts the metaphor of the spider, whose "sparkling teeth" and "wide

metallic grin" refer to the car's radiator grill. But this obviously
metaphorical mouth, followed by the other mouth of the iron
gates with its "tall fangs," makes the description of Mrs. Mgulu's
literal mouth with "pale blue teeth flashing in wide mauve lips"
doubly unreal – not only because of its improbable coloring but
because all the protagonist seems to be able to perceive before
him is a series of opening and closing mouths. Mrs. Mgulu
herself appears more like a fish in an aquarium ("blue," "floats,"
"glass globe," "cavern-blue," "purple blob," "moving bubble")
than a human being, and the perceptual intensity of this surreal
scene is conveyed through color adjectives that are often repeated
twice in the same sentence ("blares *white* as it catches the
luminosity of the *white* winter sky," "pale *blue* face floats in a *blue*
glass globe," "wide *mauve* lips under a wide *mauve* hat").
Phonetic repetitions, mostly consisting of a consonant, an /l/ and
a vowel, with additional repetitions of /b/ and /p/, further
contribute to the hallucinatory quality of the protagonist's
fleeting vision ("*close slowly*," "*pale blue* face *floats*," "*blue glass
globe*," "*blue* teeth *flashing*," "*falling plumes*," "*light reflected*,"
"*purple blob*," "*moving bubble*") that is cut short only when his
attention shifts to the numbers on the car's license plate. For the
readers, these numbers are a touchstone of reality, since they
allow them to interpret at least part of the preceding impressions
as a scene involving a vehicle passing by at some speed. But for
the protagonist afloat in a world of shifting appearances, they
promise a meaning they cannot deliver, since they – like the
numbers on his index cards – simply constitute a sequence whose
ordering does not in itself have any significance, and hence
cannot provide him with a means of deciphering the surreal
phenomena that surround him.[4]

Many of these phenomena are pathological symptoms: the
protagonist's perceptions and imagination revolve frequently
around body parts, physical deformities and diseases. From
Lilly's squint, Mrs. Ned's goiter, Mrs. Jim's gallstones and the
gnarled hands of a man who sits beside him at the Labor
Exchange, to the radiation disease whose symptoms sometimes
seem to befall Lilly and sometimes himself, the organic world

[4] In another repetition of the scene, the order of the numbers on the license plate
is in fact different (see 161).

only comes alive to him through its sicknesses.[5] This obsession informs the passage that follows, during which the protagonist sits in the sun outside his shack:

That is how the malady begins. The onset is insidious, well advanced before diagnosis. The fingers tap the smooth grey bark which remains firm on palpation and retains its characteristic notch. The imagination increases in size progressively and by no means painlessly until it fills most of the abdomen. Enlargement of the lymphatic glands may occur in the later stages of the disease, with a general deterioration to a fatal termination. The absolute knowledge . . . enters the body through the marrow bone, and up into the medullary centres, down the glosso-pharyngeal nerve no doubt or the pneumogastric, at any rate forward and down into the throat which tightens as the knowledge spreads into the chest and hurts. Sooner or later it will reach the spleen, which will increase in size until it fills the world. From ground-level on the dried-up yellow lawn the arch formed by the leaning trunk and the down-sweeping branch frames a whole landscape of descending olive groves beyond the road, which itself disappears behind the bank.   (163–64)

This paragraph forms part of what in a high-modernist novel one would no doubt refer to as the protagonist's stream of consciousness: bits and pieces of personal observations and reflections intermingled with linguistic fragments that penetrate the character's awareness from the outside or from memory, such as the sentences that appear to be taken from a medical handbook. But the technique employed here differs from Joyce's or Woolf's stream of consciousness not only in that the focal character never thinks about himself in the first person; his "thinking" also never deviates from the smooth flow of a flawless and fairly compli-cated syntax quite unlike the broken sentences and fragments scattered about, for example, Leopold Bloom's consciousness. The impression of a mind thinking is conveyed only through the shifts and substitutions by which terms and locutions that belong to one particular scene, perception or reflection move to the description of another one, altering its syntax or meaning just so much that what was familiar suddenly becomes strange or even

[5] Brooke-Rose herself has commented on the importance of disease in the novel: ". . . I began to write *Out*, which is a very 'sick' novel. I think one can feel that. . . . the reason the whites are discriminated against is because they are sick" (Friedman and Fuchs, "Conversation," 30). In another context she observes that in *Out*, "[t]he narration is both objective . . . and obsessive, sick" (Brooke-Rose, "Illicitations," 102).

unintelligible. Such a substitution is obvious in the sentences "The imagination increases in size progressively . . . until it fills most of the abdomen" and ". . . it will reach the spleen, which will increase in size until it fills the world," where it also includes a pun on the double meaning of "spleen" as either an internal organ or an *idée fixe*. This particular substitution of "imagination" for "spleen" recurs in other passages, and gradually makes one doubt one of the seemingly most "realistic" details of the plot, the susceptibility of the Colorless to a blood disease triggered by exposure to radiation. Perhaps this leukemia is, after all, only a metaphor for the protagonist's (or maybe the reader's) wildly proliferating imagination, which creates and "fills" entire worlds but may end up undermining the reality of the one who imagines.[6] This metaphor would agree perfectly with one of the novel's rhetorical leitmotifs, the insistence that "[i]t is sometimes sufficient merely to imagine an episode for the episode to occur" (21), and with other, explicitly metafictional elements which occur especially at the very beginning of the text;[7] in the course of some of the initial dialogues, for example, a voice apparently out of nowhere remarks, "Very witty. But you are talking to yourself. This dialogue does not necessarily occur" (17), or "Look, since you're inventing this dialogue you ought to give something to the other chap to say" (19), or "You're incapable of preparing any episode in advance. You can't even think" (20).[8] Although these overtly self-reflexive observations rapidly diminish in frequency after the first few sections, the word substitutions in the later passages remind the reader that even the novel's harshest realities may, after all, just be imaginary.

Substitution also accounts for the paragraph's enigmatic third sentence, "The fingers tap the smooth grey bark which remains

---

[6] In *Christine Brooke-Rose and Contemporary Fiction* (Oxford: Clarendon, 1994), Sarah Birch analyzes in detail the metaphorical superimposition of certain types of specialized discourse upon other, less specialized ones in Brooke-Rose's novels, and puts particular emphasis on the importance of medical language and its metaphorical extension to the imagination and various areas of knowledge in *Out* (54–63).

[7] Formulations which emphasize that a thought or a word is enough to make a certain event or change occur or to prevent it from occurring appear throughout the text (16, 17, 22, 28, 31, 33, 46, 59, 68, 88, 91, 101, 128, 130, 174, 185, 193).

[8] Richard Martin mentions these self-reflexive elements very briefly in "'Just Words on a Page': The Novels of Christine Brooke-Rose," *Utterly Other Discourse*, 43, as does Brian McHale (" 'I draw the line,' " 193).

firm on palpation and retains its characteristic notch," which is based on earlier passages such as "the spleen remains smooth and firm on palpation and retains its characteristic notch. The black fingers tap the flaccid white flesh" (66; see also 60, 67, 107, 168). It substitutes for the human body part the "grey bark" of the fig-tree that the protagonist is looking at, which reappears at the end of the paragraph with the "grey framework of the trunk." Similarly, the phrase concerning the "absolute knowledge" which "enters the body" amalgamates the protagonist's fantasies with the description of the malady. But in this case, it is impossible to ascertain what the medical discourse originally said: in all other passages which contain the same description of an object entering a body (85, 107, 184–85), it is already associated with an abstract concept such as "passion" or "knowledge," so that the original wording cannot be reconstituted. Finally, the protagonist's attention to which visual elements frame others points to his habit, pervasive throughout the novel, of seeing combinations of objects or persons as pictorial compositions without depth rather than as three-dimensional scenes.

As this passage demonstrates, the protagonist's perceptions are therefore conveyed not so much through a stream of consciousness as through a linguistic jigsaw puzzle in which the pieces that make up a particular scene are taken apart and recombined with pieces from other scenes. This process repeats itself so many times that almost all of the words describing the novel's main events are dislocated from their original sequence and reappear in such disparate contexts that one retrospectively wonders whether the "original" event was not just a recombination effect as well. Whether a certain event gave rise to certain perceptions and phrases or whether it arose from those phrases and perceptions becomes more and more doubtful as one reads on, and as each sentence resounds with more and more echoes from other contexts.[9] The two passages we have seen therefore illustrate two of *Out*'s most important narrative techniques: the protagonist's perceptions are highly idiosyncratic, shaping realities rather than recording them, and the words which render these impressions in

---

[9] Commenting on this narrative technique, Birch observes: "The web or network of images spun by the protagonist's discourse has subsumed all past images to its present. The past becomes a projected image created retrospectively at every moment" (*Christine Brooke-Rose*, 58).

the text lead a life of their own that is not reducible to the associative functioning of a human psyche. They are disconnected from any mental or "actual" voice that might be their origin and point of articulation, since they disintegrate and recombine in ways that cannot be explained with reference to any realistically conceived character psychology. Textual effects rather than expressions of a mind, they are as displaced from their causes as the protagonist's actions are from his intentions and his perceptions from the perceived objects.

In part, this peculiar mode of perception is due to the temporal structure of the world that surrounds the protagonist and imposes severe restrictions on knowledge. Since the past has become at least partially inaccessible, beginnings – and therefore causes – can no longer be observed under any circumstances. This is not only a peculiarity of the protagonist's – perhaps pathologically deformed – apparatus of perception, but one of the axioms or "articles of faith," as the text calls it, that the entire society he lives in is based on. For example, when he is notified that his wife has had an unexpected attack of radiation disease and confronts the doctor about the reasons for her collapse, the doctor reproaches him, "There you go again with your sick talk. Don't you understand that in paleontology the beginning of a new organism cannot be observed, because at the beginning it is not recognisable as a new organism and by the time it has become one the beginning is lost" (169). This rule, the doctor insists, applies to medicine as well as all other disciplines: a beginning can only be identified and described as such in view of some consequence or outcome it produces, but by the time such an outcome has become perceptible, the beginning is past. It can therefore only be reconstructed in an epistemological operation that effectively turns it into the result of the observation itself.[10] The notion of "displacement" describes this process in which beginnings are lost in their very reconstruction.

---

[10] Edward Saïd has analyzed this process in *Beginnings: Intention and Method* (New York: Columbia University Press, 1985), where he argues that "a beginning might as well be a necessary fiction" (50): it is always chosen from a wide range of particular phenomena by means of abstract principles that cannot be experienced directly, but are only inferred through the observation of their form and function (51–52).

The novel emphasizes this inaccessibility of beginnings up to its very last page:[11]

That is how it all began. There is a secret but it is not a story. It is not possible to witness the beginning, the first ticking of the metronome, because all you are entitled to assume is that it would have been as now described if it had been seen by minds with the kind of perception man has evolved only quite recently. Those that cannot grow with it must die. (198)

The paradoxical juxtaposition of "That is how it all began" and "It is not possible to witness the beginning" sums up the crisis of temporal and causal logic that Brooke-Rose's novel addresses. As a scenario of the past, beginnings nevertheless originate in a present perception, and therefore do not, in a sense, pre-exist the moment that they are purported to have given rise to; "the beginning is now," and "now is the time for the beginning," several of the characters insist (171, 173, 126). For those who cannot adapt to this type of thinking and still search for a beginning in the past, it turns into an ending ("Those that cannot grow with it must die"). Observer and observed, cause and effect are constantly shifted away and displaced from each other in a present that has no inlet from the past and no outlet toward the future.

This process by which observation and description effectively preclude access to causes is one of *Out*'s principal concerns and motivates several of its narrative leitmotifs, among them the speculation about what the use of a specialized instrument might reveal in a scene that the protagonist is watching merely with his bare eyes. At the very beginning, for example, he observes the copulation of two flies that have settled on his knee: "The fly on top is . . . agitated . . . A microscope might perhaps reveal animal ecstasy in its innumerable eyes, but only to the human mind behind the microscope, and besides, the fetching and rigging up of a microscope, if one were available, would interrupt the flies" (11). If this sentence gives the reader a first glimpse of the protagonist's "scientific" mode of observation and at the same time facetiously rejects narrative omniscience in favor of a more

[11] See also the following passage: "It is impossible ever to see the beginning of anything because at the beginning the thing is not recognisable as anything distinct and by the time it has become something distinct the beginning is lost" (196).

limited but more objective stance, it also immediately makes clear that such objectivity will not reveal a reality that pre-exists observation. Even to ask the question what the fly "feels" during copulation is an application of human categories to a realm in which they may be wholly inappropriate, a fact that Lilly foregrounds when she remarks, "Flies don't make love. They have sexual intercourse" (12). This misapplication of categories may be too obvious to be of much interest in itself, but it alerts the reader from the first page to the prejudices an observer brings to any situation merely through his being human: the human body, without aid from specialized instruments, can only perceive events at a certain scale and from a cultural perspective whose biases he may not be able to neutralize. In other words, the mere fact that an observer is human means that he must at least partially create the observed object in relation to his own humanity in the process of observation.[12] At the same time he observes, he also interferes with what he observes. In a narrative application of Heisenberg's uncertainty principle, then, this first paragraph defines observation as an alteration of the observed event, and emphasizes the impossibility of any perception or description that does not contain an element of self-reference to the observer as the cause of the event.[13]

Even "scientific" observation cannot give access to first causes; the act of perception and what is perceived condition each other, at the same time that the act of perception cannot be separated from the medium, linguistic or otherwise symbolic, in which it is communicated: all this is, of course, standard knowledge in twentieth-century science and scientific philosophy. Placed at the beginning of a novel and repeated periodically, such reflections might be no more than a signal to the reader that the narrator should not be understood to describe reality objectively. In *Out*, however, the issue is not so much the narrator's personal reliability as the question of how deformed any observation *must* be given that humans observe at a human scale, whereas decisive

[12] This relativity is also what the racial question in *Out* foregrounds: whether a Caucasian is called "White" or "Colorless" depends on the observers – and the color of *their* bodies.

[13] Birch comments on the importance of Heisenberg's uncertainty principle for *Out* and quotes a 1965 article by Brooke-Rose that confirms the novelist's interest in its implications (*Christine Brooke-Rose*, 56).

"events" might be taking place at a scale that is not immediately accessible to human observation. The distinction between animate and inanimate objects, for example, fundamental at the human level of concern, becomes immaterial when the focus shifts to the level of cellular biology:

The wrinkled wood is quite static in the light, as static, at any rate, as the network of minute lines on the back of the wrist. A microscope might perhaps reveal which is the more static of the two. The protozoan scene under the microscope is one of continual traffic jams and innumerable collisions. (58)

What makes this scene of "continual traffic jams and innumerable collisions" so disturbing is that it can cause profound alterations of reality not only at the scale of the individual human, but beyond it for entire human societies. This becomes clear when the protagonist's attention, shortly afterwards, focuses on Lilly's white skin:

... the mobile eye wriggles away, its blue mobility calling out the blueness of the temple veins and a hint of blue in the white skin. A microscope might perhaps reveal a striking increase in the leucocyte count, due to a myeloid hyperplasia leading to an absolute increase in the granular leucocytes. Sooner or later immature and primitive white cells appear in the peripheral blood and corresponding changes in the bone marrow. (58–59)

As the reader knows all too well by this time, the "striking increase in the leucocyte count" is one of the main symptoms of the deadly radiation disease that has altered Lilly's and the protagonist's personal lives. But beyond that, it is also the factor that led to the international geopolitical reorganization and social upheaval during which the "Melanian" races seized power and the "Colorless" were relegated to hunger and misery. The "protozoan" scene leads directly to a global scenario: developments at the scale of cells that the bare eye cannot even perceive give rise to events that affect social and political structures at a planetary scale. This causality cannot be grasped directly by humans, who must use highly specialized kinds of instruments and knowledge to understand it; their own bare-eye perceptions are useless in this context, and hence leave them, outside of specialized discourses and methodologies, floating about helplessly in a universe whose temporal and causal structure they no longer have direct access to.[14] This discrepancy of scale is the philosophical core of *Out*'s concern with time and causation and informs its choice of narrative strategies from style and viewpoint to plot.

John Barth's "Menelaiad" and particularly Pynchon's *Gravity's Rainbow*, which I discussed in Chapters 1 and 5, describe a similar junction between the world of atomic or subatomic structures, and events of a planetary scale such as world wars and explosions of nuclear bombs. *Out* investigates the same connection between the microscopic and the macroscopic; but whereas *Gravity's Rainbow* puts the main emphasis on the victimization of individuals at the hands of an international business cartel that derives its power from the manipulation of molecules, *Out* focuses on the alienation of the individual who faces social and cultural changes triggered ultimately by biological alterations in his own body. Through a cultural logic that was already operative before the "displacement" – racism and discrimination under the cloak of pluralism – these minuscule alterations become the starting point of social upheavals over which the individual has as little control as over the micro-processes of his own biology. Therefore, in the world of pathology which surrounds *Out*'s protagonist, the main characters are not really humans, but entities such as "myeloid cells, . . . polymorphonuclears and immature cells . . . myeloblasts, promyelocytes, myelocytes and metamyelocytes" (85; see also 106, 108), agents that only a microscope could reveal. Just as the universe of Tyrone Slothrop, such a world can no longer be grasped in terms of conventional notions of time and causality. For Slothrop, the only strategy to survive was paranoia, the obsessive conviction not only that everything was causally linked, but linked for the specific purpose of destroying him: a conviction which gave the world around him a definable if threatening causal structure. Not even this option is available for the protagonist of *Out*, however, for whom the universe is always on the point of disintegrating into a rush of shapes, sounds and colors. *Out*, therefore, describes a

---

[14] In this respect, *Out* complements Jean-François Lyotard's argument about the increasing specialization and fragmentation of scientific knowledge with its equally specialized "language games" (*The Postmodern Condition: A Report on Knowledge*, trans. Geoff Bennington and Brian Massumi [Minneapolis: University of Minnesota Press, 1984], 9–11, 31–41).

universe beyond paranoia, in which not even fear can make world or self cohere.

3. Diagnosis predicts aetiology

The disintegration of the self in *Out* emerges most clearly during the procedure the novel calls "psychoscopy," essentially a condensed, technologized version of psychoanalysis. At the beginning of this procedure, "[t]he microscopes are gathered all around, pointing downwards and converging" on the protagonist (134), in an inversion of the novel's initial scene in which he had imagined what similar microscopes might reveal about the flies *he* was observing. Indeed, psychoscopy, suggesting a surgical intervention by its very name, seems to have more affinities with the taking of an electroencephalogram than with classical psychoanalysis, since the protagonist is connected to a variety of machines through multiple wires and cables, and his image appears projected on an overhead monitor. At the beginning, he repeatedly looks up at this screen to observe himself, but the doctor admonishes him to keep his eyes on the interviewer or the camera in front of him because he will never be able to meet his own eyes on the screen, anyway: whenever he raises his eyes, the screen image does so, too, and all he is able to see is a "fresh white jellyfish . . . with yellowish white filaments flowing downwards and long black tentacles flowing upwards" (134). From the outset it is clear, therefore, that psychoscopy will not be a procedure in which the patient gains insight into himself, but a diagnostic whose outcome will be valuable only for the attendant doctors.

The image of the jellyfish, however, recalls several earlier scenes in which the protagonist contemplated his reflection in a glass door as a way of grasping his own identity. This mirror-image already portrayed him as radically fragmented:

The glass door of the verandah reflects a green light, in which a filmy monster shifts into view, cut into three sections. The top section frames a jellyfish, the middle section a tiered hierarchy of diagonal wobbles, the lower section two thin trunks, wavering like algae. . . . Sooner or later the identity will be called out. And here is Mr. Blob in our studio tonight. Mr. Blob, you've been cutting yourself into three sections of different wriggling shapes for twenty years now, beating your own record year

after year. . . . But isn't there a very real danger of complete disintegration?
– I might of course disintegrate, but that is a risk worth taking.   (54–55)

As opposed to the Lacanian mirror-image, which deludes the
subject into believing in his own coherence due to the way in
which he sees himself represented, this mirror turns the protagonist into a lighting effect without depth, another one of the
disjoint mirages of color and shape that constantly surround him
anyway: he is flat ("Mr. Blob"), visually fragmented into three
sections, and becomes trivialized through the imaginary
TV-studio conversation, in which Mr. Blob's only achievement is
that of beating a record for which no one else competes with him
in the first place, "standing still in near disintegration" (55). If the
fantasized TV screen here foreshadows the psychoscopy monitor,
it does so to prepare the reader for a psychoanalytical "talking
cure" in which no coherent story any longer emerges to account,
through its temporal reversal to childhood, for the discontinuous
symptoms that make up the personality of the adult.

  In fact, most of the questions that the analyst asks the protagonist during the psychoscopy session do not concern his personal
history at all, but repeat parts of a political opinion poll which
had earlier been conducted outside the Labor Exchange. One of
these questions, "Do you prefer history or progress?," is answered by the protagonist with the slogan about the non-
existence of history:

– There is no such thing as history, save in the privacy of concupiscence.
– This . . . is . . . the privacy of concupiscence. I am your doctor, father,
God. I build you up. I know everything about you. Your profile is
coming up very clearly indeed on the oscillograph, and the profile
provokes its own continuation, did you know that, the profile moulds
you as it oscillates? Diagnosis provokes its own cause, did you know
that? To put it more succinctly, diagnosis prognosticates aetiology [. . .]
(138–39)[15]

This surprising statement, which the doctor repeats to the patient
once more at the end of the session (140), applies the principle
that observation creates what it observes to pathology, thereby
again overturning conventional models of temporal and causal

---

[15] Only the elision marks in parentheses are mine; the preceding ones form part of
the text.

reasoning.[16] Psychoanalysis in its traditional form relies heavily
on causality, as we already saw in the case of Tyrone Slothrop,
since it explores past causes for present symptoms and assumes
that they have to be uncovered if the symptoms are to be cured.
Within this framework, even mere accidents and seemingly
contingent remarks become part of a tightly drawn causal
network: everything from dreams and unconscious reactions to
lapses of the tongue are assumed to occur for a determinate
reason with its roots in the remote past. Psychoscopy, however,
strips psychoanalysis of causal investigation: if there is no
aetiology before diagnosis, disease does not exist in time and has
no history, but comes into existence at the moment it is being
examined and *because* of this examination. Any search for causes
in the past would be unwarranted under such an assumption.
Diagnosis turns into self-fulfilling prophecy, and therefore psychoanalysis can dispense with time, as the doctor himself indicates: "Psychoscopy's an extracted absolute of analysis. We don't
need transference any more. We're not only able to telescope a
dependence that used to take years to build up, we telescope the
let-down as well" (140–41). Hence, a procedure that used to last
months or even years can be completed in a mere two hours and
does not pretend to reveal anything, but merely to provide the
patient with a "technique for living" (132). When the protagonist
desperately asks the doctor at the end what the "secret" or the
"answer" might be, he is handed a prescription for drugs by way
of response.

He raises the same question a little later in the presence of Joan
Dkimba, and she confirms to him that providing answers or
cures is not the object of any of the sciences as practiced in the
new society:

An answer. What do you mean, an answer? Don't be so metaphysical.
Do you mean an explanation of the origin? Or do you mean a cure?
Surely you know that diagnosis only prognosticates aetiology. . . . It's a
short way of saying that they don't claim to find either the ultimate
cause or the ultimate cure, but they do know exactly how it functions,
and can prescribe accordingly. I mean every neurosis has its mechanics,
which are absolutely predictable, they can tell exactly what anyone will
do next, it's marvellous. And it's true of everything, medicine, for

[16] See Birch, *Christine Brooke-Rose*, 59–60.

instance, . . . and of course social science, and demography, and politics, the lot. That's why the principle is so important. (151)

Scientific knowledge, in other words, has been replaced by engineering: nature, including the human body and mind, are approached as more or less mechanical devices that need to be managed rather than understood. Theories and general principles have become unimportant, since the main goal of science now is to ensure that nature and society function according to the plans of the ruling class. But not even the rulers themselves are exempt from such management: as Joan reveals, all politicians and their spouses undergo psychoscopy regularly and plan their pro-fessional agenda in accordance with the resulting biograms – biograms which, according to the psychoscopic principle, must create the psyches they are based on as much as they describe them. In the absence of temporal sequence and causal conse-quence, as these details reveal, the nature of knowledge changes radically; simultaneous with its object, it is its cause at the same time as its effect.

But in fact, the protagonist never even gets to see his own biogram. Instead, he has to answer once more the question he has already been asked dozens of times at the Labor Exchange: ". . . what is your occupation?" (139). Egged on by the doctor, he gives a series of varying answers, until the doctor urges him to leave these identities behind. "I don't know. I really don't know," the protagonist answers. "I see a huge triangle, orange, and a yellow shower, and circles, red . . . oh" (140).[17] This image resembles many of the protagonist's other visual impressions, but remains enigmatic until the very end of the novel, when he is back in Mrs. Mgulu's garden burning leaves: "The fire leaps up bright orange, with a yellow shower, circles of red, oh, close your eyes . . . under the eyelids a gold triangle, a yellow shower, circles of orange and the head goes leaden, grey . . ." (198). I will return to this final scene later, but it should already be noted here that the burning of the leaves metaphorically stands in for the protagonist's own terminal dispersion. His vision of himself during psychoscopy anticipates this final "funeral pyre" (197), and the disintegration that had already been announced comically by "Mr. Blob." Psychoscopy, as a condensed, detemporalized version of psycho-

[17] The elision marks are part of the original text.

analysis, reveals at the deepest level no longer the self but its disintegration, its implosion into a mere visual effect of shapes and colors on a monitoring screen.

So far, I have read the psychoscopy session as a "real" event within the futuristic world of *Out*. It is, however, only as real as many of the other scenes in the novel – that is, it, too, is in part made up of pieces of text that also appear elsewhere; I already mentioned that some of the questions asked by Dr. Lukulwe, the psychoscopist, are verbatim repetitions of a political opinion poll that had been taken earlier in the text. But some of them are new, such as the question, "Do you love Mrs. Mgulu or Mr. Swaminathan best?" (137), or the final, climactic question, "Will you lay down the white man's burden?", which the protagonist answers with the words, "He is dying. Absolve him . . . That are heavy laden. Take it up, take it up for me . . . Oh, father, doctor, touch me, cure me, oh Mr. Swaminathan, I love you" (140).[18] Even if one takes into account Dr. Lukulwe's remarks concerning "telescoped transference," both questions and answer are peculiar given that Mrs. Mgulu is merely the protagonist's employer and Mr. Swaminathan her majordomo, or perhaps her gardener. The fact that they are being invoked in an analytical session much like a mother and father figure would be suggests that they are perhaps mainly or exclusively figures in the protagonist's mind rather than actual characters. Rather than pointing to any psychological reality, psychoscopy turns out to foreground some of the unrealities that structure the rest of the text.

The text gives abundant evidence to bear this hypothesis out. Mr. Swaminathan is regularly described as "indwelling" and as "sharing the observation of phenomena" in the protagonist's mind (106–07, 116, 117, 122; see also 161), and the same formula is at times applied to Mrs. Mgulu (161, 184). In one scene, Mrs. Mgulu's limousine glides by "[i]nside the avenue of the mind that functions in depth" (51, 160), and in another, Mr. Swaminathan stands on the steps of a gazebo "inside the mind" (85), swaying from one foot to the other as is his usual habit. Some scenes are even more obviously fantastic: for example, when the protagonist sees or imagines Mrs. Mgulu walking along the dusty road with him in golden sandals, and he complains to her

[18] The elision marks are part of the original text.

that Mr. Swaminathan inside him spies on him and watches him desire her. She reassures him that Mr. Swaminathan has now disappeared because "I shall always be with you, talking to you and sharing your observation of phenomena, until you die, because that is the way you want it, and I am your dark reality" (161). If Mrs. Mgulu and Mr. Swaminathan seemed like reasonably plausible characters at the beginning of the plot given its social and political premises, it becomes gradually clearer that they may be only figures for certain psychological functions in the protagonist's mind: Mrs. Mgulu with her madonna-like face, who first rescues the protagonist after he has fainted in a bathroom of "pink veined marble" with a sunken bath that suggests a womb, is obviously a mother figure to her employees, trying to alleviate their misery where she can. Mr. Swaminathan, by contrast, incarnating the stern, vigilant father figure who controls access to Mrs. Mgulu, patiently explains to the protagonist why it is impossible for the Colored to love the Colorless, and refuses him even the paternal nod that would at least confirm his inferior existence. Mrs. Mgulu and Mr. Swaminathan, therefore, lead an ambiguous existence in the text: at times, they seem to be characters who exist independently of the protagonist, but at others, they appear to function principally as substitute parent figures in his imagination. If Mrs. Ned confesses that she first met her father "in the usual circumstances, as a transference" (119), it is equally unsurprising that the protagonist should turn his superiors and racial Others into parent figures with whom he enacts, perhaps mentally, perhaps in reality, elaborate scenarios of acceptance and rejection. In a world in which biological parents have been swept aside along with the past, figures from the present replace them through transferential substitution. Transference precedes the encounter with the parent: effects precede their cause, and turn into simulations of causes.

Mr. Swaminathan, in this scenario, comes to embody the ambiguity, skepticism and denial that create an atmosphere of uncertainty and unreality in the protagonist's surroundings. Persistently and ominously swaying from one foot to the other, Mr. Swaminathan hides his opinions behind cryptic remarks that leave the protagonist wondering desperately what they might mean. When he is questioned by the opinion pollsters, Mr. Swaminathan skillfully misleads them through phrases which seem to imply criticism of the government, only to deny any such criticism when he is asked directly. The protagonist also attempts to call him on some of these phrases; in response, he is simply told not to believe everything he hears on the street. But Swaminathan not only hides his own identity behind ambiguities and evasions, he also denies the protagonist his. When the latter first presents himself for his job interview, Mr. Swaminathan puts his identity in doubt even though he admits in the same breath that he recognizes him from Lilly's description. And up until the end he does not nod to acknowledge his existence although the protagonist repeatedly asks him to do so, complaining that "[t]his swaying of yours, you see, it's such a negative sort of gesture" (102). But according to Swaminathan, "to deny is the only true human power, rather than free will. . . . The reflected image of any object or notion depends on our acceptance, but we can efface it in a thought. Thus the power of negation determines the faculty of reasoning" (78–79). Swaminathan therefore embodies everything that denies the protagonist a place in society, that "displaces" him from any permanent and secure position either socially or epistemologically.

Mr. Swaminathan dominates the protagonist's imagination in the second part of the novel, while he works as an odd-job man at Mrs. Mgulu's house. But in the third part, after the psychoscopy, Mr. Swaminathan fades away: he is first declared to have left the Mgulu estate, and later a gardener unknown to the protagonist tells him that his predecessor has died.[19] Given these indications, the protagonist's exclamation, "He is dying" (140) at the climactic moment of his psychoscopy may well refer to Mr. Swaminathan, especially since the protagonist has been repeating throughout the session much of what he had heard from him. Instead of Mr. Swaminathan, the protagonist's fantasies afterwards revolve around his employer, the beautiful Mrs. Mgulu. As I already indicated, she is in some ways clearly meant to function as the opposite of her Managing Agent. She seems genuinely attached to her servants, especially Lilly, her former nanny, and is sincerely concerned to secure a job for Lilly's husband through repeated phone calls and letters to the Labor Exchange officials.

[19] This scene is also an almost identical replay of the scene in Part 1 in which the protagonist first presented himself at Mrs. Mgulu's house, so that Mr. Swaminathan appears never to have existed, except in the protagonist's fantasies.

When Lilly falls ill with the radiation disease, she offers her own blood for a transfusion, although blood transfers between the races are illegal; she takes care of the protagonist after his fall, and sends him in for psychiatric treatment when she fears he may be mentally disturbed. She converts her flower garden into a vegetable field to help end the famine, and gives a charitable ball – all apparently signs that she does what she can to provide for those in her care. Yet with all her philanthropic rhetoric and gestures, Denise Mgulu never once admits that the society she lives in might be unjust, but staunchly maintains that it is pluralist and egalitarian. Quite the "lady of the manor," as Joan Dkimba calls her with a touch of condescension, she treats her white servants well, but will not admit them as personal attendants who might come in touch with her body. Her beauty and luxurious attire – silk dresses, gold sandals and exotic jewelry – mentioned time and time again, reinforce the contrast with her impoverished domestics.

It is difficult to say how much of Mrs. Mgulu's kindness and beauty is real and how much fantasy, especially since it remains unclear whether and how often the protagonist has actually seen her; many of his fantasies may simply be kindled by Lilly's descriptions. That she passes him in her limousine may be a plausible scenario; one may doubt whether she does in fact appear in the pink bathroom just when he regains consciousness after his fall; and by the time she is described as walking along the dusty road in gold sandals just to accompany the protagonist, she definitely has turned into an unreal fairy figure. The protagonist's thoughts themselves confirm this, such as when he refers to "[t]he absolute knowledge that Mrs. Mgulu writes no notes and walks along no highway and does not nod" (163–64), or to "the heavy knowledge that Mrs. Mgulu has not nodded, nor appeared, nor given the slightest proof of her objective existence" (184). Thus, the more Mrs. Mgulu appears opposed to Mr. Swaminathan's skepticism and denial, and the more her words and actions seem to affirm the protagonist's identity and position, the more fantastic she herself becomes.

Both Mrs. Mgulu and Mr. Swaminathan, then, function on one hand as representatives of the new social and racial order, but on the other hand as sites of transference for the protagonist, (perhaps) imaginary instances of authority who "share the observation of phenomena" with him and thereby authenticate not only the accuracy of his observations, but also his very existence as an observer. The second function, however, is dependent on the first one: to be plausible witnesses to the protagonist and his perceptions, they must be authority figures independent of him. In this role, however, Mr. Swaminathan categorically denies any sort of confirmation to the protagonist, and Mrs. Mgulu becomes more and more implausible the more motherly reinforcement she lavishes on him. The complex narrative play with these two figures therefore leaves us in doubt as to the novel's focal character: if they "really" exist, he may well not exist at all; if they do not, or only in his mind, they cannot serve to confirm that he relates to his surroundings the way he claims to, and that he is indeed who he seems to be. In other words, they form part of a self-referential loop through which the protagonist, in the guise of what appears to be something like psychoanalytical transference, generates himself as the observing instance of the world he lives in. Observation generates the observer as a symptom of itself: this, ultimately, is the implication of *Out*'s medical principle that "diagnosis prognosticates aetiology."

4. The secret that is not a story

Narrative in *Out*, as we have seen, develops as a displacement of effects, rather than as a movement from cause to effect. In this constantly shifting universe, the protagonist himself seems to have no place: designated "Colorless" in a world that bursts with brilliant colors at every step, he is also stricken with an "inaudible voice" in a "condition of chronic aphonia" (89). Whirled along in a stream of words and perceptions, he occasionally attempts to go beyond the contingency that surrounds him and to discover a logic or rationale that would allow him to situate himself in his universe and to find a voice of his own. We already saw that after his psychoscopy, he asks the doctor, "Is there a secret? . . . I mean, what is the answer?" The doctor responds, "The answer's in biochemistry, of course," and hands him a prescription for drugs (140), a reaction that is quite in keeping with *Out*'s general emphasis on ultimate causes as belonging to the realm of the microscopic and phenomena at the human scale as contingent.[20]

But more importantly, it is the protagonist's transferential father, Mr. Swaminathan, who is called upon repeatedly to answer the pressing question of ultimate meaning. In a scene which amalgamates the protagonist's memory of the pollster's interview of Mr. Swaminathan in the street with his own desire for an answer, Mr. Swaminathan claims that such an answer cannot be articulated in narrative form:

– Tell me Mr. Swaminathan, will you be voting for history or for progress?
– There is no such thing as history, except in the privacy of concupiscence. That is an article of faith. Memory is a primitive organ in the left hemisphere of the brain, inscribed with sensory observations, which are reflected by the right hemisphere as the moon reflects the sun. But that's another story.
– So you will be voting for progress?
– There is no such thing as progress. There is only the Moment of Truth.
– Mr. Swaminathan help me. Is there a secret? A story behind the story?
– There is a secret. But it is not a story. (91)

In his refusal to opt for anything like either history or progress, Mr. Swaminathan confirms the irrelevance of temporal progression for the world he and the protagonist live in; and since neither past nor future can be envisioned, the only time that matters is the present, the "Moment of Truth," as he phrases it. In this Moment, all other temporal dimensions co-exist simultaneously. Sensory perception, which usually conveys the greatest sense of immediacy, amalgamates past and present, according to Mr. Swaminathan, since it originates from the impact of external circumstance as well as from the reflection of memories layered in the brain: any shape, sound or color we perceive can only be registered as such because we already have an experience of similar sensory impressions. Any observation, then, mixes the immediate with the already-experienced in an inextricable simultaneity. This underlying simultaneity of all temporal moments is the secret that cannot be phrased in a story, since a story requires

[20] Clearly, though, this scene is also meant as a critique of the depersonalized and dehumanized way in which medicine is practiced in the type of society *Out* describes.

sequence, and sequence is that which can no longer be thought in the framework outlined by Mr. Swaminathan.

Mr. Swaminathan articulates this denial of narrative possibilities again in a similar conversation which the protagonist holds, or perhaps imagines he holds, with him while he is working in Mrs. Mgulu's house:

– But Mr. Swaminathan, you did say, didn't you, that denial is the only true human power, rather than free will, and that negation is the shadow self which permits man to find unity?
– Well that's another story.
– But is there a story behind the story?
– That's a very good question. I congratulate you on having avoided the trap.
During the hammering, the conversation is one-sided. Highly intelligent questions pertinent to the conversation are posed with a rush of ease, but remain essentially unanswered, for the imagination has not sufficiently identified to compose exactly the same answers as those composed by an alien set of neural cells. This proves that the unhammered conversation has been real since unimaginable replies occurred, though difficult to reconstruct, and fading fast. (103)

Constantly plagued with doubts as to the reality of what he sees and hears, the protagonist here turns the very vagueness of his perceptions into proof of their existence; since he himself would never answer his own questions as ambiguously as Mr. Swaminathan does, it must mean that Mr. Swaminathan's replies did indeed occur independently of his own imagination – although in fact these replies are already beginning to slip his memory. This train of thought not only enacts exactly the principle of negative reasoning as the only guarantee for the subject's unity as Mr. Swaminathan had formulated it; it also foregrounds the constant slippage between self and other, and here specifically between present observation and half-remembered perception, that makes up the protagonist's universe: he himself is never entirely sure whether he actually hears Mr. Swaminathan speak, whether he is merely recalling sentences he heard him say on another occasion or what, really, these words are or were. The same slippage affects not only the form of many conversations in *Out*, but also their content. None of what Mr. Swaminathan is here purported to say really answers any of the protagonist's questions: Mr. Swaminathan neither confirms nor denies that he did indeed say what the protagonist repeats to him, and he completely evades the question of meaning that informs the urgent request for "the story behind the story." As the form of this request already indicates, Mr. Swaminathan's utterances always prompt further deferral of meaning and continued displacement.

This displacement lasts until the last pages of the novel and in fact concludes its text, since the last words refer again to a different story that might or might not be told. The protagonist is back in Mrs. Mgulu's garden, burning leaves and sprinkling the grass around it with a hose to prevent the fire from spreading:

> The fire leaps up bright orange, with a yellow shower, circles of red, oh, close your eyes, relax but grip the instrument and hold it up, well up, let it gush forth from the deep sphere of our being and reach up for the sky before it turns to spray its dust over the fire that crackles, leaps up bright orange, open your eyes . . . under the eyelids a gold triangle, a yellow shower, circles of orange and the head goes leaden, grey in a hundred and sixty microseconds, three million two hundred and thirty one thousand six hundred and forty two years one hundred and seventy three days point nine. And a billion more besides. We are merely marking time and time is nothing, nothing. A moment of agony, of burning flesh, an aspect of the human element disintegrating to ash, and you are dead. But that's another story. (198)

At first sight, the final words seem to be a meditation on the transience of human life not unlike those one finds in biblical psalms or *Ecclesiastes*.[21] But something more is at stake here. The leaf fire which turns into the protagonist's self-image repeats, as I pointed out earlier, a vision which surged up in him at the climactic moment of his psychoscopy, so that even at that point his own disintegration did not really lie in the future, but was and is woven into the temporal texture of his self-awareness at any moment. In the protagonist's mind, disparate time scales from the microscopic (microseconds) to the human (days) and the cosmological (millions of years) co-exist and annihilate each other, making the concept of time itself meaningless. But if "time is nothing, nothing," beginnings and endings also disappear; we already saw to what extent *Out* problematizes the notion of beginnings by foregrounding that a beginning, in order to be

[21] Richard Martin comments on the "hopelessness and gloom" which he finds expressed in this ending, and compares it to the pessimism of many Beckett texts ("'Just Words on a Page'," 43).

perceptible as such, needs to be envisioned in terms of a later development that at the same time obliterates it. This last paragraph of the novel emphasizes in addition the impossibility of perceiving endings: the protagonist is unable to witness his own disintegration since this would imply that he could survive his own ending in the "other story" that the last sentence hints at. Unlike *Gravity's Rainbow*, in which the reader saw Tyrone Slothrop get scattered over the post-War zone, disintegration can only be alluded to, but not included in the kind of temporality *Out* proposes. Anything as terminal as entropic dispersal would run counter to the very nature of the story *Out* tells, which is designed to exclude historical beginnings and endings at a personal as well as global scale. "[A]n aspect of the human element disintegrating to ash" is a formulation that perhaps still fits into the narrative discourse of *Out* since it assimilates the death of a human being to that of a cell in a larger organism which continues to live, but "you are dead" would quite definitely be "another story."

Like *Gravity's Rainbow*, then, *Out* explores a scenario of posthistory and its implications for knowledge, narrative and politics. Both novels use inversions of cause and effect as a central structural and thematic element so as to demonstrate the difficulties of reasoning and storytelling in the absence of historical time. But the systematic deployment of causal paradox does not lead to the same ideological and narrative consequences in the two cases. In *Gravity's Rainbow*, both the implications of the plot and the possibilities for political resistance remain indeterminate; since none of the characters can ascertain whether events are planned in advance and causally related or mere strings of coincidences, they oscillate between paranoid beliefs in the world's coherence and feelings of utter randomness. Readers, to the extent that they attempt to construe the novel as a gradually unfolding, coherent story, must ask whether the causal links they impose upon the text are as paranoid in their structure as those some of the characters discover, and whether an interpretation that leaves greater room to contingency might not be more appropriate. Through its structural indeterminacies, *Gravity's Rainbow* therefore forces characters as well as readers always to entertain at least two alternative and radically different interpretations of events side by side, without any way of deciding which provides the more adequate construction. In *Out*, causal paradox leads to a different type of indeterminacy. The political power structure and the existence of a conspiracy if not against the protagonist, then at any rate against his race in general, is not in question, but manifests itself beyond any possibility of doubt in all the major social institutions.[22] What is in doubt, however, is the daily life of the protagonist: which version of the interview with Mrs. Mgulu's gardener really took place? How many of his conversations with Mr. Swaminathan and encounters with Mrs. Mgulu actually occurred? Did he have an affair with Mrs. Ned? Was he psychoscoped at the hospital? Did Lilly come down with the radiation disease or not? The text offers some of these episodes in several alternative versions, and in other cases leaves open whether they are actual occurrences or the protagonist's fantasies. As Brian McHale points out, matters are complicated even more by the fact that the world of *Out*, even in its most realist dimension, is a futuristic one that the reader cannot judge by everyday standards of verisimilitude, so that the boundary between fact and imagination becomes even harder to draw.[23] Therefore, whereas in *Gravity's Rainbow* the profusion of facts and details precludes insights into the overall political power structure, *Out* presents a world in which the general power distribution is all too clear, but it is precisely the relentless exercise of political power by one particular group that destabilizes everyday reality for the dominated group – as well as, by extension, for the reader, who is given access only to the perspective of the underprivileged.

Through its particular deployment of causal paradox, each of the two novels assigns a different task to the reader. In *Gravity's Rainbow*, the readers must decide how to combine a wide and often contradictory variety of facts and episodes into a coherent whole; in *Out*, their major task is to select one version of events over others so as to identify a plot.[24] Since both texts system-

---

[22] Birch observes that "*Out* may be read as a dystopic version of a 'global village' in which the technology that 'wraps the earth' has disambiguated and simplified life for the privileged, who then use the founding truth of their colonial system as a weapon against the underprivileged" (*Christine Brooke-Rose*, 62).

[23] " 'I draw the line'," 194.

[24] This difference could obviously be elaborated in Jakobsonian terms such as syntagma/paradigm or metonymy/metaphor, but such an elaboration is not of crucial interest for the analysis proposed here.

atically preclude the emergence of a coherent fictional world, neither task can be accomplished without contradictions and ambiguities. Both novels therefore ultimately leave the reader facing several alternative and incompatible fictional universes in a socio-political wasteland that has come unhinged from past and future. But the evaluation of this state of affairs differs somewhat in the two cases. The loss of history in the world of *Gravity's Rainbow* is something that has simply come about, that befalls characters who have to live through the consequences, but cannot penetrate the causes of their own inability to relate to the past and plan for the future. The existence of an evil corporate network as the prime agent of history remains unconfirmed, but even if such a cartel were shown to exist, it is unclear whether the disruption of temporality that manifests itself at every level of social and cultural life in the novel is one of its goals or merely a side-effect of its manipulations. As a consequence, *Gravity's Rainbow* leaves open the possibility that the posthistorical "zone" it describes might turn into a site from which new forms of temporal reasoning and human agency can emerge, although this possibility remains admittedly undefined. No such emergence, however, seems conceivable in *Out*, where the weakening of historical thought is not a more or less random development, but a carefully planned strategy on the part of the privileged to keep other groups away from access to power. "Diagnosis prognosticates aetiology" is a slogan designed to benefit the ruling elite and to facilitate its projects of political, social and racial oppression; it does not leave any room for creative anarchy or improvised rebellion, as the aftermath of the war does in Pynchon's novel. The perspectives *Gravity's Rainbow* and *Out* take on the temporal disruptions they describe, then, to some extent resemble the theoretical approaches to the idea of posthistory that I discussed in Chapter 1. Whereas some poststructuralist theorists see the demise of historical thinking as a liberation from a philosophical tradition with oppressive tendencies, a possibility at least adumbrated in *Gravity's Rainbow*, Marxist theorists tend to associate it with a hugely diminished potential for political language and action, a view that is confirmed by the scenario presented in *Out*.

But obviously, *Gravity's Rainbow* is far from celebrating posthistory, and *Out* equally far from advocating a return to historical thinking. Like all of the other novels I have analyzed, *Gravity's Rainbow* and *Out* represent the loss of history in by and large pessimistic terms, although both texts are at the same time clearly fascinated with its consequences and the possibilities it opens up for innovating language, narrative and culture. These possibilities are explored further, and considered from a much more optimistic perspective, in a novel that I will consider in the epilogue by way of concluding my discussion: Bruce Sterling's science-fiction novel *Schismatrix* indicates by its very title that its major aim is to outline a vision of the future that overcomes the chronoschisms of posthistory.

+++

Epilogue: *Schismatrix*

+++

Bruce Sterling's *Schismatrix*, a cyberpunk novel first published in 1985, continues the exploration of alternative temporalities that underlies the narrative structure of many metafictional texts in the 1960s and 70s. But it does so in a very different vein that can no longer be considered properly posthistorical, since *Schismatrix* proposes the end of a particular history of mankind only to suggest the beginning of a new and qualitatively different type of historical development. Like *Out*, Sterling's novel projects mankind into the future and describes it as irreparably split into hostile groups; but unlike *Out*, this division does not lead to the oppression and exploitation of one group by another, but to the emergence of alternative human varieties that branch off from the mother species in an evolutionary leap that opens mankind up to a potential infinitude of future histories. This genetic and temporal split, which Sterling places into the scientific context of Ilya Prigogine's theory of non-linear dynamics, is celebrated with a futurist euphoria that fundamentally distinguishes *Schismatrix* from the more pessimistic assessments of the end of history in mainstream metafiction.

Sterling's novel focuses on a period of the future in which mankind has come under extreme forms of internal and external pressure in its development. Humans have long populated the solar system, leaving only an insignificant and retrograde civilization behind on the planet Earth. But solar mankind is deeply divided between two philosophies and ways of life that cause constant diplomatic and military confrontations between their adherents, the Shapers and the Mechanists. The Shapers have perfected genetic engineering and procreate through "gene lines," family clans that produce carefully planned and designed individuals who are adjusted further through systematic psychological training. Older Shapers, in addition, periodically undergo rejuvenation procedures which allow them to reach extreme old age. Mechanists, on the other hand, do not practice genetic planning, but rely on the fusion of the human body with mechanical and electronic technologies; through this "cyborgization," they, too, have extended the human life span considerably, but they refuse to alter body and mind as radically as the Shapers do. The ongoing conflict between the two camps is disrupted by the arrival of an alien species, the Investors, who are in contact with more than a dozen other foreign civilizations and thereby open up a completely new field of connections for humans, at the same time that unexpected external pressures begin to bear down on mankind. Hostilities between the Shapers and the Mechanists flare up again after a few decades of tenuous peace, however, and more and more subdivisions and factions begin to emerge in both populations.

Some of these newly emerging groups adhere to the theory that human life in its biological as well as social aspects develops according to levels of "Prigoginic complexity," a hypothesis that becomes standard knowledge in all of the sciences in another half-century. Proponents of the new theory argue that a species develops up to a certain point until it breaks up into different subspecies or "clades," which then follow their own evolution. This new "Posthumanist" philosophy of life transcends older divisions and leads to a new ambition among the young: the colonization of new habitats for humankind. One of these projects is presented in some detail at the end of the novel: a group of friends and relatives of the protagonist, Abelard Lindsay, decides to rebuild the Saturnian moon Europa ecologically and to convert itself through genetic engineering into the new species of "aquatic posthuman[s]" that will inhabit it:[1] with sleek black skin, gills, flukes instead of legs and flickering phosphorescent patches along the arms to communicate with visually, these new humans do not have much in common with their ancestors. The ending of *Schismatrix* suggests that they are only one of a variety of different types of posthumans that will emerge from mankind's historical crisis: the human future lies in a multitude of ever more rapidly diverging

---

[1] Bruce Sterling, *Schismatrix* (New York: Ace, 1986), 282. All future page references to the novel will be given parenthetically and refer to this edition.

Epilogue

subspecies that does away with the notion of linear and predictable historical development.

These splits in human history are impossible to predict because
major changes, such as the emergence of a new subspecies, can be
triggered by very minor causes once mankind and its environment
have been thrown off their normal balance. *Schismatrix* emphasizes
from the beginning that human society has reached an extreme
degree of instability. Although humans are dispersed all over the
solar system, they do not for the most part inhabit other planets,
but artificially created habitats which seem always prone to
ecological malfunctioning or collapse.[2] Their tenuous existence is
further threatened through political intrigue, espionage, sabotage
and military clashes between the Shapers and the Mechanists.
Even though the Investors' arrival temporarily alleviates these
pressures, it adds the strain of interaction with and adjustment to a
whole series of completely dissimilar species and civilizations. By
the end of the novel, the general disequilibrium has reached the
point where, on the basis of advanced knowledge in biological and
ecological engineering, personal rivalries, petty enmities and
minor political crises of a purely contingent sort can suddenly turn
into evolutionary branching-off points that lead to the formation of
new posthuman species. Lindsay's clique, for example, is brought
under intense political pressure through an act of treachery on the
part of one of its members, and therefore decides to leave its world
behind and colonize Europa. Schisms produce new matrices: no
longer subject only to the mechanisms of Darwinian evolution,
posthumanity in its multifarious shapes emerges explosively from
a moment of extreme instability in the history of the species.

Sterling conceived this type of historical development in
analogy to chemist Ilya Prigogine's theory of "dissipative structures," which is explicitly foregrounded in the novel. On the basis
of real but extremely limited evidence for the spontaneous self-
organization of complex patterns in certain chemical substances,
Prigogine proposed a theory to account for the behavior of
dynamical systems that won him the Nobel Prize in 1977.[3] While

[2] See Tom Shippey, "Semiotic Ghosts and Ghostliness in the Work of Bruce
Sterling," *Fiction 2000: Cyberpunk and the Future of Narrative*, ed. George Slusser
and Tom Shippey (Athens: University of Georgia Press, 1992), 218.
[3] Katherine Hayles gives a very clear account of non-linear dynamics, and of the
differences between Prigogine's branch of chaos theory and that of fractal

258

a system is in a state of equilibrium or near-equilibrium, Prigogine argues, it behaves deterministically; that is, its behavior can be predicted by applying the known laws of nature. But when it moves far away from equilibrium, its evolution can become haphazard and unpredictable; by accident, unforeseen changes can occur which introduce greater complexity into the system and thereby propel it to a higher level of internal organization. At these moments of disequilibrium, events may occur which seem to contradict the second law of thermodynamics: entropy may not increase but decrease, and new forms of order and complexity may emerge. The second law of thermodynamics, according to Prigogine, is not therefore invalid; rather, its validity is restricted to those phases during which a system is in or near a state of equilibrium. In his book *Order out of Chaos: Man's New Dialogue with Nature*, Prigogine used these findings in chemical substances to draw very far-reaching philosophical conclusions.[4] His theory, he claims, reconciles determinism and chance, causality and coincidence in the description of both natural and man-made dynamic systems, and thereby resolves the long-standing philosophical conflict between Being and Becoming. It is perhaps not surprising that these sweeping philosophical conclusions from very specialized research in chemistry have been challenged by other scientists, but the fact that Prigogine felt compelled to extrapolate a general theory of time from his findings is yet another example of the cross-disciplinary sense that conventional notions of temporality are in need of reformulation in the late twentieth century. No matter how valid or valuable Prigogine's argument may be for the analysis of natural or social phenomena in general, it provides the philosophical underpinning of Ster-

geometry in *Chaos Bound: Orderly Disorder in Contemporary Literature and Science* (Ithaca: Cornell University Press, 1990), 9–15. In general, my understanding of chaos theory as deployed in *Schismatrix* is much indebted to Hayles' lucid exposition of its scientific groundwork in both *Chaos Bound* and *Chaos and Order: Complex Dynamics in Literature and Science*, ed. N. Katherine Hayles (Chicago: University of Chicago Press, 1991), 1–19.

[4] Ilya Prigogine and Isabelle Stengers, *Order out of Chaos: Man's New Dialogue with Nature* (Toronto: Bantam, 1984). Katherine Hayles discusses the speculative nature of much of Prigogine and Stengers' discussion and observes that "this book is not . . . simply a popularized version of the new sciences. Rather, it is an ambitious synthesis that goes well beyond what many scientists working in chaos theory would be willing to grant are legitimate inferences from their work" (*Chaos Bound*, 91).

ling's novel, where it is applied to the future of mankind in an attempt to work out the consequences of a "posthistorical moment." As the novel shows, the species *homo sapiens*, brought to a stage of extreme instability through internal rifts, external pressure and the lack of suitable habitats, enters a phase of non-linear, coincidental changes from which it emerges at a higher level of complexity. The title itself indicates this transition of the system to a higher level of complexity out of a state of disequilibrium.[5]

As in most of the texts I examined earlier, the loss of causality and the multiplicity of possibilities that such a transition opens up can appear profoundly unsettling to those who are caught up in it against their will; some groups in *Schismatrix* react to the vertiginous potential of their historical situation with frenzied self-destruction, withdrawal into drug-induced calm, or general unease:

> . . . the strain was everywhere. The new multiple humanities hurtled blindly toward their unknown destinations, and the vertigo of accelera-tion struck deep. Old preconceptions were in tatters, old loyalties were obsolete. Whole societies were paralyzed by the mind-blasting vistas of absolute possibility. (238)

The narrator as well as Abelard Lindsay, the protagonist, however, embrace change. If mankind leaps into a completely new dimension of complexity, Lindsay personally undergoes a similar "phase change" into a different order of being at the very end of the novel. Rejecting the invitation of his friends and relatives to join the posthuman community on Europa, he decides instead to join an alien of an as yet unidentified species who has no visible body and is therefore referred to simply as "the Presence." As the alien Presence transforms him to its own mode

---

[5] One may wonder, however, whether the insistently foregrounded references to Prigogine really indicate the only source of the novel's philosophical structure. Another text that might provide some of its background is Jacques Monod's *Chance and Necessity: An Essay on the Natural Philosophy of Modern Biology*, trans. Austryn Wainhouse (New York: Knopf, 1971), an essay on biology which heavily stresses the role of coincidence even in Darwinian evolution. "We would like to think ourselves necessary, inevitable, ordained from all eternity. All religions, nearly all philosophies, and even a part of science testify to the unwearying, heroic effort of mankind desperately denying its own contin-gency," Monod argues (44). Causally structured, teleological narrative could certainly be thought of as such another instrument for the denial of contingency, and works like *Schismatrix* as attempts to break with this project.

of being, Lindsay leaves his body behind, a transmutation that is celebrated in almost naïvely optimistic terms in the last scene of the novel:

Lindsay perceived his new self. "I don't have any hands," he said.
"You won't need 'em." The Presence laughed. "C'mon, we'll follow [the Investors]. They'll be going someplace soon."
They trailed the Investor down the hall. "Where?" Lindsay said.
"It doesn't matter. Somewhere wonderful." (288)

Lindsay's personal history at this point splits off from that of even his closest friends and family, the new aquatic Europans, into yet another posthuman mode of existence of which he, at least as far as former humans go, is the only representative. The ending of *Schismatrix* celebrates the infinite variety of such arbitrary and random emergences in euphoric terms. Indeed, what the alien Presence Lindsay joins stands for, more than anything, is the very principle of change, and the rejection of absolute values and final answers that are not subject to further development. When Lindsay questions it about its values and goals, the Presence replies:

"My answers? I don't have 'em. I don't care what goes on beneath this skin, I want only to see, only to feel. Origins and destinies, predictions and memories, lives and deaths, I sidestep those. I'm too slick for time to grip [. . .] I want what I already have! Eternal wonder, eternally fulfilled. . . . Not the eternal, even, just the Indefinite, that's where all beauty is. . . . I'll wait out the heat-death of the Universe to see what happens next!" (287)[6]

Lindsay's transmutation, carried out by this being "too slick for time to grip," parallels one of the crucial scenes of Barth's "Menelaiad," which I discussed in Chapter 1: Proteus, whom Menelaus attempts to hold on to in spite of his prodigious abilities for metamorphosis, finally converts himself into Menelaus holding Proteus, locking both characters into a moment of self-referentiality without escape; Menelaus, as a consequence, turns into a mere voice repeating its story forever. But the differences between the two scenes are as striking as this correspondence: whereas in Barth, the presence of Proteus signals the necessary self-referentiality of a historical moment in which all

---

[6] Only the elision marks in square brackets are mine; the others form part of the original text.

metamorphoses have been accomplished and all stories told, the Protean Presence of Sterling's *Schismatrix* on the contrary opens up the moment to a variety and randomness of developments ("'Where?' . . . 'It doesn't matter'") that is envisioned with unqualified optimism ("'Somewhere wonderful'"). If post-modernist time is structured like a maze or "garden of forking paths," in Borges' metaphor, Barth's text describes a finite labyrinth and emphasizes the repetitions it imposes upon the writer and reader, whereas Sterling's novel views it as an infinite maze offering unlimited possibilities: "Futility, and freedom, were Absolute" [*sic*], the narrator affirms (273).[7]

Schismatrix differs not only from Barth's short story but from the other texts I have discussed in yet another respect. The alternative temporalities it describes are not really incompatible with each other in the way they are in Beckett's, Robbe-Grillet's or Pynchon's texts; there is nothing temporally paradoxical about the fact that some humans would convert into fish-like sea-dwellers and others into bodiless consciousnesses, since these possibilities can logically co-exist in time. *Schismatrix* does not carry temporal fracturing so far as to affirm, for example, that Abelard Lindsay transmutes into an alien presence and, in another segment, that he joins the new Europans, a combination that would correspond in its structure to those I analyzed in earlier chapters; in other words, it does not translate the time schisms it celebrates into the narrative architecture itself. By preserving a logical framework within which different histories unfold without contradicting each other, *Schismatrix* is able to emphasize the productive potential of these divisions rather than those more disturbing epistemological and ontological implica-

[7] In "The Frankenstein Barrier," *Fiction 2000: Cyberpunk and the Future of Narrative* (Athens: University of Georgia Press, 1992), George Slusser offers a different interpretation of the last scene in *Schismatrix*, arguing that the "aquatic posthumans" in Lindsay's clique symbolize mankind's cyclical return to its evolutionary beginnings in the ocean (70). This reading overlooks that the Europan sea-dwellers are only one of many posthuman species emerging from a wide range of "Terra-forming" projects (see *Schismatrix*, 280), which implies that time for mankind as a whole is neither linear nor circular but "dissipative," in Prigogine's sense of the term. Veronica Hollinger's essay "Cybernetic Deconstructions: Cyberpunk and Postmodernism," *Storming the Reality Studio: A Casebook of Cyberpunk and Postmodern Fiction*, ed. Larry McCaffery (Durham, NC: Duke University Press, 1991), which points out the extent to which *Schismatrix* emphasizes the arbitrariness of the future and the difference between past and future mankind, is closer to the analysis proposed here (208–09).

tions that many metafictional novels are primarily concerned
with.

The achievement of *Schismatrix* for the purposes of the argument that I have made throughout *Chronoschisms* is that it outlines an understanding of time, derived from a particular type of
scientific philosophy, which combines contingency and causation
without privileging causal connections, so that both continuities
and ruptures are assigned crucial roles in the texture of time. One
may regret that the novel does not propose a narrative mode to
match the complexity of its temporal philosophy, perhaps by
combining random moments and storytelling procedures with
stretches of more traditionally and causally structured narrative.[8]
But it does create a fictional universe in which neither the loss of
history due to mankind's unpredictable evolutionary leaps, nor
the discrepancy between the human time scale and that of
macroscopic or microscopic developments is experienced with
resignation or paranoia by the major characters. *Schismatrix*
thereby takes a significant step beyond the metafictional postmodernism of avant-garde narrative in the 1960s and 70s, and it
is conceivable and indeed likely that other texts will more
successfully translate this or similar temporal philosophies into
narrative form. Tom Stoppard's recent *Arcadia* provides an
example of how an innovative theory of time – in this case,
inspired by non-linear dynamics just as Sterling's novel – can
shape the architecture of a play. Whatever the usefulness of
Prigogine's brand of chaos theory may be in the context of the
natural sciences, it provides a challenging point of departure for
the innovation of narrative form when it is deployed in literature.

The interest of *Schismatrix*, however, lies not only in the
impulses it might give for the reconceptualization of narrative
structure, but in its reflection on the function of time in the late
twentieth century. As Fredric Jameson points out, the goal of

---

[8] Science fiction as the genre to which *Schismatrix* belongs may contribute to the
difficulty of developing such an innovative narrative mode, since the genre
usually relies on straightforwardly realist methods of presentation (Brooke-
Rose's *Out* is one of the few exceptions to this rule). For a discussion of realism
and science fiction, see Christine Brooke-Rose, "Science Fiction and Realistic
Fiction," *A Rhetoric of the Unreal: Studies in Narrative and Structure, Especially of
the Fantastic* (Cambridge: Cambridge University Press, 1981), 72–102; on inter-
relations between the postmodernist novel and science fiction, see Brian
McHale, "POSTcyberMODERNpunkISM," *Constructing Postmodernism* (London:
Routledge, 1992), 225–42.

Epilogue

science fiction is in the final analysis "not to give us 'images' of
the future . . . but rather to defamiliarize and restructure our
experience of our own *present*."⁹ Viewed from this perspective,
mankind's splintering into multiple subspecies as described in
Schismatrix can be understood as a reflection not only on the
implications of posthistory, but also on the multiplication of
histories that I discussed briefly in Chapter 1 as the obverse side
of the posthistorical. Even as some artists, writers and intellectuals in the 1970s, 80s and 90s explore what an "end of history"
might imply, many other writers and scholars dedicate themselves to publicizing those histories of individuals and groups
that had been ignored or repressed by the mainstream. Both
developments, as I mentioned, form part of the move away from
those nineteenth-century philosophies that conceived of history
as a linear, progressive and unified movement. Sterling's scientific philosophy logically develops the posthistorical time concept
that underlies the texts from the 1960s and 70s I analyzed earlier,
even as his re-engineered posthumans in their potentially infinite
variety stand as a compelling metaphor for the immensely
diversified construction of human histories in the late twentieth
century.

Much of the fiction that has been published in the 1980s and
90s, at least as far as the North American literary scene is
concerned, has participated in the construction of these alternative histories, and it is probably fair to say that the avant-gardist
impulse which energized various forms of metafiction in the
1960s and 70s has now passed on to narrative that is by and large
more engaged in the telling than in the questioning of such
histories. Some of these more recent texts successfully integrate
their historical projects with postmodernist strategies of storytelling, but many have reverted not only to modernist but even to
straightforwardly realist forms of narration. Considering that
these various histories are not necessarily compatible with each
other, one might argue that the alternative temporal universes
that vie with each other in postmodernist novels have now
migrated from the individual text to narrative literature as a
genre; the readers, in this view, are still confronted with a

⁹ "Progress versus Utopia; or, Can We Imagine the Future?" *Science Fiction Studies*
9 (1982): 151; original emphasis.

264

"garden of forking paths," which now spreads out over a wide variety of novels and historical texts. And even if formal innovations in narrative have not proceeded at the same pace in the last decade as they did in the 1960s and 70s, it may be that this shift away from the reconceptualization of narrative strategies is a temporary phenomenon; as Sterling's novel shows, (chrono)-schisms may give rise to new matrices, but the realist narrative mode of *Schismatrix* itself demonstrates that narrative form may take some time in catching up with innovative theories of time and causation. If the philosophy of time proposed in this novel has any validity, it would be daring to hazard a firm prediction on whether the novel will evolve in this direction in the next millennium. Whatever is left of time will (perhaps) tell.

Bibliography

Abbott, H. Porter. "Beginning Again: The Post-Narrative Art of *Texts for Nothing* and *How It Is*." *The Cambridge Companion to Beckett*, ed. John Pilling. Cambridge: Cambridge University Press, 1994. 106–23.

Adam, Barbara. "Modern Times: The Technology Connection and Its Implications for Social Theory." *Time and Society* 1 (1992): 175–91.

Timewatch: The Social Analysis of Time. Cambridge: Polity Press, 1995.

Alkon, Paul. "Alternate History and Postmodern Temporality." *Time, Literature and the Arts: Essays in Honor of Samuel L. Macey*. Victoria: English Literary Studies, 1994. 65–85.

Anderson, Sherwood. *Winesburg, Ohio*. Ed. John Ferres. New York: Viking, 1966.

Arabian Nights. Trans. Husain Haddawy. New York: Knopf, 1990.

Attridge, Derek, Geoff Bennington and Robert Young, eds. *Post-Structuralism and the Question of History*. Cambridge: Cambridge University Press, 1987.

Austen, Jane. *Emma*. Ed. Stephen M. Parrish. New York: Norton, 1972.

Pride and Prejudice. Ed. Donald J. Gray. New York: Norton, 1966.

Bakhtin, M. M. "Forms of Time and of the Chronotope in the Novel." *The Dialogic Imagination: Four Essays*. Trans. Caryl Emerson and Michael Holquist. Ed. Michael Holquist. Austin: University of Texas Press, 1981. 84–258.

Bal, Mieke. *Narratology: Introduction to the Theory of Narrative*. Trans. Christine van Boheemen. Toronto: University of Toronto Press, 1985.

Barrenechea, Ana María. "La estructura de *Rayuela* de Julio Cortázar." *Nueva novela latinoamericana*. Vol. II: *La narrativa argentina actual*. Ed. Jorge Lafforgue. Buenos Aires: Paidós, n.d. 222–47.

"Los dobles en el proceso de escritura de *Rayuela*." *Revista iberoamericana* 125 (1983): 809–28.

Barrow, John D., and Joseph Silk. *The Left Hand of Creation: The Origin and Evolution of the Expanding Universe*. New York: Basic, 1983.

Barth, John. *Chimera*. New York: Fawcett, 1988.

Lost in the Funhouse: Fiction for Print, Tape, Live Voice. New York: Bantam, 1969.

"The Literature of Exhaustion." *Atlantic Monthly* (August, 1967): 29–34.

"The Literature of Replenishment: Postmodernist Fiction." *Atlantic Monthly* (January, 1980): 65–71.

Barthes, Roland. "An Introduction to the Structural Analysis of Narrative." Trans. Lionel Duisit. *New Literary History* 6 (1975): 237–72.

"Littérature objective." *Essais critiques*. Paris: Seuil, 1964. 29–40.

Mythologies. Paris: Seuil, 1957.

S/Z. N.p.: Seuil, 1970.

Baudrillard, Jean. *Simulations*. Trans. Paul Foss, Paul Patton and Philip Beitchman. New York: Semiotext(e), 1983.

The Illusion of the End. Trans. Chris Turner. Stanford: Stanford University Press, 1994.

Beckett, Samuel. *How It Is*. New York: Grove, 1964.

Malone Dies. New York: Grove, 1956.

The Unnamable. New York: Grove, 1958.

Proust. New York: Grove, 1957.

Bell, Daniel. *The Cultural Contradictions of Capitalism*. New York: Basic, 1976.

Bender, John, and David E. Wellbery, eds. *Chronotypes: The Construction of Time*. Stanford: Stanford University Press, 1991.

Benjamin, Cornelius A. "Ideas of Time in the History of Philosophy." *The Voices of Time*. Ed. J. T. Fraser. 2nd edn. Amherst: University of Massachusetts Press, 1981. 3–30.

Benjamin, Walter. "Der Erzähler." *Illuminationen: Ausgewählte Schriften*. Ed. Siegfried Unseld. Frankfurt: Suhrkamp, 1961. 409–36.

Bents, Henri. "Computerarbeit und Lebenszeit." *Zerstörung und Wiederaneignung von Zeit*. Ed. Rainer Zoll. Frankfurt: Suhrkamp, 1988. 293–303.

Benveniste, Emile. *Problèmes de linguistique générale*. Vol. 1. Paris: Gallimard, 1966.

Bergson, Henri. *Essai sur les données immédiates de la conscience*. Paris: Alcan, 1908.

Berressem, Hanjo. *Pynchon's Poetics: Interfacing Theory and Text*. Urbana: University of Illinois Press, 1993.

Bersani, Leo. "Pynchon, Paranoia, and Literature." *Representations* 25 (1989): 99–118.

Bersani, Leo, and Ulysse Dutoit. "Beckett's Sociability." *Raritan* 12.1 (1992): 1–19.

Bertens, Hans. *The Idea of the Postmodern: A History*. London: Routledge, 1995.

Bérubé, Michael. *Marginal Forces/Cultural Centers: Tolson, Pynchon, and the Politics of the Canon*. Ithaca: Cornell University Press, 1992.

Birch, Sarah. *Christine Brooke-Rose and Contemporary Fiction*. Oxford: Clarendon, 1994.

Blumenberg, Hans. *Lebenszeit und Weltzeit*. 3rd edn. Frankfurt: Suhrkamp, 1986.

Bobko, D. J., and M. A. Davis. "Effects of Visual Display Scale on Duration Estimates." *Human Factors* 28 (1986): 153–58.

Boehm, Beth A. "Educating Readers: Creating New Expectations in *Lost in the Funhouse*." *Reading Narrative: Form, Ethics, Ideology*. Ed.

Bibliography

James Phelan. Columbus: Ohio State University Press, 1989. 102–19.

Bogue, Ronald L. "Meaning and Ideology in Robbe-Grillet's *Topologie d'une cité fantôme.*" *Modern Language Studies* 14 (1984): 33–46.

Boldy, Steven. *The Novels of Julio Cortázar.* Cambridge: Cambridge University Press, 1980.

Bolter, J. David. *Turing's Man: Western Culture in the Computer Age.* Chapel Hill: University of North Carolina Press, 1984.

Borges, Jorge Luis. "El jardín de senderos que se bifurcan." *Ficciones.* 12th edn. Madrid: Alianza, 1984. 101–16.

"Nueva refutación del tiempo." *Otras Inquisiciones.* 3rd edn. Madrid: Alianza, 1981. 170–88.

Borkin, Joseph. *The Crime and Punishment of I. G. Farben.* New York: Free Press, 1978.

Boyer, Alain-Michel. "Le récit lacunaire." *Textes et langages XII: Normes et transgressions en langue et en littérature.* N.p.: Université de Nantes, 1986. 115–23.

Brienza, Susan D. "*How It Is*: Midget Grammar." *Samuel Beckett's New Worlds: Style in Metafiction.* Norman: University of Oklahoma Press, 1987. 88–119.

Brody, Robert. *Julio Cortázar.* London: Grant & Cutler, 1976.

Brontë, Charlotte. *Villette.* Ed. Mark Lilly. Harmondsworth: Penguin, 1979.

Brontë, Emily. *Wuthering Heights.* Ed. William M. Sale Jr. and Richard J. Dunn. 3rd edn. New York: Norton, 1990.

Brooke-Rose, Christine. *The Christine Brooke-Rose Omnibus: Four Novels: Out, Such, Between, Thru.* Manchester: Carcanet, 1986.

"Conversation with Christine Brooke-Rose." With Ellen G. Friedman and Miriam Fuchs. *Review of Contemporary Fiction* 9.3 (1989): 81–90. Rpt. in *Utterly Other Discourse: The Texts of Christine Brooke-Rose.* Ed. Ellen G. Friedman and Richard Martin. Normal: Dalkey Archive Press, 1995. 29–37.

"Illicitations." *Review of Contemporary Fiction* 9.3 (1989): 101–09.

"Science Fiction and Realistic Fiction." *A Rhetoric of the Unreal: Studies in Narrative and Structure, Especially of the Fantastic.* Cambridge: Cambridge University Press, 1981. 72–102.

Brooks, Peter. *Reading for the Plot: Design and Intention in Narrative.* New York: Random House, 1985.

Brophy, Brigid. *In Transit.* New York: Putnam, 1970.

Brown, B. S., K. Dismukes and E. J. Rinalducci. "Video Display Terminals and Vision of Workers: Summary and Overview of a Symposium." *Behavior and Information Technology* 1 (1982): 121–40.

Bruns, Gerald. "The Storyteller and the Problem of Language in Samuel Beckett's Fiction." *Modern Poetry and the Idea of Language: A Critical and Historical Study.* New Haven: Yale University Press, 1974. 164–85.

Bunge, Mario. *Causality and Modern Science*. 3rd edn. New York: Dover, 1979.

Butor, Michel. *L'emploi du temps*. Paris: Minuit, 1958.

Calvino, Italo. *If on a Winter's Night a Traveler*. Trans. William Weaver. San Diego: Harcourt, 1981.

Carr, David. *Time, Narrative, and History*. Bloomington: Indiana University Press, 1986.

Carr, David, Charles Taylor and Paul Ricoeur. "Table ronde/Round Table: *Temps et Récit*, Volume I." *Revue de l'Université d'Ottawa/ University of Ottawa Quarterly* 55 (1985): 301–22.

Carter Jr., E. D. "La sombra del perseguidor: El doble en *Rayuela*." *Explicación de textos literarios* 17 (1988–89): 64–110.

Ceruzzi, Paul. "An Unforeseen Revolution: Computers and Expectations, 1935–1985." *Imagining Tomorrow: History, Technology and the American Future*. Ed. Joseph J. Corn. Cambridge, MA: MIT Press, 1986. 188–201.

Cha, Theresa Hak Kyung. *Dictée*. Berkeley: Third Woman Press, 1995.

Chambers, Judith. *Thomas Pynchon*. New York: Twayne, 1992.

Chatman, Seymour. *Story and Discourse: Narrative Structure in Fiction and Film*. Ithaca: Cornell University Press, 1978.

Chorier, Bénédicte. "Thomas Pynchon: la fin de l'histoire?" *Revue Française d'Etudes Américaines* 43 (1990): 9–17.

Clerc, Charles. "Film in *Gravity's Rainbow*." *Approaches to Gravity's Rainbow*. Ed. Charles Clerc. Columbus: Ohio State University Press, 1983. 103–51.

Cohn, Ruby. *Back to Beckett*. Princeton: Princeton University Press, 1973.
    "Comment c'est par le bout." *Samuel Beckett: The Comic Gamut*. New Brunswick: Rutgers University Press, 1962. 182–207.

Connor, Steven. *Samuel Beckett: Repetition, Theory and Text*. Oxford: Blackwell, 1988.

Conrad, Joseph. *Lord Jim*. Ed. Thomas C. Moser. New York: Norton, 1968.

Cooper, Peter L. *Signs and Symptoms: Thomas Pynchon and the Contemporary World*. Berkeley: University of California Press, 1983.

Coover, Robert. "The Elevator." *Pricksongs & Descants*. New York: New American Library, 1970. 125–37.

Cortázar, Julio. "Continuidad de los parques." *El perseguidor y otros relatos*. 5th edn. Barcelona: Bruguera, 1984. 19–20.
    Rayuela. Ed. Julio Ortega and Saúl Yurkievich. N.p.: Colección Archivos, 1991.

Cowart, David. *Thomas Pynchon: The Art of Allusion*. Carbondale: Southern Illinois University Press, 1980.

Craig, Herbert. "La memoria proustiana en *Rayuela* de Julio Cortázar." *Nueva revista de filología hispánica* 37 (1989): 237–45.

Crimp, Douglas. "Appropriating Appropriation." *Image Scavengers: Photography*. Ed. Paula Marincola. Institute of Contemporary Art/ University of Pennsylvania Press, 1982. 27–34.

Bibliography

Culler, Jonathan. "Story and Discourse in the Analysis of Narrative." *The Pursuit of Signs: Semiotics, Literature, Deconstruction.* Ithaca: Cornell University Press, 1981. 169–87.

Cunningham, Rodger. "Falling into Heaven: Pre-Adamism and Paradox in *Rayuela.*" *INTI: Revista de literatura hispánica* 34–35 (1991–92): 93–106.

Dällenbach, Lucien. *Le récit spéculaire: Essai sur la mise en abyme.* Paris: Seuil, 1977.

Dearlove, Judith. "The Voice and Its Words: *How It Is* in Beckett's Canon." *Critical Essays on Samuel Beckett.* Ed. Patrick A. MacCarthy. Boston: Hall, 1986. 102–19.

Deneau, Daniel P. "Another View of the *Topologie d'une cité fantôme.*" *Australian Journal of French Studies* 17 (1980): 194–210.

Derrida, Jacques. "*Ousia* and Gramme: Note on a Note from *Being and Time.*" *Margins of Philosophy.* Trans. Alan Bass. Chicago: University of Chicago Press, 1982. 29–67.

Speech and Phenomena: And Other Essays on Husserl's Theory of Signs. Trans. David B. Allison. Evanston: Northwestern University Press, 1973.

Dertouzos, Michael L., Richard Lester and Robert Solow. *Made in America.* Cambridge, MA: MIT Press, 1989.

Dicken, Peter. *Global Shift: Industrial Change in a Turbulent World.* London: Chapman, 1988.

Döblin, Alfred. *Berlin Alexanderplatz.* Munich: Deutscher Taschenbuch Verlag, 1965.

Docherty, Thomas. "Theory, Enlightenment and Violence: Postmodernist Hermeneutic as a Comedy of Errors." *Textual Practice* 1 (1987): 192–216. Rpt. in *After Theory: Postmodernism/Postmarxism.* London: Routledge, 1990. 37–62.

Doherty, Francis. "Breath-Clock Breath: *How It Is.*" *Samuel Beckett.* London: Hutchinson University Library, 1971. 119–31.

Dos Passos, John. *Manhattan Transfer.* Boston: Houghton, 1925.

Dowell, Coleman. *Island People.* New York: New Directions, 1976.

Dupuy-Sullivan, Françoise. "Jeu et enjeu du texte dans *Topologie d'une cité fantôme* d'Alain Robbe-Grillet." *Les lettres romanes* 44 (1990): 211–17.

Duras, Marguerite. *L'après-midi de Monsieur Andesmas.* Paris: Gallimard, 1962.

Le square. Paris: Gallimard, 1955.

Eco, Umberto. *The Role of the Reader: Explorations in the Semiotics of Texts.* Bloomington: Indiana University Press, 1979.

Elias, Norbert. *Über die Zeit.* Ed. Michael Schröter. Trans. Holger Fliessbach and Michael Schröter. 4th edn. Frankfurt: Suhrkamp, 1992.

Ellison, David R. "Reappearing Man in Robbe-Grillet's *Topologie d'une cité fantôme.*" *Stanford French Review* 3 (1979): 97–110.

Bibliography

Ermarth, Elizabeth Deeds. *Sequel to History: Postmodernism and the Crisis of Representational Time*. Princeton: Princeton University Press, 1992.

Ernst, Max. *Une semaine de bonté: A Surrealistic Novel in Collage*. Trans. Stanley Appelbaum. New York: Dover, 1976.

Fabian, Johannes. *Time and the Other: How Anthropology Makes Its Object*. New York: Columbia University Press, 1983.

Faulkner, William. *Absalom, Absalom!* New York: Vintage, 1987.

As I Lay Dying. New York: Vintage, 1987.

The Sound and the Fury. New York: Modern Library, 1956.

Federman, Raymond. *Double or Nothing*. Chicago: Swallow, 1971.

"Imagination as Plagiarism." *New Literary History* 7 (1975–76): 563–78.

Review of *How It Is*. *Samuel Beckett: The Critical Heritage*. Ed. Lawrence Grover and Raymond Federman. London: Routledge, 1979. 229–31.

Flaubert, Gustave. *Madame Bovary*. Paris: Garnier-Flammarion, 1979.

Fokkema, Aleid. "Gödel, Escher, Barth: Variations on a Triangle." *Delta* 21 (1985): 65–78.

Ford, Ford Madox. *The Good Soldier*. New York: Vintage, 1989.

Forster, E. M. *Aspects of the Novel*. San Diego: Harcourt Brace Jovanovich, 1985.

Fowles, John. *The French Lieutenant's Woman*. Boston: Little, 1969.

Franco, Jean. *An Introduction to Spanish-American Literature*. 3rd edn. Cambridge: Cambridge University Press, 1994.

Frank, Joseph. "Spatial Form in Modern Literature." *Sewanee Review* 53 (1945): 221–40, 433–56, 643–53. Rpt. in *The Idea of Spatial Form*. New Brunswick: Rutgers University Press, 1991. 3–66.

Freud, Sigmund. *Der Wahn und die Träume in W. Jensens "Gradiva" mit dem Text der Erzählung von Wilhelm Jensen*. Ed. Bernd Urban and Johannes Cremerius. Frankfurt: Fischer, 1973.

Friedman, Alan J. "Science and Technology." *Approaches to Gravity's Rainbow*. Ed. Charles Clerc. Columbus: Ohio State University Press, 1983. 69–102.

Friedman, Alan J., and Manfred Puetz. "Science as Metaphor: Thomas Pynchon and *Gravity's Rainbow*." *Critical Essays on Thomas Pynchon*. Ed. Richard Pearce. Boston: Hall, 1981. 69–81.

Fukuyama, Francis. "The End of History?" *The National Interest* 16 (Summer, 1988): 3–18.

The End of History and the Last Man. New York: Free Press, 1992.

Gallagher, Catherine. "Marxism and the New Historicism." *The New Historicism*. Ed. H. Aram Veeser. New York: Routledge, 1989. 37–48.

García Márquez, Gabriel. *La hojarasca*. 7th edn. Barcelona: Plaza, 1979.

Gass, William H. *Willie Masters' Lonesome Wife*. N.p.: Dalkey Archive, 1989.

Genette, Gérard. *Narrative Discourse: An Essay in Method*. Trans. Jane E. Lewin. Ithaca: Cornell University Press, 1980.

Gertel, Zunilda. "*Rayuela*, la figura y su lectura." *Hispanic Review* 56 (1988): 287–305.

Bibliography

Gibson, William. *Neuromancer*. New York: Ace, 1984.

Giddens, Anthony. *The Consequences of Modernity*. Stanford: Stanford University Press, 1990.

Giordano, Enrique. "Algunas aproximaciones a *'Rayuela'*, de Julio Cortázar, a través de la dinámica del juego." *Homenaje a Julio Cortázar: Variaciones interpretativas en torno a su obra*. Ed. Helmy F. Giacoman. Long Island City: L. A. Publishing, 1972. 95–129.

Gribbin, John. *In Search of the Big Bang: Quantum Physics and Cosmology*. Toronto: Bantam, 1986.

Gumbrecht, Hans-Ulrich. "Posthistoire Now." *Epochenschwellen und Epochenstrukturen im Diskurs der Literatur- und Sprachhistorie*. Ed. Hans-Ulrich Gumbrecht and Ursula Link-Heer. Frankfurt: Suhrkamp, 1985. 34–50.

Güttgemanns, Erhardt. "Die Funktion der Zeit in der Erzählung." *Linguistica Biblica* 32 (1974): 56–76.

Habermas, Jürgen. "Modernity versus Postmodernity," *New German Critique* 22 (1981): 3–14. Rpt. as "Modernity – An Incomplete Project." Trans. Seyla Ben-Habib. *The Anti-Aesthetic: Essays on Postmodern Culture*. Ed. Hal Foster. Seattle: Bay Press, 1983. 3–15.

Harasim, Linda M., ed. *Global Networks: Computers and International Communication*. Cambridge, MA: MIT Press, 1993.

Hardin, Michael. "Non-Cooperative Game Theory and Female-Readers: How To Win the Game of *Hopscotch*." *Hispanófila* 11 (1994): 57–72.

Harper, Howard. *"How It Is." Samuel Beckett and the Art of Rhetoric*. Ed. Edouard Morot-Sir, Howard Harper, and Douglas McMillan III. Chapel Hill: North Carolina Studies in the Romance Languages and Literatures, 1976. 249–70.

Harrison, Bennett. *Lean and Mean: The Changing Landscape of Corporate Power in the Age of Flexibility*. New York: Basic, 1994.

Harvey, David. *The Condition of Postmodernity: An Enquiry into the Origins of Cultural Change*. Oxford: Blackwell, 1990.

Hassard, John, ed. *The Sociology of Time*. Houndmills: Macmillan, 1990.

Hawking, Stephen W. *A Brief History of Time: From the Big Bang to Black Holes*. Toronto: Bantam, 1988.

Hayles, N. Katherine. "Caught in the Web: Cosmology and the Point of (No) Return in Pynchon's *Gravity's Rainbow*." *The Cosmic Web: Scientific Field Models & Literary Strategies in the 20th Century*. Ithaca: Cornell University Press, 1984. 168–97.

    Chaos Bound: Orderly Disorder in Contemporary Literature and Science. Ithaca: Cornell University Press, 1990.

Hayles, N. Katherine, ed. *Chaos and Order: Complex Dynamics in Literature and Science*. Chicago: University of Chicago Press, 1991.

Heidegger, Martin. *Sein und Zeit*. 16th edn. Tübingen: Niemeyer, 1986.

Heise, Ursula K. "Time Frames: Temporality and Narration in Coleman Dowell's *Island People*." *Journal of Narrative Technique* 21 (1991): 274–88.

Bibliography

Hillis Miller, J. *Fiction and Repetition: Seven English Novels.* Cambridge, MA: Harvard University Press, 1982.

Hite, Molly. *Ideas of Order in the Novels of Thomas Pynchon.* Columbus: Ohio State University Press, 1983.

Hofstadter, Douglas R. *Gödel, Escher, Bach: An Eternal Golden Braid.* New York: Vintage, 1980.

Hollinger, Veronica. "Cybernetic Deconstructions: Cyberpunk and Postmodernism." *Storming the Reality Studio: A Casebook of Cyberpunk and Postmodern Fiction.* Ed. Larry McCaffery. Durham, NC: Duke University Press, 1991. 203–18.

Horkheimer, Max, and Theodor Adorno. *Dialektik der Aufklärung.* Frankfurt: Fischer, 1988.

Hume, Kathryn. *Pynchon's Mythography: An Approach to* Gravity's Rainbow. Carbondale: Southern Illinois University Press, 1987.

"Repetition and the Construction of Character in *Gravity's Rainbow.*" *Critique: Studies in Contemporary Fiction* 33 (1992): 243–54.

Husserl, Edmund. *Vorlesungen zur Phänomenologie des inneren Zeitbewußtseins.* Ed. Martin Heidegger. 2nd edn. Tübingen: Niemeyer, 1980.

Hussey, Barbara L. "*Rayuela*: Chapter 55 as Take-(away)." *International Fiction Review* 8 (1981): 53–60.

Hutchens, Eleanor N. "The Novel as Chronomorph." *Novel* 5 (1972): 215–24.

Hutcheon, Linda. *A Poetics of Postmodernism: History, Theory, Fiction.* New York: Routledge, 1988.

Narcissistic Narrative: The Metafictional Paradox. London: Routledge, 1991.

Hutchings, William. " 'Shat into Grace' Or, A Tale of a Turd: Why It Is How It Is in Samuel Beckett's *How It Is.*" *Papers on Language and Literature* 21.1 (1984): 64–87.

Huyssen, Andreas. *Twilight Memories: Marking Time in a Culture of Amnesia.* New York: Routledge, 1995.

Huxley, Aldous. *Point Counter Point.* New York: Harper & Row, 1965.

Iñigo-Madrigal, Luis. "'*Rayuela*: Los juegos en el cementerio'." *Lo lúdico y lo fantástico en la obra de Cortázar.* Vol. III: *Estudios particulares.* Ed. Centre de Recherches Latino-Américaines, Université de Poitiers. Madrid: Fundamentos, 1986. 275–300.

Jameson, Fredric. *Postmodernism, or, The Cultural Logic of Late Capitalism.* Durham, NC: Duke University Press, 1991.

"Progress versus Utopia; or, Can We Imagine the Future?" *Science Fiction Studies* 9 (1982): 147–58.

Janelle, Donald G. "Global Interdependence and Its Consequences." *Collapsing Space and Time: Geographical Aspects of Communication and Information.* Ed. Stanley D. Brunn and Thomas R. Leinbach. London: Harper Collins, 1991. 49–81.

Johnson, B. S. *Christie Malry's Own Double-Entry.* New York: New Directions, 1985.

273

Bibliography

The Unfortunates. London: Panther, 1969.

Joyce, James. *Ulysses*. Ed. Hans Walter Gabler. New York: Vintage, 1986.

Juhnke, Ralph, and Jonathan N. Scott. "Psychology of Computer Use: V. Computer Use and the Experience of Time." *Perceptual and Motor Skills* 67 (1988): 863–70.

Kenner, Hugh. *Samuel Beckett: A Critical Study*. New edn. Berkeley: University of California Press, 1973.

——. "Shades of Syntax." *Samuel Beckett: A Collection of Criticism*. Ed. Ruby Cohn. New York: McGraw-Hill, 1975. 21–31.

Kermode, Frank. *The Sense of an Ending*. London: Oxford University Press, 1967.

Kern, Stephen. *The Culture of Time and Space 1880–1918*. Cambridge, MA: Harvard University Press, 1983.

Kidder, Tracy. *The Soul of a New Machine*. New York: Avon, 1981.

Kloepfer, Rolf. "La libertad del autor y el potencial del lector: Encuentro con *Rayuela* de Julio Cortázar." Trans. Victor Castro. *INTI: Revista de literatura hispánica* 22–23 (1985–86): 113–29.

Knowlson, James, and John Pilling. "*How It Is.*" *Frescoes of the Skull: The Later Prose and Drama of Samuel Beckett*. London: Calder, 1979. 61–78.

Koselleck, Reinhart. *Vergangene Zukunft: Zur Semantik geschichtlicher Zeiten*. 2nd edn. Frankfurt: Suhrkamp, 1992.

Kümmel, Friedrich. "Time as Succession and the Problem of Duration." Trans. Francesco Gaona. *The Voices of Time*. Ed. J. T. Fraser. 2nd edn. Amherst: University of Massachusetts Press, 1981. 31–55.

Layzer, David. *Cosmogenesis: The Growth of Order in the Universe*. New York: Oxford University Press, 1990.

Leki, Ilona. *Alain Robbe-Grillet*. Boston: Twayne, 1983.

Le Touzé, Philippe. "Aspects de l'esthétique du temps chez quelques 'romanciers de Minuit'." *Passage du temps, ordre de la transition*. Ed. Jean Bessière. Paris: Presses Universitaires de France, 1985. 187–200.

Levin, Charles. "Time and Postmodernism: A Capsule." *Communication* 10 (1988): 311–30.

Levy, Eric P. "*How It Is*: An Allegory of Time and Personal Identity." *Beckett and the Voice of Species: A Study of the Prose Fiction*. Totowa: Gill, 1980. 83–94.

Lotman, Jurij. *The Structure of the Artistic Text*. Trans. Gail Lenhoff and Ronald Vroon. University of Michigan: Michigan Slavic Contributions, 1977.

Lowry, Malcolm. *Under the Volcano*. New York: New American Library, 1971.

Luhmann, Niklas. "The Future Cannot Begin: Temporal Structures in Modern Society." *Social Research* 43 (1976): 130–52.

Lyotard, Jean-François. *The Postmodern Condition: A Report on Knowledge*. Trans. Geoff Bennington and Brian Massumi. Minneapolis: University of Minnesota Press, 1984.

"Time Today." Trans. Geoffrey Bennington and Rachel Bowlby. *Oxford Literary Review* 11.1–2 (1989): 3–20.

MacAdam, Alfred J. "*Rayuela*: La cuestión del lector." *Explicación de textos literarios* 17 (1988–89): 216–29.

Mackey, Louis. "Paranoia, Pynchon, and Preterition." *SubStance* 30 (1981): 16–30. Rpt. in *Thomas Pynchon's Gravity's Rainbow*. Ed. Harold Bloom. New York: Chelsea House, 1986. 53–67.

Maddox, Tom. "The Wars of the Coin's Two Halves: Bruce Sterling's Mechanist/Shaper Narratives." *Storming the Reality Studio: A Casebook of Cyberpunk and Postmodern Fiction*. Ed. Larry McCaffery. Durham, NC: Duke University Press, 1991. 324–30.

Madsen, Deborah L. *The Postmodernist Allegories of Thomas Pynchon*. Leicester: Leicester University Press, 1991.

Major, Clarence. *Reflex and Bone Structure*. New York: Fiction Collective, 1975.

Malone, Thomas W., and John F. Rockart. "Computers, Networks and the Corporation." *Communications, Computers and Networks*. Spec. issue of *Scientific American* 265.3 (1991): 92–99.

Marinetti, F. T. *Let's Murder the Moonshine: Selected Writings*. Ed. and trans. R. W. Flint. Los Angeles: Sun & Moon Classics, 1991.

"Zang Tumb Tuuum: Parole in Libertà." *Opere di F. T. Marinetti*. Vol. 2: *Teoria e invenzione futurista*. Ed. Luciano de Maria. Milan: Mondadori, 1968. 563–99.

Martin, Richard. "'Just Words on a Page': The Novels of Christine Brooke-Rose." *Review of Contemporary Fiction* 9.3 (1989): 110–23. Rpt. in *Utterly Other Discourse: The Texts of Christine Brooke-Rose*. Ed. Ellen G. Friedman and Richard Martin. Normal: Dalkey Archive Press, 1995. 38–51.

Mauriac, Claude. *L'agrandissement*. Paris: Albin Michel, 1963.

La marquise sortit à cinq heures. N.p.: Albin Michel, 1961.

McHale, Brian. "'I draw the line as a rule between one solar system and another': The Postmodernism(s) of Christine Brooke-Rose." *Constructing Postmodernism*. London: Routledge, 1992. 207–22. Rpt. in *Utterly Other Discourse: The Texts of Christine Brooke-Rose*. Ed. Ellen G. Friedman and Richard Martin. Normal: Dalkey Archive Press, 1995. 192–213.

"Modernist Reading, Postmodern Text: The Case of 'Gravity's Rainbow.'" *Poetics Today* 1 (1979–80): 85–110. Rpt. in *Constructing Postmodernism*. London: Routledge, 1992. 61–86.

"POSTcyberMODERNpunkISM." *Storming the Reality Studio: A Casebook of Cyberpunk and Postmodern Fiction*. Ed. Larry McCaffery. Durham, NC: Duke University Press, 1991. 308–23. Rpt. in *Constructing Postmodernism*. London: Routledge, 1992. 225–42.

Postmodernist Fiction. New York: Methuen, 1987.

McHoul, Alec, and David Wills. *Writing Pynchon: Strategies in Fictional Analysis*. Urbana: University of Illinois Press, 1990.

Bibliography

McLaughlin, Robert. "IG Farben and the War against Nature in *Gravity's Rainbow*." *Germany and German Thought in American Literature and Cultural Criticism*. Ed. Peter Freese. Essen: Blaue Eule, 1990. 319–36.

McLuhan, Marshall. *Understanding Media: The Extensions of Man*. Cambridge, MA: MIT Press, 1994.

Meltzer, Françoise. "Preliminary Excavations of Robbe-Grillet's Phantom City." *Chicago Review* 28 (1976): 41–50.

Mendelson, Edward. "Gravity's Encyclopedia." *Mindful Pleasures: Essays on Thomas Pynchon*. Ed. George Levine and David Leverenz. Boston: Little, 1976. 161–95. Rpt. in *Thomas Pynchon's Gravity's Rainbow*. Ed. Harold Bloom. New York: Chelsea House, 1986. 29–52.

Mendilow, A. A. *Time and the Novel*. New York: Humanities Press, 1972.

Metz, Christian. *Film Language: A Semiotics of the Cinema*. Trans. Michael Taylor. New York: Oxford University Press, 1974.

Meyerhoff, Hans. *Time in Literature*. Berkeley: University of California Press, 1955.

Miller, D. A. *Narrative and Its Discontents: Problems of Closure in the Traditional Novel*. Princeton: Princeton University Press, 1981.

Mistacco, Vicki. "The Theory and Practice of Reading Nouveaux Romans: Robbe-Grillet's *Topologie d'une cité fantôme*." *The Reader in the Text: Essays on Audience and Interpretation*. Ed. Susan R. Suleiman and Inge Crosman. Princeton: Princeton University Press, 1980. 371–400.

Monod, Jacques. *Chance and Necessity: An Essay on the Natural Philosophy of Modern Biology*. Trans. Austryn Wainhouse. New York: Knopf, 1971.

Moore, Thomas. *The Style of Connectedness:* Gravity's Rainbow *and Thomas Pynchon*. Columbia: University of Missouri Press, 1987.

Morrissette, Bruce. "Intertextual Assemblage as Fictional Generator: *Topologie d'une cité fantôme*." *International Fiction Review* 5 (1978): 1–14.

Intertextual Assemblage in Robbe-Grillet from Topology to the Golden Triangle. Fredericton: York, 1979.

Les romans de Robbe-Grillet. Paris: Minuit, 1963.

"Post-Modern Generative Fiction: Novel and Film." *Critical Inquiry* 2 (1975): 253–62.

"Topology and the French *Nouveau Roman*." *Boundary* 2 1 (1972): 45–57.

Morson, Gary Saul. *Narrative and Freedom*. New Haven: Yale University Press, 1994.

Morton, Michael S. Scott, ed. *The Corporation of the 1990s: Information Technology and Organizational Transformation*. New York: Oxford University Press, 1991.

Müller, Günther. "Die Bedeutung der Zeit in der Erzählkunst." *Morphologische Poetik*. Ed. Elena Müller. Darmstadt: Wissenschaftliche Buchgesellschaft, 1968. 247–68.

Bibliography

"Erzählzeit und erzählte Zeit." *Morphologische Poetik.* Ed. Elena Müller. Darmstadt: Wissenschaftliche Buchgesellschaft, 1968. 269–86.

Musil, Robert. *Der Mann ohne Eigenschaften.* 5th edn. Hamburg: Rowohlt, 1965.

Nelson, Roy Jay. *Causality and Narrative in French Fiction from Zola to Robbe-Grillet.* Columbus: Ohio State University Press, 1990.

Niethammer, Lutz. *Posthistoire: Ist die Geschichte zu Ende?* Reinbek: Rowohlt, 1989.

Nowotny, Helga. *Eigenzeit: Entstehung und Strukturierung eines Zeitgefühls.* 2nd edn. Frankfurt: Suhrkamp, 1989.

O'Donnell, Thomas. "Robbe-Grillet's Ghost Town." *Yale French Studies* 57 (1979): 195–207.

"Robbe-Grillet's *Métaphoricité Fantôme.*" *Studies in Twentieth-Century Literature* 2 (1977): 55–68.

Ong, Walter J. "A Dialectic of Aural and Objective Correlatives." *Essays in Criticism* 8 (1958): 166–81.

Ozier, Lance. "Antipointsman/Antimexico: Some Mathematical Imagery in *Gravity's Rainbow.*" *Critique* 16.2 (1974): 73–90.

Pagels, Heinz R. *Perfect Symmetry: The Search for the Beginning of Time.* New York: Simon, 1985.

Pardo Avellaneda, Rafael. "Globalización, innovación tecnológica y tiempo." *Información comercial española* 695 (1991): 77–93.

Percival, Anthony. "Reader and *Rayuela.*" *Revista canadiense de estudios hispánicos* 6 (1982): 239–85.

Perloff, Marjorie. *The Futurist Moment: Avant-Garde, Avant Guerre, and the Language of Rupture.* Chicago: University of Chicago Press, 1986.

" 'The Space of a Door': Beckett and the Poetry of Absence." *The Poetics of Indeterminacy: Rimbaud to Cage.* N.p.: Northwestern University Press, 1983. 200–247.

Petillon, Pierre-Yves. "Thomas Pynchon and Aleatory Space." Trans. Margaret S. Langford. *Pynchon Notes* 15 (1984): 3–46.

Picón Garfield, Evelyn. *Julio Cortázar.* New York: Ungar, 1975.

Plater, William M. *The Grim Phoenix: Reconstructing Thomas Pynchon.* Bloomington: Indiana University Press, 1978.

Plumpe, Gottfried. *Die I. G. Farbenindustrie AG: Wirtschaft, Technik und Politik 1904–1945.* Berlin: Duncker, 1990.

Poggioli, Renato. *The Theory of the Avant-Garde.* Trans. Gerald Fitzgerald. Cambridge, MA: Harvard University Press, 1968.

Pouillon, Jean. *Temps et roman.* Paris: Gallimard, 1946.

Poulet, Georges. *Etudes sur le temps humain.* Paris: Rocher, 1976.

Prigogine, Ilya, and Isabelle Stengers. *Order out of Chaos: Man's New Dialogue with Nature.* Toronto: Bantam, 1984.

Proust, Marcel. *A la recherche du temps perdu.* 8 vols. Paris: Gallimard, 1954.

Pynchon, Thomas. *Gravity's Rainbow.* New York: Viking, 1973.

Ramírez Molas, Pedro. *Tiempo y narración: Enfoques de la temporalidad en Borges, Carpentier, Cortázar.* Madrid: Gredos, 1978.

Ricardou, Jean. *Problèmes du nouveau roman*. Paris: Seuil, 1967.

Richard, Claude. "Causality and Mimesis in Contemporary Fiction." *SubStance* 40 (1983): 84–93.

Richardson, Samuel. *Clarissa*. Ed. Angus Ross. Harmondsworth: Penguin, 1985.

    Pamela. Ed. T. C. Duncan-Eaves and B. D. Kimpel. Boston: Houghton, 1971.

Ricoeur, Paul. *Time and Narrative*. Vols. 1–3. Trans. Kathleen McLaughlin and David Pellauer. Chicago: University of Chicago Press, 1984–88.

Rimmon-Kenan, Shlomith. *Narrative Fiction: Contemporary Poetics*. London: Methuen, 1983.

Robbe-Grillet, Alain. Interview. With Vicki Mistacco. *Diacritics* 6.4 (1976): 35–43.

    Interview. "New Novel, New New Novel." With Katherine K. Passias. *SubStance* 13 (1976): 130–35.

    La belle captive. Brussels: Cosmos, 1975.

    La jalousie. Paris: Minuit, 1957.

    La maison de rendez-vous. Paris: Minuit, 1965.

    Les gommes. Paris: Minuit, 1953.

    Le voyeur. Paris: Minuit, 1955.

    "Order and Disorder in Film and Fiction." Trans. Bruce Morrissette. *Critical Inquiry* 4 (Autumn, 1977): 1–20.

    Pour un nouveau roman. Paris: Minuit, 1963.

    Projet pour une révolution à New York. Paris: Minuit, 1970.

    Souvenirs du triangle d'or. Paris: Minuit, 1978.

    Topologie d'une cité fantôme. Paris: Minuit, 1976.

    Topology of a Phantom City. Trans. J. A. Underwood. New York: Grove, 1977.

Roland, Lillian Dunmars. *Women in Robbe-Grillet: A Study in Thematics and Diegetics*. New York: Peter Lang, 1993.

Rosen, Steven J. *Samuel Beckett and the Pessimistic Tradition*. New Brunswick: Rutgers University Press, 1976.

Sacido Romero, Alberto. "El espacio, esqueleto representacional en la crisis lúdica de la *Rayuela*." *INTI: Revista de literatura hispánica* 32–33 (1990): 79–89.

Sage, Victor. "Innovation and Continuity in *How It Is*." *Beckett the Shape Changer*. Ed. Katharine Worth. London: Routledge, 1975. 85–103.

Saïd, Edward W. *Beginnings: Intention and Method*. New York: Columbia University Press, 1985.

Sanders, Scott. "Pynchon's Paranoid History." *Mindful Pleasures: Essays on Thomas Pynchon*. Ed. George Levine and David Leverenz. Boston: Little, 1976. 139–59.

Saporta, Marc. *Composition No.1*. Paris: Seuil, 1962.

Sartre, Jean-Paul. *L'être et le néant: Essai d'ontologie phénoménologique*. Paris: Gallimard, 1943.

Bibliography

Schaub, Thomas H. *Pynchon: The Voice of Ambiguity*. Urbana: University of Illinois Press, 1981.

Schleifer, Ronald. "The Space and Dialogue of Desire: Lacan, Greimas, and Narrative Temporality." *Modern Language Notes* 98 (1983): 871–90.

Schurman, Susan. *"How It Is." The Solipsistic Novels of Samuel Beckett*. Cologne: Pohl-Rugenheim, 1987. 132–45.

Schwanitz, Dietrich. *Systemtheorie und Literatur: Ein neues Paradigma*. Opladen: Westdeutscher Verlag, 1990.

Schwarz, Cindy. *A Tour of the Subatomic Zoo: A Guide to Particle Physics*. New York: American Institute of Physics, 1992.

Seed, David. *The Fictional Labyrinths of Thomas Pynchon*. Houndmills: Macmillan, 1988.

Seidel, Michael. "The Satiric Plots of *Gravity's Rainbow*." *Pynchon: A Collection of Critical Essays*. Ed. Edward Mendelson. Englewood Cliffs: Prentice-Hall, 1978. 193–212.

Shippey, Tom. "Semiotic Ghosts and Ghostliness in the Work of Bruce Sterling." *Fiction 2000: Cyberpunk and the Future of Narrative*. Ed. George Slusser and Tom Shippey. Athens: University of Georgia Press, 1992. 208–20.

Siegel, Mark Richard. *Pynchon: Creative Paranoia in* Gravity's Rainbow. Port Washington: Kennikat, 1978.

Simpkins, Scott. "'The Infinite Game': Cortázar's *Hopscotch*." *Journal of the Midwest Modern Language Association* 23 (1990): 61–74.

Simpson, Lorenzo C. *Technology, Time, and the Conversations of Modernity*. New York: Routledge, 1995.

Singer, Alan. "The Need of the Present: *How It Is* with the Subject in Beckett's Novel." *A Metaphorics of Fiction: Discontinuity and Discourse in the Modern Novel*. Tallahassee: Florida State University Press, 1983. 115–56.

Slade, Joseph W. *Thomas Pynchon*. New York: Lang, 1990.

Slusser, George. "The Frankenstein Barrier." *Fiction 2000: Cyberpunk and the Future of Narrative*. Ed. George Slusser and Tom Shippey. Athens: University of Georgia Press, 1992. 46–71.

Smith, Frederik N. "Fiction as Composing Process: *How It Is*." *Samuel Beckett: Humanistic Perspectives*. Ed. Morris Beja, S. E. Gontarski and Pierre Astier. N.p.: Ohio State University Press, 1983. 106–121.

Stark, John O. *Pynchon's Fictions: Thomas Pynchon and the Literature of Information*. Athens: Ohio University Press, 1980.

Stempel, Wolf-Dieter. "Möglichkeiten einer Darstellung der Diachronie in narrativen Texten." *Beiträge zur Textlinguistik*. Ed. Wolf-Dieter Stempel. Munich: Fink, 1971. 53–78. Rpt. in *Zeitgestaltung in der Erzählkunst*. Ed. Alexander Ritter. Darmstadt: Wissenschaftliche Buchgesellschaft, 1978. 299–321.

Sterling, Bruce. *Schismatrix*. New York: Ace, 1986.

Sterne, Laurence. *Tristram Shandy*. Ed. Howard Anderson. New York: Norton, 1980.

Stewart, Garrett. *Death Sentences: Styles of Dying in British Fiction.* Cambridge, MA: Harvard University Press, 1984.

Reading Voices: Literature and the Phonotext. Berkeley: University of California Press, 1990.

Stoltzfus, Ben. "Robbe-Grillet's Dialectical Topology." *International Fiction Review* 9 (1982): 83–92. Rpt. in *Alain Robbe-Grillet: The Body of the Text.* Cranbury: Associated University Presses, 1985. 102–16.

Stone, Cynthia. "El lector implícito de *Rayuela* y los blancos de la narración." *Los ochenta mundos de Cortázar: Ensayos.* Ed. Fernando Burgos. Madrid: EDI-6, 1987. 177–84.

Stoppard, Tom. *Arcadia.* London: Faber and Faber, 1993.

St-Pierre, Paul. "*Comment c'est* de Beckett: production et déception du sens." *Revue des lettres modernes* 605–610 (1981): 89–113.

Strehle, Susan. *Fiction in the Quantum Universe.* Chapel Hill: University of North Carolina Press, 1992.

Sukenick, Ronald. *Out.* Chicago: Swallow Press, 1973.

Suleiman, Susan. "Reading Robbe-Grillet: Sadism and Text in *Projet pour une révolution à New York.*" *Romanic Review* 68 (1977): 43–51.

Thiher, Alan. *Words in Reflection: Modern Language Theory and Postmodern Fiction.* Chicago: University of Chicago Press, 1984.

Thompson, E. P. "Time, Work-Discipline, and Industrial Capitalism." *Past & Present* 38 (December, 1967): 56–97.

Todorov, Tzvetan. *Introduction to Poetics.* Trans. Richard Howard. Minneapolis: University of Minnesota Press, 1981.

Toffler, Alvin. *Future Shock.* New York: Random House, 1970.

The Third Wave. New York: Bantam, 1981.

Tölölyan, Khachig. "War as Background in *Gravity's Rainbow.*" *Approaches to Gravity's Rainbow.* Ed. Charles Clerc. Columbus: Ohio State University Press, 1983. 31–67.

Toolan, Michael J. *Narrative: A Critical Linguistic Introduction.* London: Routledge, 1988.

Verschueren, Walter. "'Voice, Tape, Writing': Original Repetition in *Lost in the Funhouse* (Beyond Phenomenology: Barth's 'Menelaiad')." *Delta* 21 (1985): 79–93.

Villanueva, Darío. *Estructura y tiempo reducido en la novela.* Valencia: Bello, 1977.

Virilio, Paul. *Speed and Politics: An Essay in Dromology.* Trans. Mark Polizzotti. New York: Semiotext(e), 1986.

The Lost Dimension. Trans. Daniel Moshenberg. New York: Semiotext(e), 1991.

Weinberg, Steven. *The Discovery of Subatomic Particles.* N.p.: Freeman, 1983.

The First Three Minutes: A Modern View of the Origin of the Universe. Updated edn. New York: Basic, 1988.

Weisenburger, Steven. "The Chronology of Episodes in *Gravity's Rainbow.*" *Pynchon Notes* 14 (1984): 50–64.

"The End of History? Thomas Pynchon and the Uses of the Past."

Twentieth-Century Literature 25 (1979): 54–72. Rpt. in *Critical Essays on Thomas Pynchon.* Ed. Richard Pearce. Boston: Hall, 1981. 140–56.

Wendorff, Rudolf. *Zeit und Kultur: Geschichte des Zeitbewußtseins in Europa.* Wiesbaden: Westdeutscher Verlag, 1980.

White, Hayden. *The Content of the Form: Narrative Discourse and Historical Representation.* Baltimore: Johns Hopkins University Press, 1987.

Wiener, Norbert. *The Human Use of Human Beings: Cybernetics and Society.* New York: Da Capo, 1950.

Wilczek, Frank, and Betsy Devine. *Longing for the Harmonies: Themes and Variations from Modern Physics.* New York: Norton, 1987.

Williams, William Carlos. *Paterson.* New York: New Directions, 1963.

Wolfley, Lawrence. "Repression's Rainbow: The Presence of Norman O. Brown in Pynchon's Big Novel." *PMLA* 92 (1978): 873–89. Rpt. in *Critical Essays on Thomas Pynchon.* Ed. Richard Pearce. Boston: Hall, 1981. 99–123.

Womack, James P., Daniel T. Jones and Daniel Roos. *The Machine That Changed the World.* New York: Rasson, 1990.

Wood, David. *The Deconstruction of Time.* Atlantic Highlands: Humanities Press International, 1989.

Woolf, Virginia. "Mr. Bennett and Mrs. Brown." *The Captain's Death Bed and Other Essays.* San Diego: Harcourt Brace Jovanovich, 1950. 94–119.

Mrs. Dalloway. San Diego: Harcourt, 1985.

To the Lighthouse. New York: Harcourt, 1927.

Zerubavel, Eviatar. "The Standardization of Time: A Sociohistorical Perspective." *American Journal of Sociology* 88 (1982): 1–23.

Zoll, Rainer, ed. *Zerstörung und Wiederaneignung von Zeit.* Frankfurt: Suhrkamp, 1988.

Index

Index

Culler, Jonathan 114 n.2
cyberpunk 4, 256
cyberspace 1, 45

Dalí, Salvador 37, 51
Delvaux, Paul 115
Derrida, Jacques 58 n.85
determinism 65–66, 68, 187, 208 n.43,
    215, 259
Dickens, Charles 48 n.72, 52, 150
Döblin, Alfred 82
Dos Passos, John 52, 82
Dowell, Coleman 61
Duras, Marguerite 52
duration 13, 32, 45 n.65, 61, 147–67
durée: see Bergson, Henri

Eco, Umberto 80
Eliot, George 49
endings: see closure
entropy 29, 39, 40, 204, 207–10, 252, 259
Ermarth, Elizabeth 28–29, 30, 88 n.9
Ernst, Max 153
erzählte Zeit (narrated time) 149–53
Erzählzeit (time of narration) 149–53,
    157
Escher, M. C. 61
evolution 38, 40, 207, 236, 256, 258, 259,
    260 n.5, 263

Faulkner, William 32, 33, 36, 50, 51, 52,
    77, 229
Federman, Raymond 60, 62, 153, 168
    n.43
fiction: see metafiction, novel
film 41–42, 64, 133, 135, 175, 181, 199,
    200, 201, 205, 213–14, 217, 221, 226,
    228
Flaubert, Gustave 150
Ford, Ford Madox 50, 52, 77
Ford, Henry 34
Forster, E. M. 47 n.68
Fowles, John 60
Franco, Jean 81 n.5
Frank, Joseph 63
Freud, Sigmund 35, 48, 116–17, 119–20,
    189–91
Fukuyama, Francis 19–20
futurism 34–35, 153

García Márquez, Gabriel 52
Gass, William 63
Genette, Gérard 47 n.68, 60, 148–53,
    157
Gibson, William 45

Giddens, Anthony 34 n.47
Gribbin, John 41

Habermas, Jürgen 19
Hamilton, David 115, 116, 118, 143, 145
Harvey, David 21–22, 26 n.31, 31, 34
    n.50
Hawking, Stephen 41
Hayles, N. Katherine 29–30, 73, 179 n.2,
    181–82, 207 n.42, 258–59 n.3, 259
    n.4
Hegel, G. W. F. 12, 19–20
Heidegger, Martin 36, 48
Heisenberg, Werner 237
history 124–27, 129, 145, 147, 148, 173,
    174, 175, 180, 183, 184, 185, 186,
    193, 194–95, 198, 203, 205, 214–18,
    249, 252, 256, 264
    and fiction 2–3, 216–17
    end or crisis of history 1, 11–33,
    179–80, 181, 221–28, 241, 242,
    252–55, 256, 257, 258, 263, 264; see
    also: closure of history
    personal history 72, 208, 241, 252,
    261
    plurality of histories 3, 16–17, 74,
    256, 257–58, 262, 264
    see also: closure of history,
    posthistory
Hofstadter, Douglas 59 n.87, 62
Horkheimer, Max 18
Husserl, Edmund 36
Hutcheon, Linda 2 n.1, 14–15
Huyssen, Andreas 15, 73
Huxley, Aldous 98 n.19

information technologies 22–26, 34
    computer 1, 23, 25–26, 44–46
instantaneity 22, 23–25, 44–45, 150

James, William 1, 36
Jameson, Fredric 14, 24 n.24, 27–28, 29,
    30, 39, 74, 120 n.17, 124, 173,
    263–64
Jensen, Wilhelm 116–17, 119–20, 124
Johnson, B. S. 52–53, 60, 66, 78
Joyce, James 13, 14, 36, 50, 51, 52, 63,
    82, 232

Kenner, Hugh 157 n.18, 159 n.23
Kermode, Frank 47, 48, 49, 50
Kern, Stephen 34 n.47, 34 n.49, 38 n.54
Kojève, Alexandre 20

Layzer, David 41

Index

linearity 18, 36, 37, 59, 60, 63, 65,
77–112, 137, 164, 189–90, 193, 205,
227, 258, 259, 260, 262 n.7, 264
Lotman, Jurij 96
Lyotard, Jean-François 16–17, 239 n.14

Magritte, René 115–16
Major, Clarence 53
Mann, Thomas 13, 36
Marinetti, F. T. 34, 153
Mauriac, Claude 52
McHale, Brian 2 n.1, 51 n.76, 53, 56
n.83, 60 nn.88 and 91, 68 n.100,
83–84, 115 n.6, 192 n.20, 217 n.58,
233 n.8, 253
McLuhan, Marshall 175
media 6, 37, 41, 64, 145–46, 174–75
memory 7, 13, 14–15, 26, 35–37, 50, 51,
53, 57, 58, 70, 73, 77, 88, 90, 99, 110,
137, 141, 147, 154, 163, 164–65
n.34, 169, 173, 174, 191, 193, 209,
225–27, 232, 249, 250, 261
Mendelson, Edward 179 n.2
metafiction 2, 3, 64, 66, 68, 80, 81–82,
95, 98, 105, 233, 256, 263, 264
see also: self-referentiality
metalepsis 55, 60–62, 63, 64, 98, 139
Metz, Christian 149 n.2
Miller, D. A. 48–49
mirror images 84–87, 135, 201–02,
240–41
mise-en-abyme 60, 138
Morrissette, Bruce 114, 115–16, 123
Morson, Gary Saul 65–66
Müller, Günther 149–53
Musil, Robert 51

narratology 47–51, 77, 148–53
narrators 7, 46, 50–51, 53, 56, 59, 61–62,
72, 73, 124, 126, 127–28, 129,
131–32, 133–34, 135, 136–37, 139,
140, 141, 147, 149, 153–71, 173–74,
188, 227, 237
Niethammer, Lutz 11 n.1, 18–19, 20, 73
n.108
non-linear dynamics: see chaos theory
nouveau roman 3, 32, 113–16
nouveau nouveau roman 3, 114–15
novel
late modernist 4, 52–53, 83, 115
modernist 2, 4, 5, 7, 13, 36, 50–53,
56, 63, 64, 65, 67, 68, 72–73, 77, 78,
82–83, 86–87, 90, 92, 96, 97, 98
n.19, 104, 105, 108, 111–12, 153,
232, 264

mystery novel 130–34, 137–38, 139,
141–42, 145
nineteenth-century 48–50, 52, 67, 150
postmodernist 1–3, 5, 6–7, 11, 13, 29,
31–33, 53–68, 78, 83–84, 98, 105,
111–12, 115, 116, 158, 174–75,
264–65
spy novel 183
Nowotny, Helga 29

paranoia 65, 181, 182, 183–84, 196, 197,
202, 204, 206, 211, 217, 239–40, 252,
263
pastiche 27–28, 66
Perec, Georges 64
Perloff, Marjorie 12, 163, 165, 168 n.43
phenomenology 36
plot 3, 4, 6, 7, 47, 48, 55, 56, 65, 68, 78,
83, 87–88, 89, 90, 91, 94, 96, 108,
111, 114, 119, 125, 128–37, 138, 139,
140, 144, 145, 146, 171, 179, 180,
181–86, 187 n.7, 191, 197, 206, 210,
211–12, 213, 215–17, 219, 221, 233,
245, 252, 253
Poggioli, Renato 35
posthistoire: see posthistory
posthistory 2, 4, 11–33, 70, 73, 74, 173,
179–80, 184, 185, 217–18, 219,
221–28, 229, 252–55, 256, 260, 264
postmodernism see: time and
postmodernist culture
Poststructuralism 11, 17, 254
Prigogine, Ilya 256, 257, 258–60, 263
probability 39, 185, 187, 196, 199, 202
progress 16, 18, 29, 35, 124, 185, 241,
249, 264
Proust, Marcel 13, 14, 32, 33, 36, 50, 53,
58, 77, 90 n.12, 152, 163, 172–73
psychoanalysis 222, 240–48
case study 189–91
delayed reaction (*Nachträglichkeit*)
190–91
psychoanalytical interpretation
116–17, 119–20, 123, 144–45, 216–17
transference 242, 244, 245, 247, 248,
249
Pynchon, Thomas 4, 65, 67, 170–218,
219, 239, 242, 252–55, 262

quantum mechanics 38–39
quotation 4, 69, 71, 82, 87, 88, 90, 91,
116 n.11, 147, 155, 157, 159, 160,
162, 167–71, 173, 174

Rauschenberg, Robert 115

Index

Tolstoy, Leo 52
typography 55, 62–63, 65, 148, 153, 156–60, 174–75

Valenzuela, Luisa 64
Virilio, Paul 17, 26–27

Weinberg, Steven 41
White, Hayden 93 n.15
Wiener, Norbert 187 n.9
Williams, William Carlos 82
Woolf, Virginia 13, 35 n.52, 36, 50, 51, 52, 77, 232